Mormonism
A Life Under False Pretenses

The True Story of a Mormon Bishop's
Journey of Discovery

by

Former Mormon Bishop, Lee B. Baker

Published by (Father's Press, LLC)

ISBN: 978-1-937520-75-5
(Second Printing)

Distributed by
First Edition Design Publishing, Inc.
April 2012
www.firsteditiondesignpublishing.com

LCCN: 2012937423

Copyright, 2010 by Lee B. Baker
Edited by Jarl K. Waggoner

Includes bibliographical references, notes, letters, documents and index.

ISBN: 978-0-9825321-8-8 (previous edition)

Cover Design and Artwork by Chris Beard

Cover Photographs Used by permission, Utah State Historical Society, All
rights reserved.

Grateful acknowledgement is made to the following in support of document
security and safekeeping: Patrick McGinty.

Printed in the United States of America 2010

Unless otherwise indicated, Scripture quotations are from the King
James Version of the Bible.

Scripture quotations marked NIV are from the HOLY BIBLE, NEW
INTERNATIONAL VERSION®. NIV®. Copyright © 1973, 1978, 1984 by
International Bible Society. Used by permission of Zondervan. All rights
reserved.

- Dedication -

To those followers of the Lord Jesus Christ who have the integrity and the courage to actively defend the correct purpose and potential of His true ministry.

Five years of solid research, a multitude of probing questions, and the many prayers required for this book are now dedicated to those who might find themselves asking serious questions about the Church of Jesus Christ of Latter-day Saints, the Mormons.

CONTENTS

- About the Author -

After three decades of exceptional service in many leadership positions within the Church of Jesus Christ of Latter-day Saints, Bishop Lee B. Baker found the time to actually study the official history and the core doctrines of the church. After two years of intense religious study from official church records, which centered on the early years of the Mormon Church, several hypocritical teachings became impossible to dismiss. He sincerely asked his local, regional, and then finally the national leadership of the Mormon Church for some clarification specific to the practices of polygamy, polyandry, and blood atonement among the early "saints."

He was told that many of these questions were in direct violation of church policy, procedures, and covenants. And even though he was an ordained Bishop, he was clearly warned that any further inquiries concerning these subjects would place his membership in the Mormon Church at risk. In December of 2008, Bishop Baker forced his own excommunication from the Church of Jesus Christ of Latter-day Saints by continuing to ask piercing questions about the personal character and motives of both the past and present leadership of that church.

Only a few months prior to his excommunication, several of the High Priests who conducted this mockery of a just trial had great confidence in Bishop Baker as the Sunday school teacher of their own sons and daughters. Bishop Baker participated in hundreds of Mormon temple ceremonies, some of which included the precise method of simulating the taking of a human life if particular sacred Mormon covenants were violated. His firsthand experiences and insight into the authentic teachings, policies, and practices of Mormonism provide a unique view of one of the world's fastest growing religions, which he demonstrates to be "a life under false pretenses."

Explicit details, including the actual names, dates, and statements of the leadership of the Church of Jesus Christ of Latter-day Saints shape the foundation for this incredible true story of religious deceit and deception from 1830 to the present.

As a highly decorated retired army officer, Mr. Baker held positions of trust and responsibly within the Department of Defense for nearly thirty-five years.

PREFACE

The Apostle Paul has told us, "God is not the author of confusion, but of peace, as in all churches of the saints" (1 Cor. 14:33). And James, the brother of the Lord, has counseled, "For where envying and strife is, there is confusion and every evil work" (James 3:16). After over thirty years of dedicated service in the Mormon Church, I came to know the true details of the doctrines of polygamy, polyandry, blood atonement, exaltation (to become a God), and lying for the Lord. In the depths of my depression, I could only be comforted by the words of the Master Himself:

> "And ye shall know the truth, and the truth shall make
> you free." (John 8:32)

My devotion to the Lord has become deeper, more personal, and unrestrained through a renewed appreciation of His true sacrifice for me. This demanding but spectacular gift of clarity is possible only because I no longer worship Him from behind the dark shadows of corrupt men, who have in the past and continue yet today to disgrace His ministry and His authority. Research for yourself each and every reference, every Scripture, and every Mormon doctrine described here, for what you learn may change your life forever.

As you consider the information presented in this book, I would ask you to accept the same excellent challenge given by each pair of Mormon missionaries. It is a challenge to honesty and integrity that I have offered many times myself as a Mormon Bishop: "read, study, ponder, and pray" about what you may learn here. I pray that the Holy Sprit of truth will inspire you to act, without reservation and without consideration of tradition, family, or embarrassment, upon what He may witness to your heart. May God bless you for your efforts to seek His truth, because the truth matters.

Lee B. Baker

Former Mormon Bishop and High Priest

NOTE: *Throughout this book I reference several significant and personal experiences I have had with the leadership of the Mormon Church. As I relate these experiences, I intentionally disclose the specifics of the several meetings, conversations, or written exchanges. This information includes the actual names and dates and in most cases the original correspondences referenced. The purpose of this level of detail is not to arbitrarily harass or humiliate the representatives of the Mormon Church but to establish the credibility of my position and conclusions. Additionally, I believe that how these men have dealt with me provides an outstanding real-world example of just how others might expect to be treated if they so choose to question the history, policies, and doctrine of the Church of Jesus Christ of Latter-day Saints.*

INTRODUCTION
A Personal Account of the Deception and Deceit of Mormonism

After thirty-two years, why not just walk away? Why take the time and energy to write a book and risk family relationships? Why criticize another Christian church, which obviously has done so much good for so many around the world?

These are truly valid questions, which are central to my motivation and the drive to complete this work. I completely agree that my motivation should be questioned, understood, and challenged. I will be the first to openly admit that I have not always been the best representative of the Lord Jesus Christ. I have sinned against Him and my fellow man far too often over the course of my life. And yet without hesitation I am now able to admit that some of the most distressing transgressions of my life were committed within the walls of the Mormon temples.

Hundreds of times in Mormon temples from Switzerland to Washington D.C., from Salt Lake City to England, and from Denver to Mesa, Arizona, I took sacred oaths and covenants that required the mimicking of the taking of a human life. Several years ago when I learned for certain that these acts of brutality, embedded within the Mormon Temple Endowment, represented actual murders authorized by the leadership of the Church of Jesus Christ of Latter-day Saints, I was disgusted. My wife and I not only had acted out the murder of another person but also had authorized the taking of our own life in the same manner, by the slicing of our throats from ear to ear, if we were to break the covenants we had made within the Mormon temple. This graphic example of pure evil was just one of the several doctrines of the Mormon Church I would come to more fully understand between the years 2003 and 2008. And yet this specific example completely shattered any justification that such remarkably depraved Mormon teachings were in the distant past, for I repeatedly participated in this appalling ceremony until 1990, when it was officially discontinued. The specific words and graphic motions teaching precisely how to disembowel or cut in a single slice the neck of a fellow saint can never be purged from our memories.

The men who have instructed the many generations of good Mormons to participate in this version of the endowment ceremony have done so with the unapologetic claim that the representation of these violent events is not just authorized but also absolutely required by the Lord Jesus Christ Himself, if we are to enter into the presence of the Father. As an emotional and spiritual protection strategy, many Latter-day Saints find some comfort in the belief that the several questionable doctrines of the past Prophets are not taught today. Within this strategy is found the false hope that an individual is released from any responsibility, based on his or her lack of personal knowledge or acceptance of that questionable practice or teaching.

The primary sources for this work will be the documents of the church itself and my life experiences from my two-year conversion and baptism at the age of twenty on February 17, 1977, to my excommunication on December 7, 2008. I will chronicle the words of the Mormon Prophets themselves and the specific teachings, instructions, and lectures of the Apostles and leadership of the church, as well as many meetings with the local stake and ward leaders of the church. As a former Bishop and High Priest in the Mormon Church, I will explain in detail the subtle relationships between the unique doctrines, practices, and policies, as well as the oaths and covenants, which will be second nature to the Latter-day Saint reader. Only a few hundred current members of the church will actually know of my service and remember my lovely wife and my dedicated family. Therefore, I will only briefly mention specific congregations of the church with whom we have served. As such, my primary goal is to bear witness to those whom I have not known and to those who may presuppose that what I have to say is simply a lie to damage the "good name of the Mormon

Church." I dedicated a great portion of my life to serving in the Mormon Church. There I raised my family in what I considered a nourishing Christian environment, surrounded and supported by faithful Christian brothers and sisters. I know that the fast pace of life and faithful service in the church consumes a great deal of time and energy. As a young couple with four active children, our service in the military for twenty years, as well as the constant demands associated with leadership positions in the church, left room for little else.

I completely understand how any negative information about the church, regardless of its apparent authenticity, is promptly demoted to the back of our minds as we know in our hearts that we are doing good, that we are taking part in the praiseworthy and best aspects of the church. And if, only if, the early church leaders made mistakes or took liberties with some of the teachings, then only they, and not we, are responsible for those few indiscretions. For taken on the whole, we would like to believe that the church moves forward in great ways and with enormous support within the world, across neighborhoods, and within our own families.

The Authority of the Church Leadership

In the early years of the Mormon Church, Joseph Smith Jr. taught the doctrines of polygamy and polyandry in secret, without the knowledge of the general membership of the church. If a sister in the church did not know of the teaching, that lack of knowledge on her part had absolutely no impact whatsoever on the fact that the doctrine may have been practiced next door. If last month you did not know anything about polygamy, polyandry, or blood atonement, then there was no need for you to understand just how such a teaching of the church fits within your view of the Mormon "restored gospel." Only after you are made aware of a doctrine do you then need to evaluate its application in your life, because you don't know what you don't know. But it must be plainly understood that just as in the early days of the Mormon Church, your opinions or your views on the subject are of little concern to the leadership of the church. It is the leadership of any church that establishes the relevance or application of doctrine. The social, economic, or spiritual opinions of the general membership have virtually no impact as to the application of the key doctrines of that church. If there is any considerable disagreement within the body of the church, the apostates must separate themselves or live under disagreeable or offensive doctrine.

As confirmed several times by the leadership of the Mormon Church, these several questionable or offensive doctrines have only been "suspended" and are anticipated to return in the Lord's due time.[1] If the current social or legal pressures brought upon the Mormon Church, which have led to the suspension of these doctrines, are ever removed, there is no reason to think the doctrines would not return. The vast majority of the sisters in the current Church of Jesus Christ of Latter-day Saints that I have known would not want to participate in polygamy or polyandry in any form. They should understand that the practice of these two foundational doctrines, as taught by Joseph Smith Jr., were neither started nor stopped by a vote from the dear sisters of the church. No opinion poll or vote of the sisters of the church was taken in 1831, and certainly not of Emma Smith when Joseph secretly took his first polygamist teenage wife. And I would suggest that no poll or vote will be taken from the dear sisters if the practice were to return in the future. It may be that the women of the Mormon Church today do not fully understand that the practice of polygamy is "essential to exaltation in the highest heaven," as recorded within Mormon Scriptures.[2] It is well documented that the vast majority of the plural marriages within the early church were prearranged without the consent of the women and girls involved, and there is no reason to imagine that a change would

---

[1] "The members of the Church are reminded that the practice of polygamous or plural marriage is not the only law whose suspension has been authorized by the Lord," and "The law of the United Order has likewise been suspended, to be re-established in the due time of the Lord." President Heber J. Grant, dated 13 Jan. 1914, Messages of the First Presidency of the Church of Jesus Christ of Latter-day Saints, comp. James R. Clark (Salt Lake City: Bookcraft, 1965-75), 6:327.

[2] Doctrine and Covenants sections 131 and 132.

be required when the practice returns, either on earth or in heaven.

Regarding the belief that such questionable and offensive doctrines or teachings of the early Prophets are somehow not of any interest to the current leadership of the church today, consider the following points. Within the existing curriculum of the Mormon Church, namely, The official Priesthood and Relief Society manuals (Teachings of the Prophets), Sunday school manuals, missionary instructions, the Doctrine and Covenants student manuals, Scripture topical guides, temple preparation lessons, and other official publications of the church, numerous supportive statements are made concerning the teachings, actions, and doctrines the church has supposedly abandoned. Precise and well-documented examples of this hypocritical misinformation for this current generation of Mormons will be provided throughout this book. As an overview of the principal subjects addressed, I list some of the key proposals here.

- The leadership teaches the entire church to obey the laws of the land, unless it is advantageous for the leadership to disobey it.

- The leadership teaches the entire church the will of the Lord through revelation, but the leadership may not be restricted by the same revelations.

- The leadership teaches the entire church to be honest, true, and chaste, but the leadership may not be restricted by the same virtues.

- The leadership teaches the entire church not to mingle religious influence with civil government, but the Prophet, Joseph Smith himself, can organize a theocracy and then attempt to become president of the United States.

To make clear the relationship between the intentions of the leadership of the church today and the questionable or offensive doctrines and teachings of the past Prophets, one should understand that all I have learned about these events has come from the church itself. In one sense it is extraordinary that 120 years after the doctrine of polygamy was decisively abandoned—more accurately suspended—it still remains in today's printing within Mormon Scriptures and Doctrine and Covenants. And yet of additional interest is that some of the most controversial statements of the early church leadership have also remained in print within the official history of the church and the several official lesson manuals.

When considering what the church itself has published about its own history, it should be remembered that not a single line passes without some degree of review. I have spoken with an administrative assistant from the headquarters of the church in Salt Lake City, who stated to our High Priest group Sunday class that a virtual army of writers, editors, and publishing committees take direction from the "Brethren" (a common expression for the "leadership of the church") so that every printed word is reviewed. This concept is very practical and certainly in agreement with the policy of protecting the "good name of the church," as any large organization might do. The point here is that the Church of Jesus Christ of Latter-day Saints dedicates significant resources to public relations or its public image, so that the unscripted public presentations of the church are very rare.

Recognition must be given to the Mormon Church for the enormous amount of the questionable or offensive information that remains within the archives of the church and is still reasonably available to the public. I am unsure whether the motivation for this is the deep legacy of pride and respect for the early Prophets or simply that changing what already has been published would bring immediate condemnation. Whatever the case, the spoken words of the Prophets remain for all interested parties to read and consider for themselves. That having been said, a significant effort also has been employed both by the church and organizations sympathetic to the church to excuse, rationalize, explain, or rewrite those very same questionable activities and teachings of the early Prophets.

Two very different literary strategies are quite clear within the current publications of the Mormon Church itself. It is almost as if a split personality exists within the leadership of the church concerning how best to present the modern teachings of the church. At times it is obvious that within the history of the church is the proud foundation for how far the church has come. And then at times it is equally obvious that some activities within the history of the church are clear examples of desperate acts of desperate men not in harmony with the core values of Christianity.[3]

I believe the current hypocritical defense of the more insulting doctrines that are not practiced today speaks volumes concerning the true beliefs of the current leadership of the Mormon Church. That is to say, the current leadership cannot openly endorse many of the earlier doctrines of the church, but their frustration can be seen in the several examples of diametrically opposed teachings in the modern Latter-day Saint curriculum. These examples demonstrate moments of unrestrained comments specific to what may be considered some of the more disgusting doctrines of the church, yet at the same time those doctrines are viewed as core principles of the "restored gospel," worthy of justification and defense. This, then, is the bridge between the generations of Latter-day Saints who actually practiced these principles and the current generation of Latter-day Saints, who can defend them only because of current social, political, and legal pressures to the contrary. I fully believe there exists a subculture within the Mormon Church today that sincerely anticipates the return of these morally corrupt values and teachings of early Mormonism. The real danger I see is that this subculture is also the current leadership of the church.

It has been my experience that even the titles of the leadership of the Mormon Church itself reflects the complete detachment from the Biblical and spiritual leadership of the true Christian and thus favors the secular and material leadership of the world. Not once in the Bible is there a reference to the

---

[3] See appendix B for a brief chronology of significant events in Mormon history.

"President" of a congregation or Church, yet in the Mormon scriptures over two dozen such references outline the responsibilities of the "President". The Mormons have Presidents of the several Quorums, Missions, The Women's Relief Society Organization and even the preferred title of the "Mormon Prophet" is in fact the "President". I know the duties, responsibilities and motivations of Presidents of Companies, Corporations and Countries, and with that knowledge and practical experience I am absolutely comfortable with the titles of President Joseph Smith, President Brigham Young and President Thomas S. Monson the current President of The Church of Jesus Christ of Latter-day Saints. I would ask all Christians and the Mormons as well if you can truthfully feel the enormous spiritual contrast, if we spoke of The Biblical Prophets as President Abraham, President Jacob and President Isaiah.

Asking for the Truth About the "True Church"

One of the most personal and essential elements of a fulfilling religious experience is the ability to ask questions— real questions, and at times extremely serious questions. Mormonism robs its own membership of this right. Before I had completed my journey to discover the truth about my own religion of over thirty years, I knew, as every Mormon knows, that it is wrong to criticize, much less to openly question, the leadership of the church. This uncompromising direction was clearly stated by one of the most senior Mormon leaders alive today, during an interview for a PBS documentary: "It's wrong to criticize leaders of the church, even if the criticism is true."[4] This on-camera, authoritative declaration was immediately followed by a small but very intimidating smile from Elder Dallin H. Oaks. Without question, this message was taken extremely seriously and completely understood by active Mormons watching his interview. In this same interview, Elder

---

[4] Interview of Dallin H. Oaks, "The Mormons," PBS documentary, 2008. Oaks is an Apostle and senior member of the Quorum of the Twelve and in direct line to become the Prophet of the Church of Jesus Christ of Latter-day Saints.

Oaks declared, "Not everything that's true is useful." That is an enlightening statement that is somewhat startling from what is reported to be "the only true church on the earth today."[5] But in contrast to that, the church also has stated, "The gospel of Jesus Christ embraces all truth."[6] This is yet another example of the hypocritical and deceptive official doubletalk employed by the Mormon Church to cover all options. When a Mormon is spiritually, emotionally or logically challenged by either their own Scriptures or the true Christian Scriptures, most often they retreat to how they "feel" regardless of the clear facts, to include the spoken or written doctrine in question. This is rather different than the offer presented by Mormon Apostle Orson Pratt, who in the Official Mormon Newspaper, the Seer, was issued the following challenge to non-Mormons: "...convince us of our errors of doctrine, if we have any, by reason, by logical arguments, or by the word of God, and we will be ever grateful for the information, and you will ever have the pleasing reflection that you have been instruments in the hands of God for redeeming your fellow beings from the darkness which you may see enveloping their minds."

In the November 2007 issue of the Ensign, the official magazine of the Church of Jesus Christ of Latter-day Saints, an article appeared that profoundly changed my life. The title of this sermon by Elder Scott, "Truth: The Foundation of Correct Decisions,"[7] disturbed me greatly, as I had come to know of the great depth of Mormon hypocrisy. Unquestionably, the word truth used here would only indicate the Mormon truth, or as Elder Oaks has so spitefully communicated it, "the useful truth." The subtitle, "A knowledge of truth is of little value unless we apply it in making correct decisions," represented one of the most distressing and condescending statements I had

---

[5] A common statement of belief among the Mormon Church and formally noted in over two dozen sermons given within the general conferences of the church by the Prophets and Apostles of the church.

[6] Teachings of the Presidents of the Church: Joseph Smith (Salt Lake City: Intellectual Reserve, 2007), 264.

[7] Elder Richard G. Scott, Of the Quorum of the Twelve Apostles, "Truth: The Foundation of Correct Decisions," Ensign, November 2007, 90-92.

heard from my church. Elder Scott spoke of how very confusing "carefully crafted messages" and "diametrically opposed solutions" can be. He continued by warning the faithful that "the process of identifying truth sometimes necessitates enormous effort coupled with profound faith in our Father and His glorified Son." As I read that statement over and over, I felt an overwhelming, almost suffocating, feeling of despair, for I knew that the truth itself was about to drive me out of the Mormon Church. That feeling caused me to remember what a former Mormon Stake President had warned me of when my wife and I came to him for answers to our questions. He said, "If you continue down this path of asking questions, it will lead you to leaving the church."

To reinforce the practice of "Do as I say, and not as I do," within every Mormon temple the law of the gospel[8] is taught under a strict and solemn covenant, which in part requires the membership to avoid "evil speaking of the Lord's anointed." The Lord's anointed includes, of course, the "Prophets" and "Apostles," those who have taught, practiced, or defended the doctrines of polygamy, polyandry, blood atonement, bigotry, and lying for the Lord. So to even ask if these practices are truly from the Lord is to speak evil of the Mormon Prophets themselves. I have, over the course of many years, participated in scores of such temple ceremonies that have included several specific penalties, each mimicking the taking of a human life.

At the age of fifty-three and an avid reader with a firm appreciation for all things historical, you might think I would have known better. It is not a matter of knowing better; it is essentially a matter of learning better. What will be presented here is not intended for the casual anti-Mormon researcher. Much of what I will document will be presented from an active Latter-day Saint's perspective. Given that, fundamentals of this story will touch on sensitive feelings that only a Latter-day Saint will completely understand and hopefully learn from. The principal intent of this book is not to draw Latter-day Saints

---

[8] See appendix A document number 26.

from their church but to clarify the deception they have been drawn into. My narrative is to share the true gospel of Christ in such a way that the reader might know that our relationship with the Savior is deeply personal and should not include the several appalling and spiritually suffocating Mormon doctrines, which certainly are not from Jesus Christ. For Mormonism to be true, Christ Himself must be corrupted into one who authorizes horrible behavior, thus rendering the Mormon Prophets completely blameless concerning the motivations for their unspeakable actions. If the reader of this story can comprehend and then, with a spirit of reverence for the Lord, articulate the basic questions required of the Mormon faith,[9] my responsibility to Jesus the Christ Himself will have been satisfied.

I will acknowledge at the outset of this work that the organization and efficiency of the Mormon Church is without question one of the finest support institutions in the world. With its outstanding youth programs, local and global emergency relief activities and superior training programs specific to moral and ethical behavior of its membership, the Mormon as an individual is an excellent neighbor, coworker, student and member of society in general. Yet, as contradictory and inconsistent as it may appear, without question the Mormon who both knows of his or her Church's Official Doctrine and subscribes unconditionally to its distinctive but authorized principals and teachings, cannot be considered Christian. That troublesome statement of fact is the very foundation of this book and will be clearly and convincingly substantiated by what follows.

Why Is This Story So Important?

Why is this story so important? I can put it simply. If a man or woman is to follow the "restored gospel" of the Lord, as taught by the Church of Jesus Christ of Latter-day Saints, it should be only reasonable to ask some basic questions concerning both the character and the core teachings of Joseph

---

[9] See chapter 5 for the basic set of questions that have come to represent the author's central inquiry.

Smith Jr., the first Prophet of that restoration. As a convert to the Mormon faith and as a leader in that church for over thirty years, it has been my experience that just the asking of a few fundamental questions is enough to recognize that something is wrong, very wrong, with what is reported to be "the only true church on the earth today."

In what other critical activity of your life should you not ask straightforward questions? In what other central aspect of your life should you not know all you possibly can about the subject? From Mormon Church leaders I have seen infinitely more concern and personal knowledge about their financial investments, scouting activities, sports teams, and hobbies than about the very details of exactly what guides them and their families into eternity.

One of the most depressing aspects of coming to know the truth about the Mormon faith was inadvertently causing the personal disillusionment of several of my closest friends. I became an eyewitness to several of these very short-lived but clearly visible emotional challenges. It is hard to watch when a person realizes that what is actually taught by the church is not what that person really believes. Predictably, in that brief moment of spiritual embarrassment, personal pride and family tradition most often triumph. Yet for the average member of the Mormon Church, new information about the church, however authoritative it might be, is quickly dismissed if it does not conform to the member's existing view of the church. This is because in formal teaching curricula of the Mormon Church, only a very selective segment of church history is presented, without, in my view, the liberty of the student to ask probing questions outside of the very structured set of courses. This book will accomplish that task and still remain well within the authorized, official, and approved records of the Mormon Church itself to bring the light of the truth to its teachings.

One evening after a particularly enjoyable home teaching[10]

---

[10] Home teaching assignments generally require a once-a-month visit to a designated list of families or individuals to provide general support and/or

visit with a very charming and faithful elderly couple, an unplanned "testing" of a dear friend's understanding of church history genuinely moved me. On the ride home that evening, my companion, a true intellectual and lifelong member of the church, asked what I had thought about the dear sister's comment regarding Mitt Romney being considered as a possible presidential candidate? The subject was on the minds of most Mormons, and I told him that I thought it would bring the history of the church under a microscope. He nodded his head and thought out loud, "Oh ya, that could be rough." We both knew that for many years the church was considered anti-American in both practice and principle. He then added a very unassuming but sincere comment about the Twelfth Article of Faith.[11] His statement represented one of the first times I really understood that, as Mormons, it was simply our mandatory responsibility to defend the church. He merely said, "I have never understood that period of rebellion, in view of the Scriptures." It was a simple statement by any measure, yet it overflowed with the brutal reality that here in the ultramodern twenty-first century, he and I had several 150-year-old political, religious, and ethical positions to defend, regardless of our own values and beliefs.

For those Latter-day Saints who are genuinely unconcerned with the precise impact of an outdated sermon or a Mormon doctrine from well over a hundred years ago, the fellowship of the church today provides a welcome sanctuary from the world. Without question, the current practices, principles, and standards of the Church of Jesus Christ of Latter-day Saints are very commendable. It is absolutely logical how this generation of Latter-day Saints could become sincerely and completely apathetic to the questionable doctrines of the past. These sensitive issues have virtually no impact whatsoever on choir practice next Tuesday, Samantha's baptism on Saturday, or

---

report specific needs back to the church leadership.

[11] The 12th Article of Faith is, "We believe in being subject to kings, presidents, rulers, and magistrates, in obeying, honoring, and sustaining the law." See Joseph Smith Jr., History of the Church of Jesus Christ of Latter-day Saints (Salt Lake City: Deseret Book Company, 1948), 4:541.

Aunt Karen's talk the following Sunday. I know well the speed of life as an active Latter-day Saint; I know well the indispensable companionship of wives, mothers, sons, and daughters, each with common goals and activities.

At the very foundation of the average Latter-day Saint's inability to comprehend the significance of the differences between what is taught and what is practiced is the genuine love and companionship among the members themselves. I know from personal experience that when faced with the probability that what the leadership believed was somehow different from what I believed, my viewpoint most likely did not matter. That is as it should be, because I joined them; they did not convert to my beliefs. I take full responsibility for taking over three decades to fully understand just what their beliefs really are.

When I finally came to the painful understanding that my issues with the past history and bizarre doctrines of my own church were of no concern to the leadership I had so faithfully served, it hit me that it was never their judgment or opinion I should have been seeking. It was as if for a short time I had somewhat abandoned my individual relationship with the Savior Himself. I had come to the point that I had more faith in the leadership of my church than in what I knew to be the true teachings of Jesus Christ. The Mormon teaching curriculum had slowly placed the lives of the past Mormon Prophets between my Savior and me. I had come to know much more of their teachings than of those pure teachings from the Master Himself. I had traded my personal relationship to the Savior for the outstanding social and emotional support provided to my family. I had made exceptions, offered excuses, and accepted totally unbelievable and irrational stories to explain the sins of deceitful men against the Lord.

In the fall of 2005 it became clear that the history, policies, rules, and doctrines of the Church of Jesus Christ of Latter-day Saints were not at all insignificant. It was the outstanding youth activities, the friendship, and the fellowship that had masked the very foundation of the church. Like millions before me, I had accepted the corrupt teachings of the leadership of the church in exchange for the warmth and tenderness of my fellow Latter-day Saints. It truthfully felt as if the common thread of just being "Mormon" somehow linked us to the past traditions of the early pioneer Latter-day Saints. I believe that this blanket of religious unity not only conceals the true teachings of the early Prophets; it also further restrains the individual's ability to openly compare the teachings of Christ against the traditions of Mormonism. Christ Himself warned of this very distortion when He said, "You have let go of the commands of God and are holding on to the traditions of men" (Mark 7:8 NIV).

The influence and power of church tradition, family unity, and personal acceptance cannot be overestimated within the social structure of Mormonism. In a very real sense, the spiritual distinctiveness of an individual can become completely lost within the organizations of the Mormon Church itself. This spiritual amalgamation of the Mormon faith suppresses individual thought to the point that even within the most encouraging of surroundings, individual thought is routinely held in check. I have been in countless Sunday school and priesthood classes where even the most basic questions with reference to church doctrine are met with total silence. Moreover, not a single educational forum can be found within the Church of Jesus Christ of Latter-day Saints that openly supports the unrestricted flow of even general questions concerning the foundation of the church itself. It has been my unpleasant experience that the very discovery and discussion of the truth within the "True Church" is an exceptionally rare practice indeed.

I have documented in this book a few remarkable comments from relatively intelligent Latter-day Saint men who can effectively manage a business and all the complexities of this life. But when they are confronted with the questionable actions and teachings of the Mormon Prophets, they become adolescent in both deliberation and dialogue. A few of the more popular comments I have heard from my former Latter-day Saints friends when confronted with solid questions are: "I do not know about that; I was not there"; "We do not know everything about these issues"; "I have faith that whatever the Prophets have said and done is from the Lord"; and, of course, "In that context, it all makes sense to me."

The Lie for a Friend

The initial catalyst for a more focused review of what I had not known about my own church came from a simple question from a dear friend. Due in part to my earlier church responsibilities as Bishop, Stake Young Men's President, and Elder's Quorum President, my wife and I were called as the Stake Young Single Adult leaders of the Columbia, Maryland Stake. This calling and its associated responsibilities included planning Sunday and family home evening[12] lessons, hosting activities, and caring for and reporting on the spiritual welfare of as many as sixty youth between the ages of 18 and 30.

This calling was by far one of the most rewarding responsibilities we had ever had in the church. The youth were excited about the church, spiritually vibrant and grateful for the support group we had helped cultivate among them. We shared birthdays, weddings, personal tragedies, and triumphs. One evening in our home during refreshments after the formal lesson, a dear friend and youth leader of the church group asked me the following question.

"Brother Baker," he said, "I have had a question from a coworker concerning the character of Joseph Smith. He has asked, 'Why would a true Prophet of God boast in such a manner as this?'" He then asked, "Did you know of this comment? And are you OK with it?" He then handed me the following quote from Joseph Smith himself:

> *I have more to boast of than ever any man had. I am the only man that has ever been able to keep a whole church together since the days of Adam. A large majority of the whole have stood by me. Neither Paul, John, Peter, nor Jesus ever did it. I boast*

---

12 Church leaders have instructed members to set aside Monday night as "family home evening." This is a time for families to study the gospel together and to do other activities that strengthen the family spiritually, create family memories, and increase unity and love. See lds.org.

that no man ever did such a work as I.[13]

I truly had not known of this quote. Although stunned and hopeful it was not true, I told this young man that I had known about it and that it was not an issue with me. He said, "Brother Baker, if you are OK with it, then so am I." I had just lied to defend the integrity of Joseph Smith; it would be both the first and last time that I would knowingly do such a thing. This book will document the events that followed that fateful day, as I took this very question to my church leadership, who were very much concerned that I would even ask such a question but had no concern whatsoever that it may be true. I believe that the real issue at hand was a possible assault on the character of Joseph Smith himself. In fact, character is what this book is about. The very character of the leadership of the Church of Jesus Christ of Latter-day Saints, both past and present, is paramount to this work. The many years I have endured condescending and pompous answers will be clearly documented in this book. As such, I will include the actual names, dates, locations, and exact words of those who spoke them.

The Truth Matters—It Really Does

It should be stated from the very outset of this work that what follows is not cruelly or unkindly directed toward the general membership of the Latter-day Saint faith. Rather, this effort is intended to illustrate the dishonorable motivations of the leadership of the church through their own words and deeds. The local and national leadership of the Church of Jesus Christ of Latter-day Saints, who know well the deliberate deceptions of the church, are, I believe, enemies of the Lord and thus the subject of this book. The average Latter-day Saint will never know of these disgusting and immoral events because the prescribed church study guides and formal curricula mis-represent the truth or conceal the very context of the actions themselves, and these subjects are immediately dismissed if brought up for discussion.

---

[13] Smith, History of the Church, 6:408-9.

It is a virtual certainty that any member of the Mormon Church who might ask the fundamental questions documented in this book[14] will be immediately ridiculed, viewed with contempt, and rejected by those they might now consider to be friends and devoted leaders. But the truth matters, and we are indebted only to the one who rescued us from the darkness and despair of this world through His atonement and to no one else. The truth does matter; it mattered two thousand years ago, and it matters today.

Christ Himself stated to Pilate shortly before His agonizing death, "In fact, for this reason I was born, and for this I came into the world, to testify to the truth" (John 18:37 NIV). How, then, can we not ask for the truth, not seek the truth, and then not follow the truth wherever it may lead us? You may lose friendships and possibly family ties as you experience the precise sorrow of Paul, as he stood firm in the Lord when he asked, "Have I now become your enemy by telling you the truth?" (Gal. 4:16 NIV).

As I will document in this work, the church's leaders know very well the ugly truth behind the self-serving doctrines of the Mormon Church. They know it completely, and yet they actively seek to hide, alter, or discredit its discovery at every opportunity. It is my solemn testimony that a great number of the current Mormon leadership have been corrupted by the very same desire for authority and the perception of stature among men that entirely corrupted many of the early Mormon Prophets.

The foundation of the Mormon Church cannot endure even the hint of a religious scandal or the abuse of power. A long and successful deception cannot suffer even the slightest injury to the foundation of its central lie. I believe that good men and women within the Mormon Church have been totally enveloped

---

[14] The Lorin M. Lund Questions represent the fundamental questions to be asked of the Mormon Church. See chapter 5 for the complete questions and all references and footnotes taken from authorized publications of the Church of Jesus Christ of Latter-day Saints.

by this lie and are now addicted to the need to conceal it. Although I may be despised and ostracized by my family and friends for even the suggestion that some core element of Mormonism is a lie, I stand on this simple statement: I do not believe that the Lord Jesus Christ required, recognized, or respected the Mormon doctrines of polygamy, polyandry, and blood atonement. The Mormon obsession with defending repulsive doctrine is heartbreaking on many levels. I believe the modern Latter-day Saint is now vastly superior in both character and integrity to the moral and ethical scoundrels they are compelled to defend. You may come to know, as I have, many Latter-day Saints who are trustworthy, dedicated, and beyond reproach in their character. Those are precisely the respectable Mormons who will hesitate or struggle to justify the obvious spiritual failures and bizarre doctrines of the church, because they know in their hearts that they and their families live far better Christian lives than those whom they are now required to defend. Yet there are some who delight in the deception and distortion of the Lord's gospel. They would have you believe that they believe that the perversion of lying for the Lord, the act of taking another man's wife, or taking another man's life is just another essential part of what they teach as the "restored gospel of Jesus Christ."

The Character of Joseph Smith Matters

What will be documented here is both my personal journey of discovery from the Mormon-based resources and my conclusions, from those documents, that the Church of Jesus Christ of Latter-day Saints is built on the testimonies and actions of deceitful men. Without question, character, specifically the character of Joseph Smith Jr. and generally the character of the leadership of the church, is the very foundation for much of my criticism of the Mormon faith. Both Mormons and non-Mormons alike have recognized this clear requirement of upright character from the very birth of the church in April of 1830. The Mormon Church itself recognizes and records that even the father of Joseph Smith's first wife, Emma Hale, did not trust the character of Joseph due to his "treasure hunting". The two were forced to elope and soon after married by a justice of the peace on January 18, 1827.

To illustrate the importance and implication that character really does count for something, I have quoted below a few comments from the past leadership of the Mormon Church in which they themselves emphasize the importance of the genuine character and honesty of Joseph Smith Jr. I have selected comments only from the General Authorities of the church given during general conference reports. Within this setting and under the authority of the First Presidency of the church, this instruction to the membership of the church is to be considered "Scripture."

> *Are we a mighty people? We are. 6800 men holding the priesthood were in this building last night. No other people in the world like us; no other people with the power that we have here, because we are following a prophet of the living God, the man whom God chose to organize this Church, and whom he visited and to whom he introduced his beloved Son. I have met hundreds of men who have said, "If it were not for Joseph Smith I could accept your religion." Any man who does not believe in Joseph Smith as a prophet of the true and the living God has no right to be in this Church. That revelation to Joseph Smith is the foundation stone. If Joseph Smith did not have that interview with God and Jesus Christ the whole Mormon fabric is a failure and a fraud. It is not worth anything on earth.[15]*

> *A year ago from this pulpit I spoke to the theme of Joseph Smith, the Prophet, indicating that, aside from Jesus Christ, I looked upon him as second in greatness to no other religious teacher that ever lived. And judged by the same standard used in judging greatness in men—by his works—as with Shakespeare, Washington, Lincoln, Einstein, etc. I still believe my view of him is correct and that he is the greatest man America ever produced. Hence I am convinced that he is deserving of a careful,*

---

[15] President Heber J. Grant, Conference Report, October 1939, Afternoon Meeting, 128-29. Note: All quotes from conference reports taken from LDS Collectors Library 2005. CD-ROM. Salt Lake City: LDS Media and Deseret Book, 2004.

thorough, and honest study by every person interested in his personal well-being. According to first-class evidence, Joseph Smith did actually, really see and hear the Father and the Son, two highly glorified beings, they seemed to him, in whose image man himself is made. If this is not a fact, he was the greatest religious fraud this world has ever seen. Between these two positions—prophet or fraud—there is no middle ground, or compromise. This is a strong statement, I admit, but certainly a correct one. Which of these two positions is the right one?[16]

But if Joseph Smith was not called of God, then this cause that we have espoused, and these proclamations that we make, are the greatest imposition and fraud that have been promulgated in the name of religion in the course of the history of the world. We are worse than the declining churches of the world if this cause is not true, because our proclamation is that the kingdom of God has been set up on the earth and that this very kingdom is destined to grow and increase and break in pieces all other kingdoms until it fills the whole earth.[17]

The fundamental question at hand is simply this: Do the actions, character, and demeanor of Joseph Smith Jr. and the founding fathers of the Mormon Church reflect the actions, character, and demeanor of the Lord Jesus Christ? Let me repeat that the fundamental question of this book is simply this: Do the actions, character, and demeanor of Joseph Smith Jr. and the founding fathers of the Mormon Church reflect the actions, character, and demeanor of the Lord Jesus Christ? I believe that throughout the chapters of this book you will feel the irreverence and crudeness I have felt. I believe that your soul will shiver with disgust at the very idea that the true author of the appalling doctrines discussed here, as taught by the Mormon Church, is Jesus Christ Himself. I believe that no Latter-day Saint, regardless of his or her position or prominence in the Church of Jesus Christ of Latter-day Saints can truthfully

---

[16] Elder Joseph F. Merrill, Conference Report, April 1948, Second Day—Morning Meeting, 70.

[17] Elder Bruce R. McConkie, Conference Report, October 1962, First Day—Morning Meeting, 9.

answer the charges presented in this book. I have personally endured the slow and painful education that many of these church leaders know what they do is wickedness, but the embarrassment of any change and the power of pride is apparently too high a price for them to consider any alternative. This, I believe, is the core strategy of the leadership of the Mormon Church: to protect at all costs the "good name of the church," even if that cost is the truth itself and a direct offense toward the Lord Jesus Christ.

Protecting the Good Name of the Church

One of the most important lessons of this book is simply one of life's most basic of lessons: you should not lie. Moreover, you should not lie to those whom you call brothers and sisters as you willingly take their time, their money, and their wives. It is wrong to lie about your college transcripts. It is wrong to lie about the mechanical history of a used car. And it is wrong to allow personal pride to fabricate a lie about your true beliefs. And it is particularly immoral and reprehensible to lie about any aspect of a religion in order to claim it is the only "true church" on the earth today. It is disgraceful beyond all measure to lie about a religion, promising that it is directed by those who have been given divine authority to speak for and in behalf of the Lord Jesus Christ Himself, when that is not true. True religion cannot be based on a truth that must be twisted, manipulated, or hidden in the perverted doctrines of men focused on sex, power, greed, and revenge. Truth is the core value of a religion. It can bring us to know the precise will and character of the Lord Jesus Christ. But according to Mormon doctrine, is it really, really true that Christ did not just approve of but vigorously "commanded" the doctrines of polygamy, polyandry, blood atonement, and lying on His behalf to bring forth a better people, to bring forth a better church?

I believe that much of the leadership of the Mormon Church understands completely the disgraceful actions taken by Joseph Smith Jr. and other Mormon Prophets in the name of the Lord; yet for reasons of pride and tradition, they continue under false pretense. The actual advice, official direction, and spiritual guidance from those whom I have dealt with during my journey of discovery are recorded here to stand forever as a witness to the continued defense of the immoral and arrogant leadership of the Mormon Church.

It will be extremely difficult for the Latter-day Saint reader to reflect on a number of the subjects and passages of this book without being offended or insulted. My intent is not to disrespect anyone—my own children and grandchildren, whom I love dearly, are active members of the Mormon Church. My intent is to present in the most accurate way possible—by using the exact words and teachings of the Mormon Prophets themselves—the very foundations and core values of what truly is the Mormon faith.

The narrative style of this book at times will seem very irregular, unpolished, or disorganized. All correct observations to be sure. And yet within that literary incompetence is the true reflection of my spiritual distress and my genuine frustration with the maze of treachery I have tolerated for the truth. Each of these feelings is now a deep-seated element of my personality, and the unfiltered communication of those feelings is paramount to this work. Another heartless, cynical, or disparaging review of the Mormon Church from an external perspective, from someone who has not lived it, is neither what is needed nor what this book is about.

For personal reasons, I have set very high standards for what is included here. Every quote or reference to the teachings of the Mormon leadership is authenticated from one or more official publications from the Church of Jesus Christ of Latter-day Saints. As such, I have surpassed even the accuracy standards of the church itself. The current lesson manuals of the Mormon Church confirms this bold statement. For example the manual Teachings of the Presidents of the Church: Joseph Smith, published by the Church of Jesus Christ of Latter-day Saints in 2007, notes on page 558 the following sources used in this book: "History of the Church, Sermons, Articles, Letters, Journals, Remembrances of others, and Scriptures." I have not used such independent and unauthorized sources as newspaper articles and personal journals and certainly not the remembrances of others, unless the church itself has chosen to place such comments within an official publication.

On December 7, 2008, I forced my own excommunication from the Church of Jesus Christ of Latter-day Saints for asking spiritually significant and doctrinally precise questions about the Mormon Church. That event ended thirty-two years of faithful service with a church that had profoundly changed my life—once upon entering and finally on departing. And yet on the day of my excommunication, it was obvious that the administrative action completed that morning did not remove a single fragment of my knowledge, training, or experiences within the Mormon Church. The managerial stroke of that pen did not remove in the slightest degree my understanding of the immoral history, corrupt procedures and policies, or bizarre ceremonies of the church. The events of that fateful day actually set me free—not just free from the unbearable association with the men in attendance that day, but also free from the very title of "a Mormon" and its inseparable affiliation with literally hundreds of men who have intentionally and repeatedly dishonored the very name of Jesus Christ for personal gain.

A Personal Invitation From the Author

I invite you now as a son or a daughter, as a brother or a sister in Christ, or as a total stranger, to discover the truth about Mormonism from the lessons of my life, from my true experiences as a Mormon High Priest and an ordained Bishop, and from the actual questions, letters, and conversations with the leadership of the Mormon Church, which have been documented here. This is a book about the truth, the simple truth, the plain truth, which has brought me to the very edge of life and then back again into His loving arms. I speak of a truth that will not require your deep analysis but rather a simple examination of the facts, the unquestionable facts, of the appalling doctrines and teachings of the Mormon leadership.

I speak of a truth that glorifies the very name of Jesus Christ and testifies of the breathtaking depth and mercy of His atonement. I speak of a truth that correctly places the moral responsibility of despicable acts of religious corruption and deception directly on the shoulders of the self-centered men who accomplished those acts.

I pray that the Spirit of Truth might be with you, that you might review with a ruthless skepticism each and every detail recorded here, that you might research every reference, every quote, and each of my conclusions for yourself. For what I have learned and present to you now is the well-documented fact that what a Latter-day Saint may think is "anti-Mormon" information is completely and authentically just simply "Mormon."

Lee B. Baker

Lee B. Baker, Former Mormon Bishop and High Priest

Caution: *Several derogatory terms of racial bigotry are referenced in this book. These expressions are direct quotes from the leadership of the Church of Jesus Christ of Latter-day Saints as recorded in the official church records. I express a deep regret for the use of these terms. They are used here to establish the historical demeanor of the leadership of the church and their continued and subsequent defense.*

CHAPTER ONE

The Mormon Legacy of Deflecting Dishonesty on Deity

For me to accurately relate factual and personal issues that are painful or, upon serious reflection, even embarrassing, I must and will speak from the depths of my heart with all honesty and integrity. What follows is true, simply and boldly true. I now understand and decisively believe—contrary to my thinking as a Latter-day Saint leader—that the truth matters and that the very pursuit of the truth is insincere if once truth is found no action is taken.

The primary goal of this effort is to inform, not to entertain. Represented in this book are the personal and spiritual highs and lows I experienced during my thirty-two years in the Mormon Church. Specifically, this story centers on the final and painful five-year journey of religious self-discovery in pursuit of the truth. I was an ordained Mormon Bishop,[1] a High Priest after the Order of Melchizedek; and within my priesthood line of authority,[2] the man who ordained me was ordained by the current Prophet of the Mormon Church, Thomas S. Monson. I suspect that at times this book will reflect some insensitive aspect of my character toward those in whom I once trusted. For that impression no apology will be offered, for they have intentionally and repeatedly deceived my family and me over the course of many years.

In retrospect, what follows in the next few paragraphs may be of only academic concern to the reader, but I honestly believe that a short personal history of my participation in the Mormon Church is important. The primary reason for this

---

[1] See official Bishop's Certificate, signed by the First Presidency of the Church of Jesus Christ of Latter-day Saints, appendix A document number 1.
[2] See official priesthood line of authority, appendix A documents numbers 2a, 2b and 3.

background is to establish a foundation of my activity, responsibility, and dedication to the Church of Jesus Christ of Latter-day Saints. From that perspective, the reader might better appreciate the personal injury and impact I have endured as a result of the evasive and empty promises of support, as well as the openly deceptive practices. A full disclosure of my positions and activities within the Mormon Church is provided within appendix A of this book.[3]

Again, it is important to understand at the very beginning of this ordeal that my goal was to understand the issues surrounding the history and doctrines in question. I had always considered the possibility that as a young convert to the church at the age of 19, I might have missed some basic appreciation for what was generally referred to as "anti-Mormon" subjects. My intent was to better understand these points of contention concerning the church so that I might better understand and teach the gospel, correct the lies of my critics, and support those I had baptized into the church. Because of my relatively long conversion to Mormonism, just over two years, and my extensive leadership experience in the church, I had often been asked to assist the missionaries with prospective members, known as investigators of the church.

As I came to know some of the inconsistencies of the church, I felt that with the enthusiastic spiritual support and vast knowledge of my fellow brethren, I would survive this testing of my faith. Fortunately, I did not survive that test, and that support never came. Yet I did survive this personal trial, which rapidly became the most significant spiritual and emotional event of my life, and it was worth surviving. It was worth surviving because this was the faith of my children and grandchildren. As a convert to the church and as the family patriarch, my actions alone led them into the Mormon faith. It was for the promised integrity of the Mormon faith that I had left Catholicism, the faith of my father. Mormonism was the

---

[3] For listing of ordnances, endowments, callings, and ordinations, see appendix A document number 17.

faith I had willingly donated thousands of hours and hundreds of thousands of dollars to. It was for this faith I had financed my only son's two-year mission to Brazil. I was by no means looking to tear down or expose the weaknesses of that in which I was clearly very active. I was looking for the truth, simply the truth. It eventually became clear to me from those with a strong legacy or impressive family history in the church that some subjects were never to be discussed in spite of the truth, or, more obviously, because of the truth.

Although as a Mormon High Priest I had been challenged several times in the past with these "anti-Mormon" subjects, I had always dismissed them as totally unfounded or simply invented. This was primarily due to the context of the subject matter itself. What shred of credibility could I possibly give a coworker or neighbor who would dare to accuse me, as a Latter-day Saint, of following the teachings of men who shared wives with each other, taught that Christ Himself was a polygamist, taught that the black race was here to represent the will of Satan, and that under the direction of the Mormon priesthood slicing the throat of another brother or sister (from ear to ear) was a suitable punishment for violations of the Mormon Temple Covenants? And yet that and so much more was actually taught and now defended as Mormon doctrine. I painfully came to understand exactly why others had not considered me to be Christian. Did they not understand that we as Latter-day Saints believed that Jesus Christ was at the head of our church? Did they not see the pictures of Christ in my living room or in the bedrooms of my dear children? Did they not know that the very name of Jesus Christ was in the title of the church itself? They knew all of these things, but they knew more. They knew the specific sections of the bizarre teachings within the Mormon Scriptures and within the official history of my own church, which I *did not know* of or comprehend.

Polygamy I knew to be a requirement from the Lord to care for the cherished sisters of the church who became widows on the long and dangerous Mormon Trail to Utah. The reality was far worse and far more sinister. When I came to understand polyandry, the taking of another man's wife, I became physically ill. "A common misconception concerning Joseph Smith's polyandry is that he participated in only one or two such unusual unions. In fact, fully one-third of his plural wives, eleven of them, were married civilly to other men when he married them."[4]

Over my three decades within the Mormon Church, it was not at all obvious to me that an entirely separate and much lower standard of conduct is reserved for the leadership of the Church of Jesus Christ of Latter-day Saints. The high standard of behavior for the general priesthood membership of the church, but apparently *not* for the leadership, is clearly stated as Mormon Scripture from Jesus Christ Himself:

> *That they may be conferred upon us, it is true; but when we undertake to cover our sins, or to gratify our pride, our vain ambition, or to exercise control or dominion or compulsion upon the souls of the children of men, in any degree of unrighteousness, behold, the heavens withdraw themselves; the Spirit of the Lord is grieved; and when it is withdrawn, Amen to the priesthood or the authority of that man. (Doctrine and Covenants 121:37)[5]*

As this passage from the Mormon Scriptures, Doctrine and Covenants 121:37, will be referenced many times within this book, I feel it necessary to place it within some context specific to the Mormon Priesthood. To clarify the Mormon Scripture referenced here, I will note that in teaching the men and boys who hold the Mormon Priesthood, this Scripture has been referenced over 100 times within the General Conferences of the Mormon Church as the standard of moral behavior. Specifically, the phrase: *"Amen* to the priesthood or the

---

[4] Todd Compton, *In Sacred Loneliness: The Plural Wives of Joseph Smith* (Salt Lake City, Signature Books, 1997), 15. This book was awarded the Mormon History Association's Book of the Year and is listed at lds.org. In the author's estimation, Mr. Compton's book is the definitive work on the subject of the plural wives of Joseph Smith Jr.

[5] This prophecy was given to Joseph Smith Jr. while he was a prisoner in the jail at Liberty, Missouri, dated March 20, 1839.

authority of that man" clearly indicates that the *authority* of the man who abuses that priesthood power, examples of which are provided within the Scripture itself, is as a result of such abuse rendered that priesthood totally invalid, finished, useless and thus powerless to represent the Lord. And as such, that now invalid priesthood authority caused by the self-gratifying actions of a man cannot therefore be passed to any other person in the Church.

Remarkably, the finest illustration of precisely this point comes from one of the most Senior Mormon Leaders as a clarification found within the sermon *"Many Called But Few Chosen"*, delivered by N. Eldon Tanner, First Counselor to the Prophet of the Mormon Church, as recorded within the General Conference Report of April 1970, given during the General Priesthood Meeting:

> *"I should like to read just a few words to you, taken from the Doctrine and Covenants:"*

> *"Behold, there are many called, but few are chosen. And why are they not chosen? Because their hearts are set so much upon the things of this world, and aspire to the honors of men, that they do not learn this one lesson."*

> *"That they may be conferred upon us, it is true; but when we undertake to cover our sins, or to gratify our pride, our vain ambition, or to exercise control or dominion or compulsion upon the souls of the children of men, in any degree of unrighteousness, behold, the heavens withdraw themselves; the Spirit of the Lord is grieved; and when it is withdrawn, Amen to the priesthood or the authority of that man."*

> *"I interpret that as referring to those who fail to magnify their priesthood, or who use it as it should not be used."*

As a non-Mormon, your complete understanding of this point and its associated Mormon Scripture is paramount, in that, one of the key positions of this book, as validated by my own life experiences within that Church, is that this the most serious of all warnings to honor the Mormon Priesthood is intended for all Mormon men holding the Priesthood. Yet, as this book will document time and time again, this standard and warning of moral behavior, seems not to be of any concern nor is it effectively applied to the Senior Leadership of the Mormon Faith itself.

There are only two possible options concerning exactly how and by whom the Mormon Church is directed. The first possibility is that the Mormon Prophets in the past were acting on behalf of Jesus Christ Himself, the Redeemer of all mankind, and in so doing, Christ alone is the Author of polygamy, polyandry, blood atonement, murder, and the countless lies provided to the government of the United States of America. If this is true, I have made the most horrendous mistake of my life by forcing my excommunication from The Mormon Church in December of 2008. Or is the second possibility more likely, as I believe it is: that the Mormon Prophets have acted egotistically and not on behalf of Jesus Christ? In this case, the Mormon Prophets have been enthusiastically and personally sustained by Mormon leaders like Steven T. Rockwood, Michael D. Jones, and Lorin M. Lund, who have, I believe, essentially laid these repulsive actions of the Mormon Prophets at the feet of the Savior Himself. This I believe they have done in an attempt to stain the garments of Jesus Christ, to make Him responsible for the sins of men, the very men who have used His holy name to further their own personal desires. This book will examine the specific teachings of those deceitful men and the dishonest, but very contemporary, Latter-day Saint strategy that continues to defend them to this day. It is this very practice of deflecting such deceit onto the Lord Himself that cannot be considered a legitimate principle of Christianity. As such, I believe that an individual Latter-day Saint who does not practice such disloyalty against Christ may well be considered a Christian, but the Church of Jesus Christ of Latter-day Saints as a whole, which teaches that these disgraceful actions were from the Lord alone, *cannot* be considered Christian.

In the spring of 2005 a coworker asked me, "After over thirty years in the Mormon Church, how did you *not* know about the corruption?" Although I did not have an answer then, I now understand it to be as simple as this: "You don't know what you don't know." With the extraordinary discovery of the truth and through serious reflection on my life as an active Mormon Bishop, alternate titles for this work might have been, *The Mormon Psychology of a Selective Church History* or *How the Mormons Throw Jesus under the Bus.*

In the office where I work, and especially on Fridays, some of the more enthusiastic sports supporters wear the team jerseys of their favorite players. The colors, numbers, and names span the gambit of every sport known to mankind. The deliberate and public association with a specific team clearly communicates one's allegiance and devotion to that team.

After spending over twenty years in the United States Army, serving in several overseas locations, I know well the feeling and responsibility of representing both the armed forces generally and the United States of America specifically. Observers, who may hold feelings shaped by different experiences and perceptions than ours, may view our membership in association with a particular organization quite differently. How we view our participation within any organization is dependent on what we know or perceive about that organization. Although it was somewhat belated due to my ignorance, I remember very clearly my profound embarrassment after I had spoken with several older native Hawaiians about the local history of the islands. The simple fact of history was precisely set forth by an elderly Hawaiian, who told me, "In January of 1893, our Queen Lili'uokalani was violently overthrown by very powerful and self-centered American businessmen to take this land. Any other questions, white boy?" Again, the point is that we don't know, what we don't know.

In 1831, President Andrew Jackson signed the Indian Removal Act, which began the forced relocation and horrendous suffering of the entire Cherokee Nation. The United

States government time and time again cheated this loyal and trusting tribe that once was our strong ally against the British. Once I came to know the facts and fully understood the brutal and deceptive removal of the Cherokee, as well as several other tribes along what was know as the Trail of Tears, the portrait of President Andrew Jackson on the twenty-dollar bill never looked the same again.

At times in our life, we use what we might perceive as our first-rate associations or relationships to further our own influence or respect. But we might be surprised to learn that it is the perception and impact we have on others that honestly reflects the true worth of our most treasured associations. In some intellectual or high social circles, my thirty-four-year association with the United States Military may not be considered very admirable. The sensitive individual will consider his impact on the lives of others above his own self-interest. For many years, I was not such an individual. I assumed that merely being a Mormon would project all the good points of Mormonism. I had come to believe that just being a Mormon would, by and large, communicate to those around me that I was to be considered honest, loyal, and trustworthy.

What I did not know was explicitly what, or just how much, *they* knew about Mormons. It is true that the many critics of my faith did not know the true happiness I had come to cherish within my family and the enormous improvements in my personal life, all of which were a direct result of my membership in the Mormon Church. And they could not have known that my profound love and respect for my wife was also a product of my association with good Mormon men and women who loved the Lord.

The collections of teachings that the critics of the Mormon Church knew, which I did not, were truly disturbing but certainly not the lies I had been told they were. It was the fact that these terrible things were both true and had come directly from the Prophets of my own church that left me with no pre-rehearsed denial. I was soon introduced to a strange spiritual and physiological ballet, which the leadership of the church had choreographed around, through, and over the truth of these unique Mormon doctrines. This delicate dance between the truth and the unconditional need to protect "the good name of the church" confused and insulted me on many levels.

If my non-Mormon coworkers and extended family already knew the details about the Mountain Meadows Massacre, blood atonement, polygamy, and polyandry directly from church resources, then who were the Mormon Church leaders concealing this shocking information from? It took me some time to fully understand that the restriction of such information was directed at me and others who were already members of the church who might ask for some clarification concerning the previously unknown doctrines. For a time I truly resented and then envied those non-Mormons who were free to research and discuss these topics without constraint or condemnation. As an active Mormon, I was not to question the version of Mormon history given to me. A very curious, almost self-sufficient historical logic is very common among Mormons, in that they view Mormon history as uniquely separate from American or world history. It is this independent view of history that permits the church to alter, rewrite, or retell historical events as if the church were the only participant or witness.[6] Even intelligent Mormon Leaders like Dr. Lorin M. Lund seemed to be unable to grasp the idea that Mormon history is an integral part of American history. On one occasion, I forwarded a set of questions to Dr. Lund, who was also my Mormon priesthood advisor and mentor. He had earlier said that he would help me with my questions. Although he never provided even the slightest trace of support, he did forward what would become the all-too-typical questions about the questions: "These are very interesting questions. How did they come up in your conversations? Are they reading the Journal of Discourses and searching the Utah state government historical website?"[7] I

---

[6] See appendix B for a brief chronology of Mormon history.

[7] Lorin M. Lund, e-mail message to Lee Baker, August 16, 2005. Subject: A few questions to help me out.

would come to understand that an investigator (someone interested in joining the church) or a new member of the church could ask questions for a limited time, but an active member and priesthood holder would be shunned and ridiculed for such questions.

What I have lived through, including the hundreds of Mormon temple ceremonies, and more specifically what I have witnessed and then documented from the leadership of the Mormon Church, is all here and all true. My life and what is offered here is a living testimony that the deceptions of the early church are deeply embedded in the current leadership of the Mormon Church. I have been lied to and lied about. I have been the victim of several deliberate deceptions by the leadership of the Church of Jesus Christ of Latter-day Saints, and still I count this "awakening" among the greatest blessings of my life. As an ordained Bishop and High Priest, I submitted to the leadership of the Mormon Church a list of core questions that have been the very foundation of my recognition that the church is thoroughly and completely false.[8] A summary of those questions follows.

> **Question:** Did Joseph Smith Jr. follow the Laws of the Gospel governing the plurality of wives as recorded in Mormon Scriptures, specifically the 1876 publication of the Doctrine and Covenants (canonized Scripture) of the Church of Jesus Christ of Latter-day Saints, 132:61-64?

> **Question:** Why did the 1835 to 1876 publication of the Doctrine and Covenants (canonized Scripture) of the Church of Jesus Christ of Latter-day Saints teach extremely harsh opposition to the practice of polygamy during the very height of the actual practice by Joseph Smith Jr. and so many others?

---

[8] The Lorin M. Lund questions represent the fundamental questions to be asked of the Mormon Church. See chapter 5 for the complete questions and all references and footnotes taken from authorized publications of the Church of Jesus Christ of Latter-day Saints.

Question: Were the actions of the Prophet Joseph Smith Jr., specific to the practice and teachings of polyandry (taking another man's wife), really under the solemn direction and commandment of the Lord Jesus Christ Himself, or were they simply the acts of a self-centered man?

Question: How is the general membership of the church or the public at large to decide what "officially" recorded and published teachings of the Prophets and General Authorities *is* or *is not* to be considered Scripture? How is it that the Book of Mormon teachings of Alma, Lehi, Nephi, Mormon, and King Benjamin are unquestionably Scripture, but the official teachings of the modern-day Prophets like Joseph Smith Jr., Brigham Young, John Taylor, Spencer W. Kimball, or Thomas S. Monson are *at times not* Scripture?

Question: Did Brigham Young alone initiate the restriction against blacks holding the Mormon priesthood based on his personal prejudice, or was it a legitimate commandment from the Lord Jesus Christ, which the Prophet Joseph Smith Jr. preferred neither to follow nor to record?

Question: In view of the overwhelming and clear requirement for all members of the Mormon faith to avoid any association with pornography, how can an Area Authority, Elder J. W. Marriott, of the Church of Jesus Christ of Latter-day Saints, who sits in judgment of moral and ethical church disciplinary actions, profit significantly from the sale of pornography within his hotels and resorts and yet still be allowed to continue to hold the Mormon priesthood and represent the church in a senior leadership position and, presumably, the Lord Jesus Christ Himself?

Question: With a seventy-five-year history of active opposition to the laws of the United States of America, how is the current Latter-day Saint to reconcile the history of the church in relationship to the Twelfth Article of Faith as Scripture, written in 1843 ("We believe in being subject to kings, presidents, rulers, and magistrates, in obeying, honoring, and sustaining the *law*.") and Doctrine and Covenants 58:21 ("Let no man break the *laws* of the land for he that keepeth the *laws* of God hath no need to break the *laws* of the land.") as Scripture written by Joseph Smith in 1831?

Question: If it were not true as Scripture,[9] then why within the official general conferences of the Church of Jesus Christ of Latter-day Saints would Mormon Prophets teach that:

- Jesus Christ had many wives during His mission here on earth and that by them He had several children.

- Some of the sins of men are not covered by the atonement of Christ, and as such brothers and sisters in the church could have their throats slit from ear to ear.

- Without question, there are many living inhabitants on both the moon and the sun.

- The black race is on this earth to better represent the will of Satan.

From a true Christian perspective, it is disheartening to review the numerous justifications available to those Latter-day Saint leaders who manipulate or conceal the truth, Mormon leaders like Steven T. Rockwood, Michael D. Jones, or Lorin M. Lund. I believe that one of the most corrupt, yet brilliant

---

[9] Sermons by the General Authorities of the church during general conference are to be considered Scripture. See Doctrine and Covenants 68:4: When holy men of God write or speak by the power of the Holy Ghost, their words "shall be scripture, shall be the will of the Lord, shall be the mind of the Lord, shall be the word of the Lord, shall be the voice of the Lord, and the power of God unto salvation."

and effective, strategies has been to implant deep into the Latter-day Saint leader's mind the unwavering need to "defend the Prophets." Nothing whatsoever can discourage the active Latter-day Saint leader from the passionate defense of the Prophets and pioneers or their own posterity. Not the truth, not the Scriptures, not even the tender love and divine character of the Lord Himself is of any value in opposition to the egotistical teachings of the Mormon Prophets.

To better illustrate the division of personal knowledge and responsibility that I have encountered within the Mormon Church, I have mentally organized a three-tiered "grouping" of the total membership of the church. The division into groups represented here is based on the associated knowledge of each individual within that group as it relates to their awareness and thus responsibility concerning the many deceptions of the church itself. I describe these groups so that you might understand that not all Latter-day Saints are aware of all aspects of Mormonism. I know very well specific Latter-day Saints in each group described here. I have watched some of my dearest friends move spiritually from one uninformed and blissful, cheerful group of members in the church to a position of sure knowledge that something was very wrong, yet sincerely not knowing exactly what to do about it.

Group One—Doing the Right Thing Before the Lord

The average members of the Church of Jesus Christ of Latter-day Saints are kind, considerate of others, and faithful to what they know to be the character and teachings of the Lord Jesus Christ. They are devoted to the core values of the family and to the truthfulness of the church. In all aspects of life, they strive to do the right thing before the Lord.

This group, who by my estimation represents the majority of the Mormon Church, simply does not know, and may not want to know, of the shocking actions and teachings of the church leadership. They believe and act on the well-known and exceptionally good principles of the church that are taught today. There are many outstanding examples of community service, neighborly compassion, and true Christian values at work within this, the most wholesome group of Latter-day Saints. In a very real sense, their total devotion to the "restored gospel" has caused them to be uniquely oblivious or selectively ignorant of the distasteful doctrines of the "restored gospel," regardless of the authenticity or true history of those appalling doctrines.

This collection of genuinely pleasant and spiritually uncompromising Latter-day Saints is most often used by the leadership to characterize the *entire* church. It is my belief that the average member of the Church of Jesus Christ of Latter-day Saints is vastly superior to the leadership of the church, both past and present, in regard to individual character, morality, and honesty. This observation comes from over thirty years of membership in the Mormon Church, holding many leadership positions, and most importantly from my personal dealings with the senior leadership and management of the church itself.

Simply stated, the majority of the general membership of the Church of Jesus Christ of Latter-day Saints has been intentionally and systematically deceived. This deception has fashioned the ultimate "sheep's clothing" from under which the "wolves" can maneuver without detection. Within the Mormon Church the beliefs of the average member, when plainly spoken, are morally and spiritually incompatible with the teachings of the leadership.

One of the greatest injustices against the average Latter-day Saint is that corrupt men use the lives of these tender and compassionate people as examples to the world of just how good they, the leaders, are. Time and time again the average Latter-day Saint is left alone to explain, defend, or justify the questionable actions of their own leaders. These are disgraceful actions, which the general members find very hard to discuss, not because they know them to be true doctrine from the Lord, but because they maintain a much higher standard of integrity and character than those whom they are now asked to defend.

Why would a young Latter-day Saint woman hesitate to ask her mother, her sister, or her grandmother to explain why Joseph Smith took the wives of other men without telling his first wife, Emma, about it, if the action were truly from the Lord?

Group Two—Doing the Right Thing Within One's Calling

In the Church of Jesus Christ of Latter-day Saints, men and women are "called" to a specific position of leadership or service in the church. Often the responsibilities of the "calling" include an accountability to represent both the standards of the Lord and of the church. Generally this group consists of the local leadership of the church. They are very dedicated to their callings and are only vaguely aware of the peculiar teachings or questionable events in church history. This group is uniquely compelled by their position in the church to defend the church above and beyond normal spiritual or emotional rationale, for they are functionally a part of the very organization responsible for any potential deception. I believe that by whatever method we become aware that an insulting doctrine, teaching, or action has been taken in the name of Jesus Christ, we are responsible to correct or identify the offense; if we do not, we personally become an accomplice to some degree in that sin against the Lord. Several local leaders of the church have told me directly that they either did not want to know any more about such offenses against the Lord or that it was not their position to cast judgment on the "Prophets of the Lord." This extremely popular position is the very foundation of the "Mormon psychology of a selective church history."

Some years ago a former Stake President of ours told me and my wife during an interview in his office, "I have wondered if the Lord took Joseph [Smith] early in life because he may have taken liberties within the practice of polygamy." His comment was very sincere but seemed to include just a hint of anxiety. It was as if he were saying, "It might be true, but what can really be done about it?" I believe that whatever station or position we might think we occupy in this life, at the very moment we accept the Lord Jesus Christ as our personal Savior, no other loyalty or allegiance should overshadow the depth of our obligation to Him. I have often been disgusted that the lack of commitment to doing the right thing before the Lord is driven by potential embarrassment or a passionate dedication to the Latter-day Saint family or the legacy of the Latter-day Saint pioneer spirit, which has been venerated well beyond reason. In another heartbreaking example of seriously misplaced loyalties, a Bishop of ours, during one of the very first reviews of these sensitive questions, stated, "I do not want to know any more; it really scares me."

Group Three—Defending the Good Name of the Church

Within the organizational structures of the Mormon Church, there are administrative directives that on occasion require a consideration of the events at hand and how these events might reflect on the "good name of the church." As a Bishop or as a member of a stake High Council, I personally participated in at least a dozen required disciplinary actions against members of the congregation who had violated one or more standards of the church. In each case, a portion of the proceedings dealt with the consideration and assurance that the "good name of the church" had been protected. A serious evaluation of any real or perceived injury to the "good name of the church" is taken prior to any final judgment or verdict. I have often contemplated just who looks after the "good name of the Lord" within these proceedings and why there is not an administrative directive to consider His potential injury by the very teaching of the church.

No church administered by men, even the best of men, is without mistakes or without some degree of scandal or criticism. Even the frailties and failures of the first Apostles who walked and talked with the Savior Himself are recorded in the Scriptures, Peter chief among them. We know of these weaknesses, because they are documented in the Holy Scriptures themselves. These examples have been preserved, so that we, in our hour of weakness, might learn from them and be inspired by the enormous strength and recovery of these great men.

We know of and deal with the failures and lies of our political and civic leaders, as well as our own family members, but among the past and present leadership of the Latter-day Saint faith, no such imperfection can be admitted. To me, the complete and utter tenacity applied to the defense of the questionable actions of the Mormon Prophets and Apostles is essentially an acknowledgment of events far worse than what we know of now.

This group, the very leadership of the Mormon Church, are simply wicked in that that they would have the Lord Jesus Christ Himself take full, absolute, and complete responsibility for the self-centered and morally depraved actions of the Mormon Prophets. This they do effortlessly rather than admit that they too have suffered at times from the mistakes of men, the desires of men, and the disappointment common to the leadership of men. They would have us believe that the frustrations known throughout the world, throughout all known history, concerning the corruptness of men with any degree of power and prestige has *never* been an issue within nearly 180 years of Mormon leadership.

As a former Latter-day Saint Bishop and an active member of the church for over thirty years, I understand with the utmost clarity that two essential elements of defense will be paramount to the Latter-day Saint reader. First is the position or opinion that this book, its research, and its primary goal are obviously "anti-Mormon." Second is the claim that what is referenced here specific to the Mormon Prophets of the past is just that— "in the past"—and that we should not attempt to play the teachings of the past Prophets against the teachings of the living Prophet. I understand fully and totally agree that in Mormon teaching and practice the guidance of the living Prophet surpasses the direction of all previous Prophets.

As a final preparation to invite you to honestly consider the several points of this book, I would like to address each of these assertions in some detail.

These Subjects and Comments Are Obviously Anti-Mormon

On many occasions I have cautioned my coworkers, friends, and Catholic family members that anti-Mormon remarks are offensive. I remain committed to that declaration to this very day. Further, I believe that my resolve is even stronger after coming to an understanding of what is genuinely anti-Mormon and what is simply Mormon. As this is such a critical element in the defense of the church—that is, to simply and completely dismiss any disagreeable subject as "anti-Mormon"—consider the following examples in contrast.

The denial of Christ by Peter is no abstract example of a total and complete spiritual failure. Not only did Peter deny Christ, but he also began to curse and to swear to those who accused him of any association with the Galilean criminal now under arrest. He emphatically claimed that he did not know this man. Simon Peter walked with the Lord Jesus Christ, and the Master taught him personally. Peter witnessed firsthand the most significant events of the life of the Savior, and yet he failed. Not only did he fail, but his total spiritual collapse also was to be recorded for all mankind to consider. His failure to stand by Jesus in His hour of need is graphically documented by Matthew, Mark, Luke, and John. Who among us has not felt the complete and utter despair of Peter? Yet, we know in our hearts that this horrific event was both acknowledged and then recorded in the Holy Scriptures so that we might have hope in our weaknesses and some measure of trust in the mercy and forgiveness of the very Master who forgave Peter.

I ask this question: Who among us would call this account of Peter's denunciation of Christ "anti-Christian"? Who among us could call Matthew, Mark, Luke, and John irresponsible, dishonest or "anti-Christian" for recording this graphic account of a truly heart-wrenching event? Who among us would consider the Holy Scriptures complete without this example of a chosen Apostle of the Lord, who failed and yet was redeemed?

When Stephen Ambrose, Gore Vidal, or Norman Mailer teaches us the accurate history of our country, its leaders, and general and social reformers with their associated great successes and miserable failures, is this then called anti-American literature? When we come to know the truly inspirational and the truly disgraceful details of the significant political and military events that have shaped this great country, neither that knowledge nor those who communicate it to us are called anti-American. Yet the culture of Mormonism labels any disclosure of dishonorable truth within its own history as anti-Mormon. Within the traditions and society of Mormonism, the truth, however well documented, is censored, altered, or labeled as anti-Mormon to keep the membership ignorant of the facts. The self-centered and self-preserving motivations and deceitful tactics of the early Mormon leadership are alive and well in this current generation of local and national Mormon leaders. They have distorted and concealed their own teachings to better blend into the Christian mainstream, but they are no more Christian now then they were when Joseph Smith Jr. boasted of doing more than Christ Himself.

> *I have more to boast of than ever any man had. I am the only man that has ever been able to keep a whole church together since the days of Adam. A large majority of the whole have stood by me. Neither Paul, John, Peter, nor Jesus ever did it. I boast that no man ever did such a work as I.* [10]

Author's Note: "For by grace are ye saved through faith; and that not of yourselves: [it is] the gift of God: Not of works, lest any man should boast" (Eph. 2:8-9).

I submit to you that the words, actions, and teachings of the Mormon Prophets, when taken from the official and authoritative documents of the church itself, cannot be anti-Mormon; they are simply Mormon. How is it that one generation of

---

[10] Smith, *History of the Church*, 6:408-9.

Mormons can attend the official semi-annual general conference of the church, listen in fervent admiration to the teachings of the living Prophet of God, and then a second generation of Mormons has both the audacity and ignorance to label the very same teachings of that day as anti-Mormon? This dilemma is especially perplexing if no succeeding Prophet of the church has corrected the earlier teachings, which are now viewed as anti-Mormon. The inconsistency is not the teachings of the Prophets, not the subject of the revelation, and certainly not the authority by which it was delivered to the faithful of the church. The only variable is why and who is quoting the Prophet. As an active Bishop in Hawaii, and as the High Priest Group Leader in Columbia, Maryland, I have quoted Brigham Young as stating, "I have never yet preached a sermon and sent it out to the children of men, that they may not call Scripture."[11] Yet, when I quote the very same words of Brigham Young from the very same resource, now it becomes just another typical anti-Mormon statement, as I am at present an "excommunicated" Bishop.

It is obvious to me now that the selective, subjective, and diversionary comments of many Latter-day Saints, from the leadership in Salt Lake City to your next-door neighbor, are representative of a culture of deception. I have witnessed both an astonishing and frightening transformation concerning the teachings of the Mormon Prophets, related not to what those teachings are but to *who* quotes from those teachings. As an illustration of hypocrisy or false pretense, I would like to document a few examples of valid points of instruction, which instantly become "anti-Mormon" when a non-Mormon uses the exact same passages.

> *We believe in being subject to kings, presidents, rulers, and magistrates, in obeying, honoring, and sustaining the law. (Twelfth Article of Faith)*

---

[11] President Brigham Young. *Journal of Discourses*, 1870, 13:95. Note: Quotes from *Journal of Discourses* are taken from *LDS Collector's Library* 2005 CD-Rom.

If the above were a true principle, how could the following come about?

"In 1882, The United States Congress passes the Edmunds Bill, making plural marriage a felony and prohibiting polygamists from voting, holding public office or performing jury duty."[12]

Note: Polygamy continued within the Mormon Church from 1831 on, despite the fact that the Illinois State Law of Bigamy, 1833 (Section 121, pages 198-99), specifically prohibits the act.

***

"We believe in being subject to kings, presidents, rulers, and magistrates, in obeying, honoring, and sustaining the law."

If the above were a true principle, how could the following come about?

President John Taylor "receives word during a visit to California that federal officials have ordered his arrest for practicing polygamy. Returns to Salt Lake City on 27 January. On 1 February 1885, preaches his last public sermon and, in hopes of limiting the persecution against the Church by federal authorities, goes into hiding."[13]

Author's Note: Polygamy continued unabated within the Mormon Church.

***

"We believe in being subject to kings, presidents, rulers, and magistrates, in obeying, honoring, and sustaining the law."

If the above were a true principle, how could the

---

[12] *Teachings of the Presidents of the Church, Wilford Woodruff* (Salt Lake City: Intellectual Reserve, 2004), xiii.

[13] *Teachings of the Presidents of the Church, John Taylor* (Salt Lake City: Intellectual Reserve, 2001), x.

following come about?

"*Many of America's religious and political leaders became very angry when they learned that Latter-day Saints living in Utah were encouraging a marriage system that they considered immoral and unchristian. A great political crusade was launched against the Church and its members. The United States Congress passed legislation that curbed the freedom of the latter-day Saints and hurt the Church economically. This legislation ultimately caused officers to arrest and imprison men who had more than one wife and to deny them the right to vote, the right to privacy in their homes, and the enjoyment of other civil liberties.*[14]

Author's Note: Polygamy continued unabated within the Mormon Church.

***

"*We believe in being subject to kings, presidents, rulers, and magistrates, in obeying, honoring, and sustaining the law.*"

If the above were a true principle, how could the following come about?

"*The United States Congress passes the Edmunds-Tucker Act, another anti-polygamy law, allowing the federal government to confiscate much of the Church's real estate. The act becomes law on March 3, 1887.*"[15]

Author's Note: Polygamy continued unabated within the Mormon Church.

***

"*We believe in being subject to kings, presidents, rulers, and magistrates, in obeying, honoring, and sustaining the law.*"

If the above were a true principle, how could the following come about?

---

[14] *Our Heritage: A Brief History of the Church of Jesus Christ of Latter-day Saints* (Salt Lake City: Church of Jesus Christ of Latter-day Saints, 1996), 97.

[15] *Teachings of the Presidents of the Church, Wilford Woodruff*, xiii.

"Part of the difficulty, of course, was the natural aversion Americans held against 'polygamy.' This new system appeared to threaten the strongly entrenched tradition of monogamy and the solidarity of the family structure."[16]

Author's Note: Polygamy continued unabated within the Mormon Church.

***

"We believe in being subject to kings, presidents, rulers, and magistrates, in obeying, honoring, and sustaining the law."

If the above were a true principle, how could the following come about?

"The Mormon Church not only offends the moral sense of manhood by sanctioning polygamy, but prevents the administration of justice through ordinary instrumentalities of law."[17]

Author's Note: Polygamy continued unabated within the Mormon Church.

***

"Polygamy in the Territories, destructive of the family relation and offensive to the moral sense of the civilized world, shall be repressed."[18]

Note: Polygamy continues within the early Mormon Church.

***

"Throughout the paper (Nauvoo Expositor [June 1844]) they accused Joseph Smith of teaching vicious principles, practicing whoredoms, advocating so-called spiritual wifery, grasping for political power."[19]

---

[16] *Church History in the Fulness of Times* (Salt Lake City: Church of Jesus Christ of Latter-day Saints, 1989), 256.

[17] President James A. Garfield, Inaugural Address, March 4, 1881.

[18] President Grover Cleveland, Inaugural Address, March 4, 1885.

[19] *Church History in the Fulness of Times*, 275.

Author's Note: The church manual quoted above implies that the *Nauvoo Expositor* wrongly accused Joseph of "spiritual wifery," and yet the Doctrine and Covenants records below the doctrine of "plurality of wives."

Section notes, Doctrine and Covenants, Section 132: *"Revelation given through Joseph Smith the Prophet, at Nauvoo, Illinois, recorded July 12, 1843, relating to the new and everlasting covenants, including the eternity of the marriage covenant, as also plurality of wives. HC 5:501-507. Although the revelation was recorded in 1843, it is evident from the historical records that the doctrines and principles involved in this revelation had been known by the Prophet since 1831."*

***

"The brethren unanimously sustained a motion to propose their own ticket with Joseph Smith as their candidate for president."[20]

Author's Note: The church manual implies that the *Nauvoo Expositor* wrongly accused Joseph of "grasping for political power." Yet the very same manual, only six pages previously documented that Joseph was in fact "grasping for political power" seeking to become the president of the United States.

***

"We must not treat lightly the counsel from the President of the Church."[21]

If the above were a true principle, how could the following come about?

"Do not, brethren, put your trust in man though he be a Bishop, an Apostle, or President; if you do, they will fail you at some time or place; they will do wrong or seem to, and your

---

[20] Ibid., 269.

[21] *Teachings of the Presidents of the Church, Wilford Woodruff,* 201.

support be gone; but if we lean on God, He never will fail us. "[22]

Author's Note: A search of conference addresses and lessons within church publications on the theme of "Follow the Prophet" number nearly five hundred. Was President Cannon, who served as a counselor to Presidents Brigham Young, John Taylor, Wilford Woodruff, and Lorenzo Snow, wrong in his recommendation not to trust these men?

The above represents only a small collection of obvious examples of selective hypocrisy and diametrically opposed, but official, statements by the church leadership on identical subjects. This strategy not only speaks to the inconsistency of the church doctrine, but it also provides the opportunity for deception by quoting multiple sources of opposing positions, a very versatile technique for teaching depending on the audience and the message required at the time.

Teachings of the Past Prophets and the Value of a Living Prophet

Within the Church of Jesus Christ of Latter-day Saints, the current and living Prophet of the church is both the president of the corporation of the church and the only man on the earth who holds all the keys of the priesthood and is authorized to receive revelation for the entire church. Below is a typical affirmation of that belief, as stated during one of the many semiannual general conferences of the Church of Jesus Christ of Latter-day Saints:

> *I move that, recognizing Wilford Woodruff as the President of the Church of Jesus Christ of Latter-day Saints, and the only man on the earth at the present time who holds the keys of the sealing ordinances, we consider him fully authorized by virtue of*

---

[22] President George Q. Cannon, *Gospel Truth: Discourses and Writings of President George Q. Cannon,* 2nd ed. (1957; repr., Salt Lake City: Deseret Book, 1987), 249. Originally published in the *Millennial Star* 53 (October 1891).

his position to issue the Manifesto which has been read in our hearing and which is dated September 24th, 1890, and that as a Church in General Conference assembled, we accept his declaration concerning plural marriages as authoritative and binding.[23]

Formalities notwithstanding, as polygamy continued long after the first manifesto denouncing the practice in 1890, this church-wide recognition of the power and authority of the President of the church is sufficient for the discussion at hand. I have been told several times by Stake President Michael D. Jones, of the Arvada Colorado Stake, that I should "follow the keys, follow the keys," meaning the keys of the priesthood. This reprimand was in reference to my inability to understand the Mormon philosophy that whatever the Prophet says or does is of the Lord. My rebuttal to President Jones, a large and powerful man, was that my issue was with the teachings of the past Prophets that had not been corrected by the succeeding Prophets. An example of how that can happen follows.

You see some classes of the human family that are black, uncouth, uncomely, disagreeable and low in their habits, wild, and seemingly deprived of nearly all the blessings of the intelligence that is generally bestowed upon mankind.[24]

Shall I tell you the law of God in regard to the African race? If the white man who belongs to the chosen seed mixes his blood with the seed of Cain, the penalty, under the law of God, is death on the spot. This will always be so.[25]

I remind you that no man who makes disparaging remarks concerning those of another race can consider himself a true

---

[23] President George Albert Smith, Conference Report, October 1947, Afternoon Meeting, 165. He is reviewing what President Lorenzo Snow stated in 1890.

[24] President Brigham Young, General Conference, October 1859. *Journal of Discourses* 7:291. Quotes from the *Journal of Discourses* taken from *LDS Collector's Library 2005.*

[25] President Brigham Young, Salt Lake Tabernacle, March 1863. *Journal of Discourses* 10:110.

disciple of Christ.[26]

In this case, President Hinckley in 2006 clearly and concisely corrected the earlier teachings of Brigham Young in both 1859 and 1863. It was straightforward and the right thing to do. And yet the church did not collapse the next day. I believe that it is possible for any organization, especially a religious organization that claims to be the "only true church on the earth today," to correct irregularities or mistakes in doctrine. In the case of Mormonism, it is the foundation itself, specifically the early years of the church, that is suspect, and with each passing year, the modern Church of Jesus Christ of Latter-day Saints endeavors to assimilate more to the mainstream of Christianity. It has been my observation that no other reportedly Christian church has undergone more changes in such a shorter period of time than Mormonism. In the early years of the church, being different was a hallmark to be proud of. Today, however, the unique and peculiar doctrines of the church have been pushed backstage or de-emphasized whenever possible.

Not the least among these potentially embarrassing doctrines is the fact that Joseph Smith as a Prophet of the Lord issued an unfulfilled "Prophecy" which remains in the Mormon Doctrine and Covenants (84:1-5). This "Prophecy" clearly states that the New Jerusalem and its Temple will be built in Missouri in "*this*" (the current) generation. So confident of this "Prophecy" was the church, that even the Mormon Apostle Orson Pratt decisively affirmed in 1870 that: "*The Latter-day Saints just as much expect to receive a fulfillment of that promise during the generation that was in existence in 1832 as they expect that the sun will rise and set tomorrow. Why? Because God cannot lie. He will fulfil all His promises.*" As neither the city of New Jerusalem nor its Temple was ever built, as Joseph's "Prophecy" claims, we should then turn to Deuteronomy 18:22 for the following guidance from the Holy

---

[26] President Gordon B. Hinckley, General Conference. *Ensign,* April 2006, 58.

Scriptures: *"When a prophet speaketh in the name of the Lord, if the thing follow not, nor come to pass, that is the thing which the Lord hath not spoken, but the prophet hath spoken it presumptuously: thou shalt not be afraid of him."*

> *The Latter-day Saints possess the truth, and have many principles of truth in addition to what is possessed by the people of the world. Of course, we are peculiar for a number of reasons. It is our peculiarities that make us different from other Christian people.*[27]

> *In contemplating the remarks of Elder McKay yesterday, with regard to the Latter-day Saints being a peculiar people, I am reminded that we are peculiar in this particular, that, unlike all other "orthodox" Christians, we believe that men must be called of God to preach the gospel and officiate in the ordinances thereof.*[28]

> *It is said that this is a most peculiar doctrine that we preach, a most peculiar religion that we have embraced. The fact is this is the religion of Jesus Christ, the Church that He established. That is the reason it is regarded as a peculiar religion.*[29]

With regard to the teachings of the past Prophets and the value of a living Prophet, I would like to make a few observations here, while specific examples will be provided in chapter 4 concerning the leadership of the church. To recognize the most obvious change of a single doctrine in the Mormon faith, one only has to look at polygamy, which began within one year of the organization of the church in 1830, and by association polyandry. Although the transformation itself was preceded by unclear guidance to the church,[30] several federal

---

[27] President Francis M. Lyman, Conference Report, October 1905, First Day—Morning Session, 97.

[28] Elder Joseph Eckersley, Conference Report, October 1911, Outdoor Meeting. 107-8.

[29] Joseph A. McRae, Conference Report, October 1908, 50.

[30] See the OFFICIAL DECLARATION-1, October 6, 1890, Doctrine and Covenants, in which President Wilford Woodruff, speaking "to whom it may

laws, prison sentences, the potential loss of statehood, and even the Prophet John Taylor himself becoming a fugitive from the law until his death on July 25, 1887, when it finally came, the change seemed firm and unyielding.[31]

It should be plainly understood that the two major splits within the Church of Jesus Christ of Latter-day Saints were in the 1840s and 1890s. Both divisions were centered on the doctrines of polygamy and polyandry. The first division came when a large number of the Saints would not accept polygamy, and the second division was when a large number of the Saints would not stop participating in polygamy. The issue of polygamy within the Mormon Church continued long after the first manifesto of 1890. In 1905 two members of the Twelve, Apostles in line to be the Prophet of the church, John W. Taylor and Matthias F. Cowley, resigned as they had been reprimanded for performing plural marriages. It was generally thought that these two Apostles were exposed only because of the 1904 to 1906 United States congressional hearings on an Apostle who was nominated to the Senate, Elder Reed Smoot.[32] During the first two weeks of the hearing in March of 1904, the then Prophet and President of the Church of Jesus Christ of Latter-day Saints, Joseph F. Smith, a practicing polygamist, was called to testify before the Congress and the people of the United States. Even later, Apostle Richard R. Lyman was excommunicated from the church on November 12, 1943, for practicing polygamy.[33] The significance of three members of the Quorum of the Twelve Apostles—men who were in line to become the Mormon Prophet—leaving the church over

---

concern," provided his "advice" for the church to "refrain" from polygamy. Note: A Second Manifesto was required in 1904 due to the Reed Smoot Congressional Hearings as polygamy continued after 1890.

[31] See Michael H. Paulos, ed., *The Mormon Church On Trial – Transcripts of the Reed Smoot Hearings* (Salt Lake City: Signature Books, 2007). Of note is the testimony of the Mormon Prophet Joseph F. Smith to the Congress of the United States.

[32] Ibid.

[33] The First Presidency: Heber J. Grant, J. Reuben Clark, Jr., and David O. McKay.Conference Report, April 1944, 1.

polygamy is astonishing and a sure testimony that the first manifesto of 1890 to end the practice was not taken very seriously by the church.

The official church history confirms that the first printing of Doctrine and Covenants section 132, which supports polygamy, was in the year 1876. The heading of this section documents that the revelation was recorded in 1843 but known (practiced) by the Prophet in 1831. Even more disturbing is the fact that the 1835 printing of the Doctrine and Covenants, specifically section 101, *denied* the practice[34] in the harshest of terms:

> *As to the charge of polygamy, I will quote from the Book of Doctrine and Covenants, which is the subscribed faith of the church and is strictly enforced. [Doctrine and Covenants 101:4, says,] "Inasmuch as this church of Christ has been reproached with the crime of fornication and polygamy, we declare that we believe that one man should have BUT ONE WIFE, and one woman but one husband except in case of death when either is at liberty to marry again."[35]*

Few modern Latter-day Saints entirely understand that the copy of the Doctrine and Covenants that they take to church each Sunday is *not* the version, specific to polygamy, the early Latter-day Saints took to church each Sunday, as noted above. Even fewer modern Latter-day Saints have understood the truly sinister motives and personal wickedness behind the need to maintain two sets of Scriptures dealing with polygamy. In 1835 the church publicly denounced the practice of polygamy within the canonized set of Scriptures, only to secretly practice the doctrine without the knowledge of the majority of the members at the time. The only purpose for such a deception of the early

---

[34] Polygamy continued in the Mormon Church from 1831 on, despite the fact that the Illinois State Law of Bigamy, 1833 (Section 121, pages 198-99), specifically prohibits the act.

[35] Joseph Smith Jr., "On Marriage," *Times and Seasons,* vol. 3 (November 1841-October 1842), no. 23 October 1, 1842, p. 939; see also, Joseph Smith Jr., *History of The Church of Jesus Christ of Latter-day Saints,* 2:247. As a mockery to the reality of practice of polygamy, the church printed the words "BUT ONE WIFE" in all capital letters.

Saints would have been for the personal gain of Joseph Smith Jr. The Apostle Paul warned against this very perversion within the church: "But among you there must not be even a hint of sexual immorality, or of any kind of impurity, or of greed, because these are improper for God's holy people" (Eph. 5:3 NIV). Again, I would ask the reader to consider the authority of such a man to continue to direct the church on behalf of the Lord Himself, if even a shadow of the following "Scripture" is true:

> *That they may be conferred upon us, it is true; but when we undertake to cover our sins, or to gratify our pride, our vain ambition, or to exercise control or dominion or compulsion upon the souls of the children of men, in any degree of unrighteousness, behold, the heavens withdraw themselves; the Spirit of the Lord is grieved; and when it is withdrawn, Amen to the priesthood or the authority of that man. (Doctrine and Covenants 121:37)*[36]

As a member of the Church of Jesus Christ of Latter-day Saints, I was taught to look upon the early Prophets and Apostles of the "Restoration" with the same degree of admiration and respect I would have for those disciples who were called by Jesus Christ Himself in Judea. To me, the differences between the two groups of "Prophets" and "Apostles" with regard to the personal application of honesty, integrity, and unwavering devotion to the truth appears to be more than a little obvious.

The graphic below represents information from documents of the Church of Jesus Christ of Latter-day Saints. From the section heading of Doctrine and Covenants 132, we learn "that the principles involved in this revelation had been known by the Prophet since 1831," yet the revelation was not recorded until *July 12, 1843* and was not in print for the early Saints to read until 1876. From the history of the church, we learn the following:

---

[36] This prophecy was given to Joseph Smith Jr. while a prisoner in the jail at Liberty, Missouri, dated March 20, 1839.

The first publication of the Revelation received by Joseph Smith was attempted in Independence, Missouri, in 1833, but was destroyed by a mob before it was completed. Only a few copies were saved. The first edition of the Doctrine and Covenants, printed in 1835, contained 103 sections. A subsequent edition was printed in 1844 in Nauvoo, Illinois, and in 1845, a Liverpool, England, edition was published. Subsequent editions were published in 1876, 1879, 1921, and 1981.[37]

This information confirms that the current edition of the Doctrine and Covenants, with section 132 *supporting* polygamy, was printed in 1876, and the 1835 edition of the Doctrine and Covenants, with section 101 *denying* polygamy, was in use for some 41 years prior to that, apparently as a decoy Scripture to appease the United States government. While the modern printing of millions of Doctrine and Covenants continues today, the revelation of section 132, which provides the details of polygamist marriages, remains in print some *120* years *after* it was abandoned and the practice intensely rejected by the Mormon Church in 1890. I have, in vain, asked church leaders, if not for deception alone, the purpose of printing as Scripture a "revelation" that was never employed (section 101) or the purpose of the continued printing as Scripture of a "revelation" that has been repeatedly and severely rejected (section 132).

---

[37] S. Kent Brown, Donald Q. Cannon, and Richard H. Jackson, eds., *Historical Atlas of Mormonism* (New York: Simon and Schuster, 1994), 36.

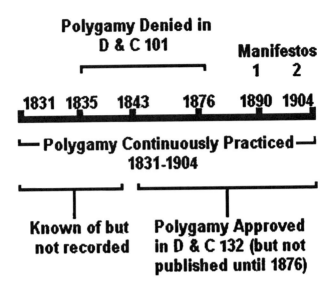

To promote the deception of both the public and the members of their own church, the following statement was issued in the official newspaper of the church in 1844.

> *As we have lately been credibly informed, that an Elder of the Church of Jesus Christ, of Latter day Saints, by the name of Hiram Brown, has been preaching Polygamy, and other false and corrupt doctrines, in the county of Lapeer, state of Michigan. This is to notify him and the Church in general, that he has been cut off from the church, for his iniquity; and he is further notified to appear at the Special Conference, on the 6th of April next, to make answer to these charges.* [38]

Nevertheless, when the practice was publicly and finally denounced, it demonstrated that the living Prophet could alter the direction of any previous Prophet and thus be both relevant to the issues at hand and responsive to the will of the Lord. Many in the church did not accept this change in direction, and several breakaway groups were formed. They believed then, as they do now, that the "everlasting covenant" was just that—

---

[38] *Times and Seasons,* vol. 5, No. 3. Nauvoo, Illinois, Feb. 1, 1844.

everlasting. They believed that the will of the Lord should not have been altered by extreme political pressure from the Untied States Congress, its laws, or the offer of statehood. Specifically, the position of the "fundamentalist" churches rests on the exact same set of Scriptures that the Latter-day Saints use today, for virtually none of the actual Scriptures dealing with polygamy have been changed in 120 years. The perplexing consequence is that the current practice of abstaining from polygamy is *not* reflected in the current *Scriptures* of the Mormons in Utah. Rather, their *Scriptures* reflect the polygamous practice of the fundamentalist Mormons in Texas. However, the Utah Mormons' *Web site*, which is *not* to be considered Scripture, has been updated to reflect what their printed *Scriptures* is missing as noted below.

Mormon Official Scripture

And again, as pertaining to the law of the priesthood—if any man espouse a virgin, and desire to espouse another, and the first give her consent, and if he espouse the second, and they are virgins, and have vowed to no other man, then is he justified; he cannot commit adultery for they are given unto him; for he cannot commit adultery with that that belongeth unto him and to no one else. (Doctrine and Covenants 132:61)

Mormon Non-Scripture Internet Information

Polygamy (Plural Marriage)

The family is ordained of God. Marriage between man and woman is essential to His eternal plan. At certain times and for His specific purposes, God, through His prophets, has directed the practice of plural marriage (sometimes called polygamy), which means one man having more than one living wife at the same time. In obedience to direction from God, Latter-day Saints followed this practice for about 50 years during the 1800s but officially ceased the practice of such marriages after the Manifesto was issued by President Woodruff in 1890. Since that time, plural marriage has not been approved by The Church of Jesus Christ of Latter-day Saints and any member adopting this practice is subject to losing his or her membership in the

Church.[39]

I believe that the *suspension* of this doctrine is only temporary. This is based on what I personally have been told by both local leaders of the church and, more authoritatively, on what was issued by the Prophet of the Church of Jesus Christ of Latter-day Saints in 1914. This official statement was made just as the majority of the church was coming to terms with the agonizing reality of the defeat of a key doctrine of exaltation and needed some reassurance of its eventual return.

> *The members of the Church are reminded that the practice of polygamous or plural marriage is not the only law whose suspension has been authorized by the Lord. The law of the United Order has likewise been suspended, to be re-established in the due time of the Lord.*[40]

Central to the proposal that the doctrine of polygamy has only been suspended are the following statements from Mormon Apostle Orson Pratt, who has never been considered a "fundamentalist" or anything other than an honored Apostle of the church, who was called and set apart as a Prophet, Seer, and Revelator by Brigham Young.

> *All these principles that I have treated upon, pertaining to eternal marriage, the very moment that they are admitted to be true, it brings in plurality of marriage, and if plurality of marriage is not true or in other words, if a man has no divine right to marry two wives or more in this world, then marriage for eternity is not true, and your faith is all vain, and all the sealing ordinances and powers, pertaining to marriages for eternity are vain, worthless, good for nothing; for as sure as one is true the other also must be true. Amen.*[41]

Begrudgingly or not, inspiration or not, revelation or not,

---

[39] Gospel Library, Gospel Topics, A-Z Index, Polygamy, www.lds.org.

[40] President Heber J. Grant, dated January 13, 1914, *Messages of the First Presidency of the Church of Jesus Christ of Latter-day Saints*, 6:327.

[41] Apostle Orson Pratt, July 18, 1880, Tabernacle Salt Lake. *Journal of Discourses* 21:286.

polygamy was ended—or at least suspended—and the prohibition has been enforced by the living Prophets and Apostles of the church. Again, this demonstrates that the will and the ability of the living leadership of the church is supreme. Following is one of the clearest examples of such modern-day direction and clarification from a living prophet of the church.

> *Inasmuch as laws have been enacted by Congress forbidding plural marriages, which laws have been pronounced constitutional by the court of last resort, I hereby declare my intention to submit to those laws, and to use my influence with the members of the Church over which I preside to have them do likewise.*[42]

This issue was settled. No further debate would be required or even considered with regard to the practice of polygamy among the members of the church. Now that it has been established and clearly demonstrated that the current living leadership of the church unquestionably has the right, the power, and the authority to correct, as directed by the Lord, any necessary modification or amendment to any doctrine, let us now consider several points of Mormon doctrine that have *not* been so altered.

During my service around the world in many leadership positions with the Church of Jesus Christ of Latter-day Saints, I have known good men and good women who were quite aware of what is called the "peculiar doctrines of the church." I have participated in several relatively quiet discussions concerning this collection of unique doctrines, teachings, or comments by those in authority. This almost dejectedly orphaned collection of teachings seems to have been delivered to the church in the same manner as the more accepted or conventional doctrines. The issue at hand is simply this: if a given prophet or Apostle speaks to the church as a whole at an officially sanctioned meeting, such as the semiannual general conference of the church, are his words to be considered Scripture? Is this not the

---

[42] President George Albert Smith, Conference Report, October 1947, Afternoon Meeting, 165.

appropriate forum for the leadership of the church to communicate the will, the mind, and the direction of the Lord as His Prophets, Seers, and Revelators?

To clarify the issue of what is or is not Scripture, I am once again compelled to reference the following direction from the church leadership itself, on this important subject.

I have never yet preached a sermon and sent it out to the children of men, that they may not call Scripture.[43]

> *When holy men of God write or speak by the power of the Holy Ghost, their words "shall be scripture, shall be the will of the Lord, shall be the mind of the Lord, shall be the word of the Lord, shall be the voice of the Lord, and the power of God unto salvation" (Doctrines and Covenants 68:4).[44]*

> *We believe what Jesus taught, and in this we rely on scripture, including the Bible, which we believe as it came from the mouths of the prophets. We believe also other works, given to other peoples anciently and modernly, in addition to that word given to ancient Israel—works, which are consistent with and complementary to the Bible. In addition, we believe in the words of the living prophets. We believe in continuous revelation, for we feel that a Loving Father still gives divine guidance, and would not leave his sincerely seeking children alone without counsel or direction-and him whose countenance you have seen this morning in conducting this conference—President David O. McKay—we accept and sustain as a prophet of God, as we accept Moses and Abraham, and Peter and Paul, and Isaiah and Elijah or any such others.[45]*

> *We quote from a living prophet to explain one of the major distinguishing features of the Church. President David O.*

---

[43] President Brigham Young. *Journal of Discourses* (1870), 13:95.

[44] The official, canonized Scriptures of the church, often called the standard works, are the Bible, the Book of Mormon, the Doctrine and Covenants, and the Pearl of Great Price. See "Scriptures," as listed on lds.org Gospel Library, A-Z, Gospel Topics.

[45] Elder Richard L. Evans, Conference Report, April 1962, Third Day—Morning Meeting, 97.

McKay has said, ". . . we believe in divine authority by direct revelation rather than by descent." The power and authority came to this Church through the visitation of angelic messengers: Peter, James, and John, the Apostles of old who as resurrected beings, conferred their authority and power upon Joseph Smith and Oliver Cowdery in this dispensation. We explained that this doctrine is both scriptural and logical, for the Bible itself is a compilation of revelations. They were given at different periods of time through various prophets over approximately 4,000 years. Just as each prophet in times past left scripture as evidence of the divinity of his calling, so we offer to the honest in heart today additional scriptures, both ancient and modern. These additional revelations form the scriptural basis for the doctrine of The Church of Jesus Christ of Latter-day Saints.[46]

One of the major beliefs of the Church of Jesus Christ of Latter-day Saints is continuing revelation. If that revelation is based on the power of the Holy Ghost, then indeed, "we must not treat lightly the counsel from the President of the Church."[47] One of my continuous questions over a five-year period to the senior leadership of the Mormon Church, was basically, what happens to those lesser-known, unique, or peculiar teachings of the Prophets and Apostles of the church? Do they simply fade away? If an authorized representative of the Church of Jesus Christ of Latter-day Saints addresses the body of the church by the power of the Holy Ghost within an officially sanctioned forum, and it is then recorded by church historians,[48] is this not Scripture? How can it simply fade away?

As an amateur historian, I have come to a deep appreciation for how the meaning and presentation of mere words can shape

---

[46] Elder A. Theodore Tuttle, Conference Report, April 1964, First Day— Morning Meeting, 8-9.

[47] *Teachings of the Presidents of the Church, Wilford Woodruff*, 201.

[48] To ensure the accuracy of the text, all references and quotes of the LDS Prophets, Apostles, or General Authorities of the church have been taken from the *LDS Collectors Library 2005* (Salt Lake City: LDS Media and Deseret Book, 2004). LDS Media and Deseret Book is owned by the Deseret Management Corporation, which is owned by the Church of Jesus Christ of Latter-day Saints.

a nation, arouse the soul, and awaken a great excitement and passion. More than the subject of politics, a superbly delivered religious oratory can literally change the course of a person's life. The impact of mere words are transformed into divine guidance when the speaker is believed or known to be one of the authorized representatives of the Lord Jesus Christ.

> *They ignore the great witness that comes from these conferences. We ought to, indeed we must, heed the counsel of these men, for the Lord said, "What I the Lord have spoken, I have spoken, and I excuse not myself; and though the heavens and the earth pass away my word shall not pass away, but shall all be fulfilled, whether by mine own voice or by the voice of my servants, it is the same."*[49]

Concerning what might be called the questionable issues of doctrine, a devout and knowledgeable former High Priest and dear friend of mine, and also one of my trusted counselors, said, "There is no such thing as questionable doctrine in the church. If an Apostle or Prophet said it, it stands." I then asked if that were true concerning doctrine of the church spoken of just once and has not been repeated or validated by other prophets in more recent times. It was his conviction that a given doctrine did not become "more valid" if it were spoken of or discussed by the Brethren more often than any other officially decreed doctrine of the Lord. His logic and commitment were both flawless. If a true prophet of God had brought the doctrine forth, it was true.

The following day I researched the definition and then the process by which revelation becomes authorized Scripture and by implementation formal doctrine of the church. No matter the authority of the several corroborating sources, the definitive Scripture on the subject was consistently this:

> *When holy men of God write or speak by the power of the Holy Ghost, their words "shall be scripture, shall be the will of the Lord, shall be the mind of the Lord, shall be the word of the*

---

[49] Elder Boyd K. Packer, Conference Report, October 1968, Afternoon Meeting, 76 (quoting Doctrine and Covenants 1:38).

Lord, shall be the voice of the Lord, and the power of God unto salvation." (Doctrine and Covenants 68:4).

Within a few days of that conversation, I was impressed to write the following to the first presidency of the church.[50]

> The Church of Jesus Christ of Latter-day Saints
>
> Office of the First Presidency
>
> President Thomas S. Monson
>
> 50 East North Temple Street
>
> Salt Lake City, Utah 84150
>
> 30 January 2006
>
> Dear President Monson,
>
> After 30 years of faithful service… I only ask for 30 minutes of consideration by someone, <u>anyone</u> in authority who could answer one personal question. Thus far the silence concerning this question has been very demoralizing.
>
> Over the past two years it has become obvious, both when sharing the Gospel and now on a personal level… that a number of subjects found to be in the "anti-Mormon" category, are in fact, <u>True</u> and <u>Accurate</u> accounts of the actual teachings of the Prophets and General Authorities as documented within the authorized Church publications.
>
> As only one example, the Journal of Discourses (issued under the authority of the First Presidency) has long been the single most referenced source of General Conference talks and official teachings of the early Prophets, Apostles and General Authorities.
>
> How am I to explain or understand the <u>selective</u> use of the Journal of Discourses, in contrast to the simultaneous <u>rejection</u> of "some" of the teachings from

---

[50] For original letter, see appendix A document number 12.

the same Prophet or Apostle during the same time on the same subject presumably under the same inspiration of the Spirit also recorded in the Journal of Discourses?

With sincerity and respect,

Lee B Baker

Brother Lee B. Baker

High Priest

Membership Nr. 000-3443-8033 (Provided for identification purposes)

As no answer came to this or any of the other eight letters to church officers, friends, and fellow members of the church, I began to review with much more uncertainty the value and validity of questionable Mormon doctrine. As I studied the matter further, it became clear that the church had actively censored the complete and authorized history of the church by filtering any reference to the questionable subjects through secondary authors who were not firsthand witnesses to the event or sermon referenced. The official Priesthood/Relief Society manual, *Teachings of the Presidents of the Church, Brigham Young,*[51] frequently cites *Discourses of Brigham Young* (DBY).[52] In fact, DBY accounts for a full 95 percent of this official church manual. That book (DBY) opens in the preface with this statement:

> *This book was made possible because Brigham Young secured stenographic reports of his addresses. As he traveled among the people, reporters accompanied him. All that he said was recorded. Practically all of these discourses (from December 16, 1851 to August 19, 1877) were published in the Journal of Discourses, which was widely distributed. The public utterances of few great historical figures have been so*

---

[51] *Teachings of the Presidents of the Church – Brigham Young* (Salt Lake City: Church of Jesus Christ of Latter-day Saints, 1997).

[52] John A. Widtsoe, *Discourses of Brigham Young* (Salt Lake City: Deseret Book, 1941).

faithfully and fully preserved.

I have a full and complete copy of the *Journal of Discourses*, and I have never yet found a single misused quote or mistake in any wording that has been used as a reference by the church in any official manual. The obvious question, then, is, why not use the *Journal of Discourses* itself, which was issued not only under the authority of the first presidency but also included a letter of introduction, which testified to the accuracy of the work and bears the signature of all three members of that presidency: Brigham Young, Heber C. Kimball, and Willard Richards? The answer is equally as obvious. The *Journal of Discourses* contains the questionable doctrine of the church that has fallen out of favor with the church—but apparently not to the point that it would require any correction by the living Prophet. Without censorship, the *Journal of Discourses* is an embarrassment to the church. It is also noteworthy that the *Journal of Discourses* has been selectively used in a wide variety of church publications beyond the student manuals mentioned earlier. The point here is that the *Journal of Discourses* is anything but an "anti-Mormon" guidebook. Although it may serve that purpose well, it was intended as a faithful and authoritative "reporting [of] the public Sermons, Discourse, Lectures, &c., delivered by the Presidency, the Twelve."[53] In addition, here are a few references from the *Journal of Discourses* when it has been freely used within current official publications of the church for non-controversial statements, and thus openly acknowledged as the recognized source of the quote.

Our Heritage: A Brief History of the Church of Jesus Christ of Latter-day Saints (1996). Chapter 2, footnote 8; chapter 3, footnote 4; chapter 7, footnote 1 and footnote 14.

Church History in the Fulness of Times, Religion

---

[53] Recognition of the efforts of Elder George D. Watt and the purpose of the *Journal of Discourses,* as signed by the first presidency, page 1 of the *Journal of Discourses.*

341-43 (1989). Chapter 27 endnotes, page 351; chapter 30 endnotes, page 391; chapter 31 endnotes, page 405; chapter 32 endnotes, page 421; chapter 34 endnotes, page 450.

Doctrine and Covenants and Church History, *Gospel Doctrine Teacher's Manual* (1999). Lesson 14, page 68, paragraph 4 and page 78, paragraph 3; lesson 24, page 135, paragraph 7; lesson 27, page 153, paragraph 4.

It may seem that I have spent an inordinate amount of time establishing the authority of the reference materials for this next section. This will be the standard by which all references and quotes are chosen throughout the entire book. This is important for two reasons. First, as a self-defense mechanism, most Latter-day Saints assume, suggest, or conclude that the offensive words or actions of the prophets and other leaders of the church are not genuine but simply lies created by critics, or they wildly contort the facts to fit an implausible premise.[54] And, second, I was wrongly accused and then excommunicated for "distributing packets of statements which contained information that is not Church doctrine," when in fact those were the precise actions of the Stake President who excommunicated me.[55] What Stake President Michael D. Jones did not even vaguely comprehend when he provided his unauthorized and irresponsible packet of information to me was the depth of my research, as well as the accuracy and consistency of my documentation.

Following will be a limited collection of the questionable doctrines or teachings spoken of earlier. As a member of the church, I was constantly probing how other leaders and members of the church categorized the bizarre teachings noted here. Due in part to a policy of "no comment," I came to be

---

[54] See chapter 2, "Following the Prophet: The Art of Personal Responsibility and Discernment."

[55] See chapter 4, "The Leadership of the Church: A Lower Standard of Conduct."

very skeptical and distrustful of the local and national leadership of the church. Indeed, the "leadership laryngitis" fostered varying beliefs among the general membership concerning these well-documented but peculiar statements of the prophets and General Authorities. Without some authoritative comment, position, or guidance specific to these statements, the individual member is left to both rationalize and then defend these teachings to himself or herself or any investigator of the church. I came to be part of that point of the spear, which would deal with the issues that the leadership of the church has effectively insolated themselves from at the expense of the members. As a former Army officer, I remember well the desperate feeling of being assigned a task with neither the training nor the support and equipment to complete the task. Fortunately, in the Army we invariably overcame any obstacle, but there the eternal salvation of my family did not hang in the balance.

I have assigned general subject headings below, but short of that, each of these teachings from the Mormon Prophets, Apostles, or others given within an official and public meeting, will meet the criteria outlined in Doctrine and Covenants 68:4 to qualify as Scripture.

> *When holy men of God write or speak by the power of the Holy Ghost, their words "shall be scripture, shall be the will of the Lord, shall be the mind of the Lord, shall be the word of the Lord, shall be the voice of the Lord, and the power of God unto salvation.*

Given the teachings of the Mormon Church and the ability of the living prophet of that church to correct, remove, or receive true Scripture, I have asked the leadership of the Mormon Church from Arvada, Colorado to Salt Lake City, Utah, under what condition the following *is not* Scripture.

Joseph Smith will judge who may or may not enter into heaven

> *Joseph Smith holds the keys of this last dispensation, and is now engaged behind the veil in the great work of the last days.*

I can tell our beloved brother Christians who have slain the Prophets and butchered and otherwise caused the death of thousands of Latter-day Saints, the priests who have thanked God in their prayers and thanksgiving from the pulpit that we have been plundered, driven, and slain, and the deacons under the pulpit, and their brethren and sisters in their closets, who have thanked God, thinking that the Latter-day Saints were wasted away, something that no doubt will mortify them— something that, to say the least, is a matter of deep regret to them—namely, that no man or woman in this dispensation will ever enter into the celestial kingdom of God without the consent of Joseph Smith.[56]

Note: True Christians believe that only the Lord judges who enters heaven:

"Jesus saith unto him, I am the way, the truth, and the life: no man cometh unto the Father, but by me" (John 14:6).

Jesus Christ practiced Polygamy during His ministry on earth

I discover that some of the Eastern papers represent me as a great blasphemer, because I said, in my lecture on Marriage, at our last Conference, that Jesus Christ was married at Cana of Galilee, that Mary, Martha, and others were his wives, and that he begat children.[57]

God the Father had sexual intercourse with Mary to conceive Jesus

When the Virgin Mary conceived the child Jesus, the Father had begotten him in his own likeness. He was not begotten by the Holy Ghost. And who is the Father? He is the first of the human family; and when he took a tabernacle, it was begotten by his Father in heaven, after the same manner as the tabernacles of Cain, Abel, and the rest of the sons and daughters of Adam and Eve; from the fruits of the earth, the first earthly tabernacles were originated by the Father, and so on in

---

[56] President Brigham Young, Tabernacle, Great Salt Lake City, October 9, 1859. *Journal of Discourses* 7:282.

[57] President Orson Hyde, president of the Quorum of the Twelve Apostles, General Conference, October 1854. *Journal of Discourses* 2:210.

succession. I could tell you much more about this; but were I to tell you the whole truth, blasphemy would be nothing to it, in the estimation of the superstitious and over-righteous of mankind.[58]

The birth of the Savior was as natural as are the births of our children; it was the result of natural action. He partook of flesh and blood—was begotten of his Father, as we were of our fathers.[59]

Racism and bigotry against the black race is of the Lord

You see some classes of the human family that are black, uncouth, uncomely, disagreeable and low in their habits, wild, and seemingly deprived of nearly all the blessings of the intelligence that is generally bestowed upon mankind. The first man that committed the odious crime of killing one of his brethren will be cursed the longest of any one of the children of Adam. Cain slew his brother. Cain might have been killed, and that would have put a termination to that line of human beings. This was not to be, and the Lord put a mark upon him, which is the flat nose and black skin.[60]

Shall I tell you the law of God in regard to the African race? If the white man who belongs to the chosen seed mixes his blood with the seed of Cain, the penalty, under the law of God, is death on the spot. This will always be so.[61]

When he destroyed the inhabitants of the antediluvian world, he suffered a descendant of Cain [blacks] to come through the flood in order that he [Satan] might be properly represented upon the earth. And Satan keeps busy all the time, and he will until he is bound; and I expect they will then have good times

---

[58] President Brigham Young, General Conference, April 9, 1852. *Journal of Discourses* 1:51.

[59] President Brigham Young, Salt Lake City, July 8, 1860. *Journal of Discourses* 8:115.

[60] President Brigham Young, General Conference, October 1859. *Journal of Discourses* 7:291.

[61] President Brigham Young, Salt Lake Tabernacle, March 1863. *Journal of Discourses* 10:110.

until he is loose again.[62]

Yet Cain continued to love Satan more than God. He entered into a secret covenant with Satan to murder his brother Abel for gain. "And he gloried, [so the scripture says], in his wickedness." (Ibid., 5:31.) And after this terrible crime had been committed, Cain received his "wages from him whom he listeth to obey." He was cursed by the Lord with a dark skin. He lost the Holy Priesthood. He lost his eternal soul, becoming a son of perdition. Thus, he was turned over to Satan—his master.[63]

The atonement of Jesus Christ did not apply to all the sins of man

Will you love your brothers or sisters likewise, when they have committed a sin that cannot be atoned for without the shedding of their blood? Will you love that man or woman well enough to shed their blood?[64]

I say, that there are men and women that I would advise to go to the President immediately, and ask him to appoint a committee to attend to their case; and then let a place be selected, and let that committee shed their blood.[65]

You may think that I am not teaching you Bible doctrine, but what says the apostle Paul? I would ask how many covenant breakers there are in this city and in this kingdom. I believe that there are a great many; and if they are covenant breakers we need a place designated, where we can shed their blood.[66]

We have those amongst us that are full of all manner of

---

[62] President John Taylor, Discourse delivered at Grantsville, Sunday Evening, October 29, 1882. *Journal of Discourses* 23:333.

[63] Elder Milton R. Hunter, Conference Report, April 1952, Afternoon Meeting, 123.

[64] President Brigham Young, Salt Lake Tabernacle, February 1857. *Journal of Discourses* 4:220.

[65] President Jedediah M. Grant, Second Counselor to President Brigham Young, Father to Heber J. Grant, delivered in the Bowery, Great Salt Lake City, September 21, 1856. *Journal of Discourses* 4:49-51.

[66] Ibid.

abominations, those who need to have their blood shed, for water will not do, their sins are of too deep a dye.[67]

Brethren and sisters, we want you to repent and forsake your sins. And you who have committed sins that cannot be forgiven through baptism, let your blood be shed, and let the smoke ascend, that the incense thereof may come up before God as an atonement for your sins, and that the sinners in Zion may be afraid.[68]

Oath of Vengeance remains in a Mormon song of today

You and each of you do covenant and promise that you will pray and never cease to pray to Almighty God to avenge the blood of the prophets upon this nation, and that you will teach the same to your children and to your children's children unto the third and fourth generation.[69]

Sacrifice brings forth the blessings of heaven;

Earth must atone for the blood of that man.

Wake up the world for the conflict of justice.

Millions shall know "Brother Joseph" again.[70]

Only those who participate in polygamy may become a God:

The only men who become Gods, even the Sons of God, are those who enter into polygamy. Others attain unto a glory and

---

[67] Ibid.

[68] Ibid.

[69] Temple Oath of Vengeance, 1845 to 1927. See David John Buerger (1987), "The Development of the Mormon Temple Endowment Ceremony." *A Journal of Mormon Thought* 20, no. 4 (Winter 1987): 33–76, http://content.lib.utah.edu/u?/dialogue,20139; *U.S. Senate Document 486 (59th Congress, 1st Session) Proceedings Before the Committee on Privileges and Elections of the United States Senate in the Matter of the Protests Against the Right of Hon. Reed Smoot, a Senator from the State of Utah, to hold his Seat.* 4 vols. [+1 vol. index] (Washington: Government Printing Office, 1906).

[70] William W. Phelps, "Praise to the Man," *Hymns of The Church of Jesus Christ of Latter-day Saints* (Salt Lake City: Church of Jesus Christ of Latter-day Saints, 1985), number 27.

may even be permitted to come into the presence of the Father and the Son; but they cannot reign as kings in glory, because they had blessings offered unto them, and they refused to accept them.[71]

A lie by Joseph Smith is recorded in the official church history

What a thing it is for a man to be accused of committing adultery, and having seven wives, when I can only find one.[72]

The moral character and importance of Joseph Smith is established

When a man places himself in a position to receive a testimony that Joseph Smith was a prophet of God, he is in a position to demand recognition from our Father in heaven, and our Father in heaven will listen to him.[73]

Joseph Smith was a man of unblemished character. His veracity was never impeached. His honor in religion, in morality, and in business transactions, as attested by friend and foe, was unsullied to the end of his mortal career.[74]

---

[71] Remarks by President Brigham Young, in the Bowery, in Great Salt Lake City, August 19, 1866. *Journal of Discourses* 11:269.

[72] Joseph Smith Jr., *History of the Church*, 6:411. In addition to numerous other men's wives, Joseph took three sets of sisters, a mother and her daughter, several teenagers, and two fourteen-year-old girls as wives when he was thirty-seven. One was the daughter of Heber C. Kimball. It also should be noted that Joseph did not tell his first wife, Emma, of over half of his thirty-three recorded marriages and she threatened to leave him on at least two occasions. See Todd Compton's *In Sacred Loneliness: The Plural Wives of Joseph Smith*, 4-9. On the official church site (lds.org) is recorded the fact that this book "was recently honored with the annual best book award from the Mormon History Association. This recognition is deserved because it is the most detailed study of the lifetime experiences of the women sealed to Joseph Smith." **Warning from the Scriptures**: "Now the Spirit speaketh expressly, that in the latter times some shall depart from the faith, giving heed to seducing spirits, and doctrines of devils; Speaking lies in hypocrisy; having their conscience seared with a hot iron" (1 Tim. 4:1-2).

[73] Elder Ben E. Rich, Conference Report, April 1913, Afternoon Session, 24-26.

[74] Elder John Longden, Assistant to the Council of the Twelve, Conference

I close with the thought that Joseph Smith, his claims, his teachings, and his achievements are so very remarkable in character that they challenge every normal human being able to do so, to make an honest and thorough investigation of them. A refusal to do this is likely to bring sometime, somewhere, painful regrets and handicaps as a consequence.[75]

To the divine help, the life of Joseph Smith was confined; to the bringing of that higher truth and moral light which could not be developed except by some divine message from heaven. He brought to light the nature of God, man's immortality, and the highest elements of moral character.[76]

Despite the touching statements by those who may have known him, I believe that after my thirty-two years of service within the church he founded, I have good reason to question the character, morals, and motives of Joseph Smith Jr., as well as several of his successors as Prophets and Presidents of the Church of Jesus Christ of Latter-day Saints. Again, I must state that I have found it remarkably hypocritical that the following Mormon Scripture applies *only* to the average member of the church and not at all to the behavior of the church leadership and definitely never to the "Prophet."

That they may be conferred upon us, it is true; but when we undertake to cover our sins, or to gratify our pride, our vain ambition, or to exercise control or dominion or compulsion upon the souls of the children of men, in any degree of unrighteousness, behold, the heavens withdraw themselves; the Spirit of the Lord is grieved; and when it is withdrawn, Amen to the priesthood or the authority of that man. (Doctrine and Covenants 121:37)

Report, October 1966, Afternoon Meeting, 35.

[75] Elder Joseph F. Merrill, Conference Report, April 1947, Morning Meeting, 137.

[76] Elder Levi Edgar Young, of the First Council of the Seventy, Conference Report, October 1948, Afternoon Meeting, 93.

A Selective Lack of Knowledge

The final chapters of this book are uniquely focused on Mormon readers. For them, there is not a personal feeling, family emotion, or spiritual challenge associated with this discovery of the truth that I have not endured myself. We who have been baptized in the holy name of Jesus Christ are indebted only to Him. It may be exceptionally harsh to consider, but the very certainty of our salvation is *not* dependent on the selected doctrines of any one church. Our salvation is based on our acceptance of Jesus as the Christ. In this there is no middle ground and no compromise. It is completely illogical and against the teachings of Jesus Christ Himself to consider that we may be entirely devoted to a few aspects of any church and yet be at liberty to dismiss other teachings or doctrines of the same church. How is it that within the "only true church," some Latter-day Saints accept all the teachings of the prophets, some accept the majority of the teachings, and still others view those teachings within a personal "context" before the principle is applied? His truth is constant; His truth can withstand the review of all questions and the light of complete and clear knowledge without deception, deceit, or dishonesty.

In the past I have found myself attempting to justify the offensive and questionable doctrines of the Mormon Church. I have done this in consideration of the incredible youth programs of the church and the exceptional focus on family relationships and many other outstanding programs. Nevertheless, whatever elements of the Church of Jesus Christ of Latter-day Saints I may have been peculiarly enthralled with, the fact remains that as a member I owned *all* the doctrines of the church, not just the splendid ones. I could not plead a selective lack of knowledge concerning what was certainly offensive to the Lord. To do so would be to carelessly turn away from the truth and place the church above my personal relationship with my Savior.

The sometimes disagreeable but unshakably true fact remains that your membership in a church, any church, is not validated by your personal opinion. Your opinion or disagreement with church doctrine is completely irrelevant in that you have joined the church's viewpoint; the church has not joined your viewpoint. A responsible and rational adult who claims to follow the teachings of Jesus Christ or any given Christian church cannot simply state, "Well, I really do not know about that." It is truly insincere to the Lord Jesus Christ to be an uninformed or apathetic Christian. In the same way, I have come to believe that it is equally insincere and spiritually risky to be an uninformed or apathetic Mormon.

The Fundamental Conclusions of This Chapter

As an overview of this book, this chapter highlights the true-life experience of a Mormon Bishop who was exceptionally active in the Church of Jesus Christ of Latter-day Saints for over three decades. What this book is *not* is nearly as important as what it *is*. This book is not an external or detached review of the clinical or even theoretical reasons why the Mormon Church is wrong on so many levels. It is the honest representation of one man's agonizing journey of religious discovery with all the required facts, dates, and formal Mormon Church documents to substantiate its claims. At risk were my family, my marriage, and my personal relationship with my Lord and Savior.

The central point of this chapter is the clear illustration that the "Jesus Christ" of the "Mormon faith" has been reduced in His character, principles, and morals in order to shield the egocentric desires of the Mormon Prophets. Additionally, this chapter reviews the overwhelming evidence from the Mormon Church itself that exposes several core Mormon doctrines and teachings as unmistakably anti-Christian in both concept and practice. Finally, this chapter provides an examination of the intentional deception that has been poured upon the ordinary members of the Mormon Church in order to distract their attention and restrict their knowledge of the truth.

CHAPTER TWO

Following the Prophet: The Art of Personal Responsibility and Discernment

In that context it all makes sense to me.

Steven T. Rockwood, Arvada, Colorado, October 17, 2008

Not only does the foundational statement above expose a high degree of self-justification, but it also captures the fundamental nature of the modern Mormon thought process. Throughout the history of the Mormon Church, non-Christian doctrine has been found acceptable within the self-justified "context" in which it was practiced. In this way, the Lord Himself becomes the author of the questionable doctrine,[1] and not the kindhearted "Prophet" of the church. The Lord Himself becomes a personal shield, and securely behind the Son of the living God, one can do no wrong. When Joseph Smith Jr., the founding Prophet of Mormonism, proposed the concept of plural marriages to women who were already married and to the fathers of several young girls, he assured them all that it was not *his* idea but a true commandment from Jesus Christ Himself. When I questioned a former friend, Mormon High Priest Steven T. Rockwood, about Smith's motivations and his own apparent failure to follow the specifics of that "commandment," Mr. Rockwood provided what I now consider to be the finest written example of Mormon self-justification: "In that context it all makes sense to me."[2]

In my view, Steven T. Rockwood is much like the early Mormon priesthood holder who could effortlessly and piously justify illegal or immoral activities based on the "context" in

---

[1] Namely, polygamy, polyandry, blood atonement, bigotry, and lying for the Lord.

[2] E-mail sent to the author by Mr. Rockwood on October 17, 2008. See the original in appendix A, document 19.

which a specific doctrine was given or "viewed." An even more adaptable strategy, as demonstrated by Mr. Rockwood, is the combination of both how you "view things' (laws, commandments, or divine guidance) and the "context" of the specific instruction. I have come to label this strategy the "Rockwood Doctrine."

The establishment of the Rockwood Doctrine came from an exchange of e-mails between Mr. Rockwood and myself in the fall of 2008. At the very depth of my depression, when I finally came to recognize that my thirty-two years in the Mormon Church was most likely based on the lies and deceptions of "Prophets," Steven Rockwood offered to help. As a former member of the Arvada Colorado Stake Presidency[3] and an employee of the church itself, "Brother" Rockwood was a well-respected figure of some authority and certainly very knowledgeable of Mormon doctrine and Scripture.

To fairly represent the exchange of thoughts, I will present the e-mails in time order and exactly as sent. I have underlined the key statements to give some emphasis as to the significant points of the exchange.

E-mail to Lee Baker from Steven T. Rockwood, former First Counselor to the Stake President, Arvada Colorado Stake of the Church of Jesus Christ of Latter-day Saints

> Subject: How are you?
> Date: Wed, 15 Oct 2008
>
> Hi Lee,
>
> I haven't seen you for a while. How are things and is there anything I can do for you?
> Steven

E-mail from Lee Baker to Steven T. Rockwood

---

[3] For the hierarchy of the Church of Jesus Christ of Latter-day Saints, see the outline in appendix A document 20.

Subject: RE: How are you?
Date: Wed, 15 Oct 2008

Steven,

Thank you for the email and the offer.

How are things?

The very worst year of my life, and Kathy's and now also for my four Children.

What can you do for me?
Simple, tell me again how what is clearly called a Law in the canonized Scriptures of the Church, became diluted into something... anything less.

As clearly recorded by Joseph Smith in Doctrine and Covenants 132:61-64, the Lord sets <u>three</u> conditions (under the heading of a Law) which are required for a member of the Priesthood who desires to take other wives: She must be 1) "**a virgin**", 2) "**the first to give her consent**", and 3) "**vowed to no other man**", "**belongeth unto him and to no one else**".

"All these principles that I have treated upon, pertaining to eternal marriage, the very moment that they are admitted to be true, it brings in plurality of marriage, and if plurality of marriage is not true or in other words, if a man has no divine right to marry two wives or more in this world, then marriage for eternity is not true, and your faith is all vain, and all the sealing ordinances and powers, pertaining to marriages for eternity are vain, worthless, good for nothing; for as sure as one is true the other also must be true. Amen. *Apostle Orson Pratt, 18 July 1880, Tabernacle Salt Lake, JoD, v21, p.286*

Thanks again for your thoughtfulness... but I really do believe that even with your kind heart and true consideration... it is not your calling or your responsibility to address my Spiritual issues. But I am very interested in your thoughts on the above items, as they seem to me to be clear and free from any need of analysis or debate as do the vast majority of my questions.

Thanks again.

Lee

E-mail to Lee Baker from Steven T. Rockwood

Subject: RE: How are you?
Date: Fri, 17 Oct 2008

Lee,

I am truly sorry to hear of the affect your questions are having on you and your family. While I know these questions are very important to you, I am sure you are considering if they are worth the pain they seem to be causing. Their fruits don't seem to be the fruit of the Spirit as described in Galatians and Ephesians.

I have learned that it is important to become source sensitive. What are the sources of our questions and answers? I also know that the Lord always requires faith as we seek after truth, so I wonder if it is worth considering that perhaps the great purpose in this whole process is to exercise your faith and move on, follow the counsel of your leaders and friends, trusting that the questions have been answered or will be answered in due time, but not to let them cause harm to you in the mean time. I had an experience six years ago that I still don't understand, still doesn't make sense to me, still seems very wrong, but I had to drop it before I let it consume me. I still don't have the answers, but I am at least not entangled with the pain and the consequences of that pain anymore. I learned that what the Lord was not going to give me the answers I wanted and instead was going to require me to drop it and exercise my faith, let it go, and in due time perhaps I might get the answers and justification I seek. The confusion, anger and inequity of the situation still creep into my mind once in awhile, but I have to remember to leave it alone, it does me absolutely no good, no matter how I feel about it. I can't tell you how free I felt when I forgave the individuals and the situation involved and finally realized my personal role, responsibility and contribution to the situation and let it go. There are so many examples of how rather then [sic] resist something or relentlessly pursue something that doesn't seem to bring forth good fruit, no mater [sic] how important or right it seems to be to us at the moment, we need to just let them go and trust that the Lord in his wisdom will reveal to us the why's and how's when he deems fit.

In regards to the scripture you mention. I don't view those three things as absolute conditions. I view them as one example of many possible scenarios. In that context it all makes sense to me. I also concentrate on verse 60. Since it is not mine to know everything that went on in those infant years of the Church, I know that Joseph was sustained and justified by God and that the fruits of his works the last 170 years since then prove to me that Joseph was a prophet of God in good standing with God and therefore should be with me. Evidently, as he struggled to fulfill his mission assigned to him by God, he had challenges, mistakes, struggles, and triumphs along the way, but in the end seemed to satisfy is [sic] Father and therefore deserves nothing less than my satisfaction and thanks. [Emphasis added]

I am praying that peace will come to you and that you will stay close and united with the gospel and the saints whom you love and who love you.

My sincerest hopes,

Steven

As demonstrated by Mr. Rockwood, to avoid any possible judgment of the church leadership, the modern Mormon must maintain multiple standards of personal behavior. One standard must be preserved for the common member of the church and a second (much lower) standard for the leadership of the church. A serious temple violation,[4] which would certainly negate the priesthood power and authority of the average member, would not have the same impact on the "Prophet" or other high-ranking leaders of the church. The juvenile literary deflection Mr. Rockwood attempted was to dismiss the "absolute conditions" that were in fact recorded in the noted Scripture. As stated in my question they are:

> *As clearly recorded by Joseph Smith in Doctrine and Covenants 132:61-64, the Lord sets <u>three</u> conditions (under the heading of a Law) which are required for a member of the Priesthood who desires to take other wives: She must be 1) "**a virgin**", 2) "**the first to give her consent**", and 3) "**vowed to no other man**", "**belongeth unto him and to no one else**.*

The three requirements given by the Lord specific to "a member of the Priesthood who desires to take other wives" simply and undoubtedly still remain. Under the Rockwood Doctrine, one may state that what is known may not be an "absolute condition," but does that make the "absolute conditions" that *are* recorded irrelevant or simply disappear? It is true that one may add to the known conditions the Lord has set. For example, one might add that she must be of a specific height, weight, hair color, or ethnic background. But how, then, would any of those new additions change the known conditions already set by the Lord? Knowing that the vast majority of Joseph's thirty-three wives did not meet these "absolute"

---

[4] Adultery, fornication, and others noted within the Endowment; see appendix A document number 26.

conditions set by the Lord makes for a short conversation with a Mormon High Priest.

With my frustration at an all-time high, I sent an admittedly sarcastic and immature letter to Mr. Rockwood in the fall of 2009. As he is a very intelligent man and an employee of the Mormon Church, I proposed the following question and offered a follow-up assessment of his absurd reading of the Mormon Scriptures.

> *Are you any "more" or "less" flexible with Official Golf Rules than you are the Laws of the Priesthood? If you play the 9th hole at the local club and you really, honestly, truly and passionately don't "view" the Par 3 as an absolute, because it may be just one of "many possible scenarios". You might just "view" it as a Par 5, and in that "context" you can say: "it all makes sense to me.*

> *What a charming life you must have. But I freely admit that this is only an imaginary tale, for who would or who could question the Official PGA Rules in that way? But for **you**, it seems that with the Commandments from the Lord, you can question, you can manipulate, you can change or you can view, as you wish. Can I just say that in that context "none of that makes any sense to me."*

Given the liberal parameters of the Rockwood Doctrine, polygamy, polyandry, blood atonement, bigotry, murder, revenge, deceptions, and lies can all be "viewed" as truly sacred elements of Christianity. Throughout Mormon history, and as reflected in the current literature of the church, such appalling activities were and still are justified by the teachings of the Mormon Prophets. It is my opinion that Steven Rockwood is a reasonably typical modern Mormon leader. He may find himself in a different era, but he is perfectly synchronized with the early Mormon core values as they relate to following the "Prophets."

As a member of the Church of Jesus Christ of Latter-day Saints, how much official history or authorized doctrine can one subjectively discard for personal reasons? At some stage, individual membership in a church, any church, becomes pointless when a significant collection of doctrine is personally rejected. This is exactly the painful process I underwent with only the support of my wife. I came to understand that no brother or sister in a leadership position could answer my questions, for the answers would contradict the very teachings of the Lord Himself, as they understood it. I completely believe now that the leadership of the Mormon Church is permanently and irreversibly locked into a 180-year history of problematic theology that cannot be corrected without a total collapse of the church. And still, one of the most bewildering facts I have yet to comprehend is that this "new age" generation of Mormons, who contort the teachings of the early Mormon Prophets, would in fact be soundly rejected and perhaps killed by the very men they now struggle to defend. Neither Joseph Smith Jr. nor Brigham Young were of the temperament to have others offer explanations, excuses, or apologies for them. They knew very well what they taught, and it is only this new softer, milder, and more politically correct generation of Mormon leaders that finds such teachings an embarrassment and struggle with great difficulty to force such doctrine into a perverted form of Christianity.

On a personal level, I have asked many Mormon leaders just how to manage or teach the rejection of unpleasant doctrine. What specific set of doctrines is actually required to be accepted by the membership of the church? Who actually establishes any list of required doctrines if the membership of the church, like Mr. Rockwood, is at liberty to pass judgment on the Scriptures themselves? If the practice of selective acceptance or rejection of official doctrine is reasonable, then certainly unpleasant or older doctrine can simply fade away. Likewise, any doctrine that others may reject can become a central pillar of your distinctive expression of faith within the very same church.

When confronted with lesser-known but official doctrines of the church, I have known Mormon Bishops and Stake leaders who have stated: "I do not want to know anymore, even if it is true." A lack of knowledge, intentional or unintentional, with regard to the authorized history or doctrines of the church does not make any teaching less valid or reduce the purpose or intent of the Prophet who received the "revelation." Yet many Mormons seem to fear that too much knowledge of Mormon history and teaching will create disharmony with the Brethren in Salt Lake and jeopardize their standing in the church. I believe that members of the Church of Jesus Christ of Latter-day Saints, more than any other religious group, deliberately restrict the information they acquire and then process to sustain their faith. On the few occasions when members of the church would speak with me concerning these issues of doctrine, most would appear to be very confused that I, as a Bishop, would be considering such questions.

CHAPTER THREE

Read, Study, Ponder, and Pray: The Trauma of Learning the Truth

And Jesus answered and said unto them, Take heed that no man deceive you.

Matthew 24:4

And ye shall know the truth, and the truth shall make you free.

John 8:32

The Truth Matters

A common thread woven throughout some of life's most intensely traumatic and sincerely enlightening events is simply the truth. Although tremendously powerful, the simple and straightforward truth can destroy a family, rescue a marriage, or satisfy a lifetime of misplaced resentment. The value placed on the truth is an accurate measure of one's own character and integrity. Discovery of the truth can be one of the most powerful motivations in one's life; it can be invigorating or devastating, but it is always better than a lie.

I remember well a valuable education concerning the truth that I received in Hawaii. Before I knew the full history of Hawaii, our family occasionally would take visitors to the Dole Pineapple factory just outside of Honolulu. The tour was always excellent, and the cheap knick-knacks and free pineapple juice were very popular with our guests. The Dole multimedia presentation of the history of the islands and the importance of the pineapple harvest, complete with classical Hawaiian music in the background, was first-class. The bus tour of an operational pineapple field, regularly hosted by a young Polynesian, persuaded me that the Dole operations were thoroughly Hawaiian.

In the second of our five years living in Hawaii, I began a more serious review of the history of the islands. My interest was due in part to a story told by one of the local Hawaiian families at church. It was reported that a niece was totally disowned by the elderly patriarch of the family when she went to work at the Dole factory. A minimal amount of research confirmed the fact that Sanford B. Dole, an American businessman, led a bloody rebellion in 1887, in which the Hawaiian monarchy was placed under house arrest and Dole was declared, first, the president of Hawaii and, later, the territorial governor.

By any standard of respectable national conduct, an armed rebellion against native peoples for the expressed purpose of capital gain and personal power is unacceptable. Yet it has been a hallmark of Western modernization. I came to better understand the thinly veiled racial comments towards the whites, and more so the military in Hawaii, as massive tracks of once private land still remain under the control of the United States government. I remember one of the wittier, but utterly true, comments on a bumper sticker I once saw at a North Shore gift shop, which read, "Don't complain about the Japanese, at least they are Paying for the Land." The obvious point of this personal education was that my ignorance had no affect whatsoever on the truth itself! Without knowing the truth, nothing in my life had or would change. Likewise, with or without my knowing the truth, nothing in the lives of the descendants of those Hawaiians who had been victimized had or would change either. This, then, is the very point of the disgusting doctrines of the Mormon Church. Just because I did not know of the early teachings or actions of the "Prophets" did not change the reality of the events themselves or my unquestionable association with them.

It is reasonable to assume that we may disagree with several aspects of our preferred political party or certain elements of our trade union or even fundamental policies of our homeowners association. But religion is a choice like no other in our lives. We may have been born into a specific religion, but as an adult no other choice reflects who we are and what we believe more than what religion we follow. I do not believe that there is such a thing as "limited membership" in any religion a responsible adult willingly joins. If you disagree with or oppose the *fundamental* doctrines of a religion, you should separate yourself from that group.

In my view, the essential survival strategy within Mormonism is the intentional decision to be selectively ignorant of the bad elements of the church, thus preserving only the superior qualities of the church. Ironically, at times the leadership of the Mormon Church has been very open about the several peculiar teachings and bizarre doctrines of the church. It is the general membership of the church that employs personal filters on the information available. This was the primary reason why my questions could not be answered—simply because most Latter-day Saints cannot know the details of a true event because they have incorrectly ruled out the possibility that the general concept could be true. For them the truth is too unattractive, uncomfortable, and difficult to fit into their personal view of reality.

As a Mormon Bishop, I came to understand that I owned a portion of all the doctrines of the church and I shared, to some degree, in the total history of the church as well. As an active member, and certainly as a leader in the Church of Jesus Christ of Latter-day Saints, I was responsible for at least an understanding of the complete history of the church. It would be wrong to have answers or opinions on just the segments and subjects of the church that I had adopted as *my* version of Mormonism and remain willfully ignorant of the church's true teaching and history. Yet this is exactly how typical Latter-day Saints operate, and a perfect example of this can be found in their views regarding the practice of polygamy.

Even today a large segment of the Mormon Church believes, in complete disagreement with the formal teachings of the church, that the sealing of a man and a woman conducted within the temple does *not* involve the potential of polygamy. Although each couple is encouraged to return home and read

Doctrine and Covenants, section 132 in order to understand the fullness of the blessings they have just participated in, not one of them will be instructed to "skip over" the "plural marriage sections." The instruction is clear, the commandment is unambiguous, and 120 years after the practice of polygamy was suspended, the original demand from the Lord remains in print for the modern Latter-day Saint to contemplate.

> *And again, as pertaining to the law of the priesthood—if any man espouse a virgin, and desire to espouse another, and the first give her consent, and if he espouse the second, and they are virgins, and have vowed to no other man, then is he justified; he cannot commit adultery for they are given unto him; for he cannot commit adultery with that that belongeth unto him and to no one else. (Doctrine and Covenants 132:61)*

> *All these principles that I have treated upon, pertaining to eternal marriage, the very moment that they are admitted to be true, it brings in plurality of marriage, and if plurality of marriage is not true or in other words, if a man has no divine right to marry two wives or more in this world, then marriage for eternity is not true, and your faith is all vain, and all the sealing ordinances and powers, pertaining to marriages for eternity are vain, worthless, good for nothing; for as sure as one is true the other also must be true. Amen.[1]*

I think of the millions of women in the church today who openly have "issues" with sharing their husbands with another wife, especially those new converts in foreign lands who have never even heard of polygamy and polyandry. I believe that the leadership of the church is totally indifferent to the tender feelings of those women. I have found it somewhat confusing that the Utah Mormons do not practice polygamy as it is printed within their current Scriptures, yet the fundamentalist Mormons in Texas do, and they are rebuked by the Utah Mormons for doing it.

---

[1] Apostle Orson Pratt, July 18, 1880, Tabernacle Salt Lake. *Journal of Discourses* 21:286.

It is *not* the responsibility of the leadership of the church to educate all members of the Church concerning every detail of his or her own religious beliefs.

The members of the Church are reminded that the practice of polygamous or plural marriage is not the only law whose suspension has been authorized by the Lord. . . . The law of the United Order has likewise been suspended, to be re-established in the due time of the Lord.[2]

The members of any church have freely and willingly chosen to be associated with the complete teachings, doctrines, and policies of that church. As much as I might have wanted to disagree with the deplorable elements of the Church of Jesus Christ of Latter-day Saints or to distance myself from the offensive doctrines, the fact remains that my association was subject to *their* standards, not mine. In no other aspect of life is our complete understanding and acceptance of our deliberate association with a group more important than in what religious organization we unite with.

As a novice writer, the most demanding part of this story has been accurately communicating the brutality of total spiritual abandonment. I can describe with ease the obvious inconsistencies of the several "peculiar" Mormon doctrines. I can effortlessly illustrate the examples of hypocrisy and specific cases of deception by the leadership of the Church of Jesus Christ of Latter-day Saints. Descriptions of the many appalling abuses against the fundamental teachings of the Lord Jesus Christ do not present even the slightest issue. But the emotional and spiritual torment I went through was overwhelming, considering that challenging the church potentially could have meant losing my sweet wife of thirty-three years to a "better, more faithful, eternal Mormon companion," along with losing my son, my daughters, and my many grandchildren.

Through the use of the Temple Covenants, the clear spiritual intimidation of those who might question the church is that the

---

[2] President Heber J. Grant, dated January 13, 1914. *Messages of the First Presidency of the Church of Jesus Christ of Latter-day Saints,* 6:327.

loss of their family is the ultimate price for opposition or apostasy in the church. The totally fabricated but brilliantly applied dogma of the Mormon Church is that those family members who "fall away" from the faith simply will be replaced by a more faithful Mormon husband or wife to ensure the eternal progression of the remaining members of the family. This then sets the stage for the very real potential of a permanent spiritual strain between family members of varying activity levels. This lie was used many times by the early leaders of the church, who persuaded dozens of women that the men they were currently and civilly married to were not truly the right "eternal partners." Often this instruction was only a precursor to a proposal of plural marriage, without the need of a civil divorce from the current husband.

It is nearly impossible to fully comprehend the great risks a devoted Mormon Bishop takes by suggesting that some elements of the Mormon faith might be inconsistent with the teachings of Jesus Christ. Without actually being an indoctrinated Mormon, it is even more impractical to truthfully describe the many consequences outright opposition implies. One's own acceptance of the Lord Jesus Christ as his or her personal Savior, Lord, and Redeemer is of little relevance to the unity of the family. The overwhelmingly accepted measure of the sanctity of the family unit is the several required Temple Ordinances, which "seal" a family together forever. It is not uncommon to know of families who have been "sealed" together, yet one or more of the family members have been unfaithful to each other or to the church. Still, the "sealing" is considered to remain valid. It is as if without a written judgment from the officers of the church, the actions of the individual will not alter the "sealed" relationships.

Some declare as a statement of rationalization—but without any church authority—that the Lord Himself, setting all things in order, will deal with those who have violated their Temple Covenants. I believe that to be true. I believe that most Mormons believe that to be true as well. What I do not understand or believe is how most Mormons will *not* apply the same religious declaration of integrity and justice to the leadership of the church. Generally speaking, as members of the Church of Jesus Christ of Latter-day Saints come to the knowledge of even a potential indiscretion, much less the obvious sins of the leadership, a very composed but somewhat disturbing childish tranquility delivers a few set phrases of sympathy: "We do not understand all things"; "What the Lord has asked of the Prophets is not for us to question"; and "All knowledge will be restored in the Lord's time." To even question the character or actions of a church leader is strictly against the teachings of the church. I am again reminded of the practically sinister reprimand provided by one of the Apostles of the Mormon Church. Dallin H. Oaks, who is considered to hold the same authority and responsibility as any one of the original Apostles of Jesus Christ, declared during an interview on PBS, "It's wrong to criticize leaders of the church, even if the criticism is true."[3]

What may be only slightly more tragic, but certainly more significant as it applies to the history of the church and the actions of its leadership, is what Oaks said concerning the value of the truth. To maintain the integrity and the context of the following interview, the reference below was taken directly from the official newsroom Web site of the Church of Jesus Christ of Latter-day Saints.[4]

> **[Helen Whitney]:** *You used an interesting phrase, "Not everything that's true is useful." Could you develop that as someone who's a scholar and trying to encourage deep searching?*

> **[Elder Dallin H. Oaks]:** *The talk where I gave that was a talk on "Reading Church History" — that was the title of the talk. And in the course of the talk I said many things about*

---

[3] Interview of Dallin H. Oaks, "The Mormons," PBS documentary, 2008.

[4] Ibid. The interview transcript can be found at http://www.newsroom.lds.org/ldsnewsroom/eng/news-releases-stories/elder-oaks-interview-transcript-from-pbs-documentary (accessed October 6, 2009). Boldface added for emphasis.

being skeptical in your reading and looking for bias and looking for context and a lot of things that were in that perspective. But I said two things in it and the newspapers and anybody who ever referred to the talk only referred to [those] two things: one is the one you cite, "Not everything that's true is useful," and that [meant] "was useful to say or to publish." And you tell newspapers any time (media people) [that] they can't publish something, they'll strap on their armor and come out to slay you!
[Laughs.]

I also said something else that has excited people: that it's wrong to criticize leaders of the Church, even if the criticism is true, because it diminishes their effectiveness as a servant of the Lord. One can work to correct them by some other means, but don't go about saying that they misbehaved when they were a youngster or whatever. Well, of course, that sounds like religious censorship also."

But not everything that's true is useful. *I am a lawyer, and I hear something from a client. It's true, but I'll be disciplined professionally if I share it because it's part of the attorney-client privilege. There's a husband-wife privilege, there's a priest-penitent privilege, and so on. That's an illustration of the fact that not everything that's true is useful to be shared.*

In relation to history, I was speaking in that talk for the benefit of those that write history. In the course of writing history, I said that people ought to be careful in what they publish because not everything that's true is useful. See a person in context; don't depreciate their effectiveness in one area because they have some misbehavior in another area—especially from their youth. I think that's the spirit of that. I think I'm not talking necessarily just about writing Mormon history; I'm talking about George Washington or any other case. If he had an affair with a girl when he was a teenager, I don't need to read that when I'm trying to read a biography of the Founding Father of our nation.

The manner in which Elder Oaks makes a comparison to George Washington in his youth as having a *hypothetical* affair is disgusting, for he knows full well that Joseph Smith Jr. in *reality* took two fourteen-year-old girls as wives when he was thirty-seven and had a total of thirty-three wives. And yet Oaks demonstrates very clearly the core values and strategy of what I have called the "Rockwood Doctrine" in chapter 2 of this book, which I believe is employed throughout the Church of Jesus Christ of Latter-day Saints. I must state yet again that this policy of selective acceptance and representation of the truth from the leadership of an organization that proudly declares itself to be the "only true church on the earth" is one of the best possible indicators that their claims are anything but true. At every turn the leadership, media, and publications of the Mormon Church frustrates the spirit of truth as one attempts to navigate through the maze of contradictory positions, hypocritical actions, and misleading practices of such a disingenuous organization.

Anti-Mormon or Simply True?

On Sunday, January 22, 2006, I was asked to the home of Richard B. Cannon, the Maryland Baltimore Mission President of the Church of Jesus Christ of Latter-day Saints. I had considered President Cannon a good friend and dear brother in the church. I was asked to give a lesson on the First Council of Nicaea, held in AD 325, as I had completed considerable study of the event and its impact on the formation of the Bible. In attendance that evening was Sister Cannon, a former Mission President and his wife, a number of senior missionaries, my teenaged daughter, and a new member of the church. The new member was from my ward, Columbia Second, and I knew her daughter very well as she was active in our youth group. I had no idea that what would happen that evening would haunt me for the rest of my life.

As I was organizing my several posters concerning the events of the Council at Nicaea, the small group of guests was visiting before we started the lesson. Just then I heard this new sister to the church ask one of the young missionaries about the doctrine of blood atonement as taught by Brigham Young. She was a nurse at an area hospital and said that a coworker had questioned her about the matter. She was politely told by one of the more senior guests that the question was well off the subject of the evening. She asked again whether the doctrine was in fact taught by Brigham Young. This time her chastisement was much more abrupt: "That is just an anti-Mormon lie." Undaunted, she asked again, "Did he or did he not teach the principle?" The discouragement in her voice was unmistakable. The simplicity of her question was fresh, and it cut me to the core of my soul that she was again rejected. She began to cry. She asked for her coat and then departed, and I did nothing. I will answer for my silence someday, because I knew better. Months earlier I had read and reread the sermons of Brigham Young of which she spoke, and I did not come to her aid. I knew that Brigham Young had taught such a thing, and yet I kept quiet. I knew that he taught that the atonement of Christ did not, in his view, atone for all the sins of this world and that in some cases the blood of the sinner was to be spilt in this life.

> *Will you love your brothers or sisters likewise, when they have committed a sin that cannot be atoned for without the shedding of their blood? Will you love that man or woman well enough to shed their blood?[5]*

> *I say, that there are men and women that I would advise to go to the President immediately, and ask him to appoint a committee to attend to their case; and then let a place be selected, and let that committee shed their blood.[6]*

> *You may think that I am not teaching you Bible doctrine, but what says the apostle Paul? I would ask how many covenant breakers there are in this city and in this kingdom. I believe that there are a great many; and if they are covenant breakers we need a place designated, where we can shed their*

---

[5] President Brigham Young, Salt Lake Tabernacle, February 1857. *Journal of Discourses* 4:220.

[6] President Jedediah M. Grant, Second Counselor to President Brigham Young, Father to Heber J. Grant, delivered in the Bowery, Great Salt Lake City, September 21, 1856. *Journal of Discourses* 4:49-51.

blood.[7]

I often think of the comments and the tenderness of that sweet sister as a portion of my motivation to complete this book, because I did not defend her right to ask a simple and important question. I think of the fact that she was right, not only to ask the question but also to confront those who should have supported her search for the truth. She was new to the Mormon faith and was still accustomed to asking questions as a new member or investigator of the church. This may have been the first time that a question was rejected; she later left the Mormon Church.

Two years later, I discovered the correlation involving the doctrine of blood atonement as taught by Brigham Young and the hundreds of Mormon temple ceremonies my wife and I had participated in. I finally understood that I too had mimicked in the temple the very practice of taking a human life as taught by Brigham Young, precisely that doctrine the woman was asking about. I also have considered the words of James, specific to what I consider the hateful words of the Mormon Prophets quoted above, and found his assessment of such men completely truthful and accurate: "If any man among you seem to be religious, and bridleth not his tongue, but deceiveth his own heart, this man's religion is vain" (James 1:26).

That evening at the home of the Mission President my harsh education concerning what was truly "anti-Mormon" and what was truly just plain Mormon began. It was disheartening to consider that virtually all the promises, priorities, standards, and goals taught to my family and me were now deteriorating under the weight of the simple truth. Even more depressing was the casual and disinterested attitude that was repeated many times when I too asked for help.

---

[7] Ibid.

Spiritual Loyalty—to My Church or My God?

The fabric of the "restored Mormon gospel" is woven throughout every aspect of the life of one who holds the Mormon priesthood. The principles of honesty, devotion, fidelity, and loyalty are drilled deep into a man's character and temperament. The fundamental problem, which cannot be discovered while under the influence of the priesthood, is that these loyalty traits are primarily directed toward the church and the family but not toward Jesus Christ. In Mormon thought and culture, there is a very distinctive and unique relationship between the church and the family. To the Latter-day Saint, the family unit is neither complete nor entirely independent of the organization of the church. In Mormonism, the power and authority of the priesthood is the common thread that unites throughout all eternity the individuals of the family to each other. It is taught that the influence and authority of that priesthood is without limits both in this world and the next. As will be discussed in chapter 4, the priesthood power and authority of the average member answers to a much higher standard of conduct than the priesthood power and authority of the leadership of the church. In fact, the following Mormon Scripture, if applied to the actions of Joseph Smith Jr., Brigham Young, John Taylor, and many other leaders of the Mormon Church, would completely and absolutely negate the ability of these men to either lead the church or pass on their priesthood authority.

> *That they may be conferred upon us, it is true; but when we undertake to cover our sins, or to gratify our pride, our vain ambition, or to exercise control or dominion or compulsion upon the souls of the children of men, in any degree of unrighteousness, behold, the heavens withdraw themselves; the Spirit of the Lord is grieved; and when it is withdrawn, Amen to the priesthood or the authority of that man. (Doctrine and Covenants 121:37)*

Amazingly, there is a wealth of positive and remarkably Christian-based aspects of the church. I have stated many times that without the disgraceful or even the questionable elements of the Mormon Church, it would reflect, at least outwardly, one of the most accurate recreations of the earliest Christian churches. Yet, with all its family values and remarkable organizational achievements, the repulsive and deeply offensive fact remains that the leadership of the Mormon Church has taught and continues to teach that the Son of the living God, Jesus Christ Himself, and *not* the Mormon Prophets, is the true author of polygamy, polyandry, blood atonement, and the nearly 150 years of lies, deceit, and deception against the United States of America.

This complete and total hypocrisy is thoroughly indifferent to the Latter-day Saint's own Twelfth Article of Faith, Doctrine and Covenants 58:21, and numerous official sermons by the Prophets and General Authorities regarding the law of the land. Without question, early church officers clearly and consistently disobeyed both the territorial and federal laws of the United States of America. And yet the written, if not actually practiced, doctrines of the church present a much more obedient and submissive faith.

> *We believe in being subject to kings, presidents, rulers, and magistrates, in obeying, honoring, and sustaining the law. (Twelfth Article of Faith)*

> *Let no man break the laws of the land for he that keepeth the laws of God hath no need to break the laws of the land. (Doctrine and Covenants 58:21)*

To better clarify the spiritual impact and personal management of the several major contradictions and hypocrisies the Latter-day Saint is required to manage, I would like to highlight a few examples, which were significant in my life as a Mormon. To be fair and honest, I could never deny that many of the most sought after values and traits of Mormonism are worthy of admiration. Chief among these are the central importance of the family, outstanding youth programs, personal preparedness, and the authentic desire to provide meaningful service to others.

To be equally fair and honest, the educated Latter-day Saint must recognize that some of the darkest events in American religious history are likewise to be owned by the Mormon Church. Foremost among these are the introduction, proliferation, and passionate defense of polygamy and by association polyandry; the foundation of a religious culture dedicated to the belief that the United States of America has been chosen by God to become a theocracy; and finally the detailed planning and deceptive cover-up of the Mountain Meadows Massacre of September 11, 1857.[8] The history and impact of each of these events will be addressed in other chapters of this book. Of concern here are the several contradictions and hypocrisies openly taught by the leadership of the Church of Jesus Christ of Latter-day Saints, which the general membership must then defend, develop, dismiss, or embrace without further clarification from those who advocate such doctrine without any associated responsibility.

The moral challenge to the average Latter-day Saint is one of spiritual loyalty. If the Mormon Prophets, Apostles, and General Authorities of the church are in fact the very mouthpieces of the Lord Himself, then they should *not* be questioned or criticized, as I have done as both a High Priest of the Mormon Church and now as a recovering Christian and an excommunicated Mormon Bishop. For Mormonism to be true, Christ Himself must be corrupted into one who authorizes horrible behavior, thus rendering the Mormon Prophets completely blameless concerning the motivations for their unspeakable actions. This I believe has been clearly demonstrated by words and actions throughout the history of the Mormon Church. To more efficiently attribute the corrupt actions of a man directly to Jesus Christ Himself, the leadership of the Mormon Church has attempted to diminish the righteousness of Deity itself. The central pillar of this unjust strategy of personal justification has been the often-quoted comment by the fifth Prophet of the Mormon Church, Lorenzo Snow.

---

[8] See appendix B.

We believe that God is a personal being. By a personal being, we mean that he is a man—an exalted man. Approximately one hundred years ago, soon after Lorenzo Snow became a member of the true Church of Jesus Christ, he formulated a remarkable couplet, which has since that time become famous. He said: "As man is, God once was; as God is, man may become."[9]

Think of it, brethren and sisters, sons and daughters of God inheriting from Him through our spiritual birth the very attributes and qualities of Deity, which in our Father in heaven are perfect and make Him what He is. We are placed here upon the earth for the purpose, in part, of improving, magnifying and perfecting those qualities and attributes; so that, while we are now but gods in embryo, having been born of God, in His likeness, in His image, and having received from Him the attributes of Deity, through perfecting those attributes in time and in eternity we will be like Him in very deed, and be glorified with him in His kingdom.[10]

With this "Mormon perspective" that God came from a common man, it is much easier to accept that Christ Himself may have been motivated by the same base desires as an ordinary man and as such has directed His Prophets to fulfill those apparently sensual desires. We have been asked to suppose that only a true nonbeliever would not comprehend this foundational Mormon doctrine. Please excuse my obvious sarcasm; I have challenged this, the most pretentious of all Mormon doctrine because I have come to know the personalities and motivations of Joseph Smith Jr., Brigham Young, John Taylor, and many others whom I would in no way consider gods "in embryo." The Mormon God, who is an exalted man like us, is even capable of directing others to lie on His behalf. In the Mormon Scriptures, specifically the book of

---

[9] Elder Milton R. Hunter, Conference Report, October 1948, First Day—Morning Meeting, 15 (emphasis added). See Lorenzo Snow, *The Millennial Star* 54:404.

[10] Elder George F. Richards, Conference Report, October 1914, First Day—Morning Session, 16 (emphasis added).

Abraham 2:24 we find this instruction from the Mormon God: *"Let her say unto the Egyptians, she is thy sister, and thy soul shall live."* This is completely, fundamentally and authoritatively different from the Genesis version of the story where Abraham, not God, tells Sarai to lie. In the original Genesis (20:1-2) the text clearly places the lie with Abraham: *"Now Abraham moved on from there into the region of the Negev and lived between Kadesh and Shur. For a while he stayed in Gerar, and there Abraham said of his wife Sarah, "She is my sister." Then Abimelek king of Gerar sent for Sarah and took her."*

More to the point, I will discuss here the challenges of the Latter-day Saint specific to the several major contradictions and hypocrisies regarding the truth. The truth may require some discussion, as even the word itself has several meanings within the vocabulary of the modern Latter-day Saint. When one speaks of the "true church," it is a direct reference to the restored gospel and by association the restoration of the only authorized priesthood on the earth today. When speaking of an official doctrine or teaching that may be "true," the application of the term begins to distort somewhat into an individual acceptance through a private confirmation known as a personal revelation. This is not simply a strategy invented by the general population of the church but is a practice officially taught by the leadership to ensure all members of the church have a personal testimony of what has been taught and might know for themselves what is or is not the will of the Lord. I believe this strategy provides some measure of distance between the potentially offensive or violent teachings of the church leadership and the individual member.

A recent example of this was in the September 2007 issue of the official magazine of the church, the *Ensign*, specifically in the article "The Mountain Meadows Massacre" by Richard E. Turley Jr. on pages 14 to 21. As I was still an active High Priest in the Mormon Church at the time and had read several books on the massacre,[11] just how my church would address the 150th anniversary of the tragedy was of some interest to me. I was both shocked and embarrassed at how the church yet again passed an opportunity to take responsibility for the murder of some 120 unarmed men, women, and children on that September 11th in southern Utah. On page 16 of the magazine was one of the most offensive and misleading statements concerning the tragedy at Mountain Meadows:

> *He, Brigham Young, and other leaders preached with fiery rhetoric against the enemy they perceived in the approaching army and sought the alliance of Indians in resisting the troops.*

This statement is a carefully crafted message to the current members of the church, those who might be learning about the Mountain Meadows Massacre for the first time. It suggests to the modern reader that those early church members who heard Brigham Young and the other leaders at the time of this crisis lecture on the subject of "the enemy" apparently should have considered such preaching from the living Prophet of God, the governor of the territory, and the commanding general of the militia as just "fiery rhetoric." The point of this message, printed some 150 years after the event, is to place the responsibility directly on the early congregation of the church to disregard such rhetoric. Is it possible that the church leadership today would have us believe that the congregation at the feet of the living Prophet of God was to dismiss his violent instructions as only rhetoric? This is precisely where the traditional teaching of a "personal testimony" through "personal revelation" had failed these early members of the church. The average member of the church should have known not to kill those 120 unarmed visitors from Arkansas, for President Brigham Young, President George A. Smith, Elder John D. Lee, Stake President Isaac C. Haight, and Bishop Klingensmith, along with many other church leaders—well—they were all just kidding that day! I apologize for the sarcasm, but it is beyond

---

[11] By far the best-researched book on the subject is Will Bagley's *Blood of the Prophets, Brigham Young and the Massacre at Mountain Meadows* (Norman, OK: University of Oklahoma Press, 2002).

all reason that the Mormon Church today would have us believe that the average hardworking members in 1857 should have known those instructions were only fiery rhetoric.

I suggest that at no other time in the history of the Church of Jesus Christ of Latter-day Saints has an official publication presented to the membership of the church, and to the world, that the preaching (Scripture by his own account) of a past living Prophet was in fact nothing more than *"fiery rhetoric."* The message is offensive twice, once to the generation who sat at the feet of President Young and simply misunderstood the living Prophet of God, and to us who are now instructed to believe that it was their responsibility to "filter" his formal, more solemn sermons from his fiery rhetoric. Following are a few statements from President Brigham Young, the "authorized representative of the Lord Jesus Christ, holding all the keys of the priesthood." These statements might fall into the category of "fiery rhetoric" to which the congregation of the time was to pay little or no attention. But just how was it that the congregation of that time was *not* to believe the words of these leaders? This passionate instruction came from the very men who were to inspire, motivate, and lead with words and actions men and women to greatness and glory. And yet, the current leadership of the church would have us believe that at times these same men delivered passionate, yet empty rhetoric that the membership was not to act on at all.

> *To diverge a little, in regard to those who have persecuted this people and driven them to the mountains, I intend to meet them on their own grounds. It was asked this morning how we could obtain redress for our wrongs; I will tell you how it could be done, we could take the same law they have taken, viz., mobocracy, and if any miserable scoundrels come here, cut their throats. (All the people said, Amen.)*[12]
>
> *I will tell you a dream that I had last night. . . . With that, I took my large bowie knife that I used to wear as a bosom pin*

---

[12] A Discourse by President Brigham Young, Delivered in the Tabernacle, Great Salt Lake City, July 8, 1855. *Journal of Discourses* 2:311.

*in Nauvoo, and cut one of their throats from ear to ear, saying,
Go to hell across lots. The other one said, You dare not serve me
so. I instantly sprang at him, seized him by the hair of the head,
and, bringing him down, cut his throat, and sent him after his
comrade.*[13]

To further make certain that we today completely understand that the membership of the church, and *not* the leadership of the church, was responsible for the Mountain Meadows Massacre, a modern-day Prophet, Seer, and Revelator provided the final coaching. At the massacre site itself, Elder Henry B. Eyring, then the Second Counselor in the First Presidency, stated, "The responsibility for the massacre lies with local leaders of the Church of Jesus Christ of Latter-Day Saints in the regions near Mountain Meadows who also held civic and military positions and with members of the Church acting under their direction."[14] That is to say that we are to believe that some one hundred local church members and their leaders (only one of whom was ever prosecuted for the crime) could follow regional direction to commit mass murder, but they would not be influenced *whatsoever* by the preaching and direction of the living Prophet of God.

Here one of the great dichotomies of Mormonism is exposed. Hundreds if not thousands of formal sermons have been given declaring that there is great safety in following the guidance of the living Prophet of God. And yet, the individual Latter-day Saint also is admonished to validate that guidance through a personal witness and testimony as given by the Holy Spirit. How often could the two directions be at odds with each other? If the Holy Spirit directs the living Prophet of God and he has been called and sustained to provide guidance for the entire church, then how often could the Holy Spirit then witness to the individual member that the Prophet was wrong in his

---

[13] An address delivered by President Brigham Young in the Tabernacle, Great Salt Lake City, March 27, 1853. *Journal of Discourses* 1:83.

[14] Elder Henry B. Eyring's remarks at the Mountain Meadows Massacre Sesquicentennial on September 11, 2007, in Washington County, Utah. Newsroom.lds.org.

direction? How can both be true? I believe I have had a sure witness and testimony that the practice of taking either the wife or life of another man is wrong, yet this contradicts what was taught by the living Mormon Prophet as being from God. So again the leadership issues officially conflicting guidance to both follow the Prophet and yet validate that direction for yourself. Brigham Young said that he never gave a sermon to the church that should not be considered Scripture, but then he also stated that it might *not* be a good thing to blindly follow that Scripture.

I have never yet preached a sermon and sent it out to the children of men, that they may not call Scripture.[15]

What a pity it would be if we were led by one man to utter destruction! Are you afraid of this? I am more afraid that this people have so much confidence in their leaders that they will not inquire for themselves of God whether they are led by Him. I am fearful they settle down in a state of blind self-security, trusting their eternal destiny in the hands of their leaders with a reckless confidence that in itself would thwart the purposes of God in their salvation, and weaken that influence they could give to their leaders, did they know for themselves, by the revelations of Jesus, that they are led in the right way. Let every man and woman know, by the whispering of the Spirit of God to themselves, whether their leaders are walking in the path the Lord dictates, or not. This has been my exhortation continually.[16]

"If any man will do his will, he shall know of the doctrine, whether it be of God, or whether I speak of myself" (John 7:16-17). Every living soul in this world who will abide the law that entitles him to know by personal revelation from the Holy Ghost of the divinity of this work, of the stability and destiny of this kingdom, can get that knowledge, and I for one have that knowledge and so certify to you in sincerity and solemnity, in the

---

[15] Brigham Young, January 2, 1870 in the Tabernacle in Salt Lake. *Journal of Discourses* 13:95.

[16] Remarks by President Brigham Young, made in the Tabernacle, Great Salt Lake City, January 12, 1862. *Journal of Discourses* 9:150.

name of Jesus Christ. Amen.[17]

How Can We Come to Know Something Without Asking?

A pivotal experience for me was a regularly scheduled Priesthood stewardship meeting on the evening of Thursday July 15, 2004. During these meetings we are asked to report on our responsibilities and stewardships in the church. As the High Priest Group Leader of our ward, I reviewed our several accomplishments and challenges of the past few months. At the conclusion of this meeting, when asked if there were any outstanding issues not discussed, I asked President Lorin M. Lund, member of the Columbia Maryland Stake Presidency, for his help: "President, I have had some questions from coworkers and visitors to our meetings, and I also have some questions." I provided only the general headings of polygamy, blacks and the priesthood, and blood atonement without any details. He answered very politely, "Well, there is an answer for everything." with one hand raised as if to say, "But not now." At approximately 5:00 in the afternoon the next day, President Lund called my house and said, "Brother Baker, I did not appreciate you waiting for an audience to bring those issues up." I hung up the phone; I knew instantly that he probably had never really been challenged in his faith, and that he did not understand the truthful history of the church. If there really is an answer for everything as President Lund stated, he has never once communicated even a hint of such to me.

The "audience" President Lorin Lund spoke of that night was two other leaders in the church. The four of us, all long-time holders of the Melchizedek Priesthood, all ordained leaders of the church who were sealed to our families in the temple, were considered an "audience" to President Lund. I had been challenged dozens of times in public and at work about these

---

[17] Elder Bruce R. McConkie, Conference Report, October 1958, Afternoon Meeting, 117.

issues, and I would never have considered three of my "brethren" secluded away in a locked room within a Mormon Church an audience! The subjects I wished to speak about to my priesthood leader, my spiritual mentor who was called and set apart to support me, included polygamy, blacks and the priesthood, and blood atonement, but I could not have known then that after some five years of questions Lorin Lund would not offer a *single word* concerning these issues. As has been recorded and will be discussed later, I was being introduced to a long-standing Mormon leadership strategy, which I have come to describe as "leadership laryngitis." This peculiar strategy is based on the presumption that if one does not acknowledge or comment on a given issue, it will simply fade away. It is my sincere opinion that of all the Mormon leaders I have ever had the displeasure of being associated with, Dr. Lorin M. Lund of the Columbia Maryland Stake, is the supreme example of conceit, hypocrisy, and arrogance.

My questions did not fade away, but I was left on my own to research or place in context the teachings of Brigham Young concerning the doctrine of blood atonement. I began to review stories, which I generally believed to be invented by "anti-Mormon" elements of other Christian churches. The primary mention of this subject, which was given to me by a coworker, was:

> *All mankind love themselves, and let these principles be known by an individual, and he would be glad to have his blood shed. That would be loving themselves, even unto an eternal exaltation. Will you love your brothers or sisters likewise, when they have committed a sin that cannot be atoned for without the shedding of their blood? Will you love that man or woman well enough to shed their blood? That is what Jesus Christ meant. He never told a man or woman to love their enemies in their wickedness, never.*[18]

We need to stop here for a moment and comprehend exactly

_____

[18] President Brigham Young, Salt Lake Tabernacle, February 1857. *Journal of Discourses* 4:220 (emphasis added).

what President Brigham Young had just instructed those within the tabernacle in 1857. He informed the faithful Mormon community that Jesus Christ Himself has authorized taking the life of another human being by slicing the person's throat from ear to ear, for Christ's sacrifice was not sufficient. Additionally, it is important to understand that none of the fourteen subsequent "Prophets" of the Church of Jesus Christ of Latter-day Saints ever revised his comment, "That is what Jesus Christ meant." It is true that in 1978 the church issued a letter by Elder Bruce R. McConkie, member of the Quorum of the Twelve Apostles, in which he rejects the practice of blood atonement:

> *There simply is no such thing among us as a doctrine of blood atonement that grants a remission of sins or confers any other benefit upon a person because his own blood is shed for sins. Let me say categorically and unequivocally that this doctrine can only operate in a day when there is no separation of Church and State and when the power to take life is vested in the ruling theocracy, as was the case in the day of Moses.[19]*

I believe this attempt to deflect any legitimate criticism is betrayed by three noteworthy facts. First, the doctrine was clearly taught throughout dozens of Mormon communities by Brigham Young himself, who stated that all of his sermons should be considered Scripture. Second, the McConkie letter referenced above clearly indicates that the doctrine can operate only within a theocracy, but it should be remembered that both Joseph Smith Jr. and Brigham Young presided over a theocracy. Elder McConkie has not lied; he has only assumed that the reader would not know of the Mormon theocracies in the past. Third, millions of Mormons have participated in exactly what my wife and I participated in on hundreds of occasions a full decade *after* the McConkie letter, namely, the graphic

---

[19] Letter dated October 18, 1978, to Mr. Thomas B. McAffee from Elder Bruce R. McConkie. Photocopy at http://www.shields-research.org/General/blood_atonement.htm. It should be noted that the practice of demonstrating blood atonement within the Mormon temples continued until 1990.

representation of this exact practice, the authorized taking of a human life as described by Brigham Young and other leaders of the church. The exact wording and actions involved in this Mormon temple ceremony, which was practiced up until 1990, will be covered later in this chapter.

The few examples I have noted here are not the only teaching on the subject of blood atonement, but these represent the most popular among those teachings I had wrongly considered to be anti-Mormon, until I realized that the teachings were from the Mormon Prophets themselves. In a letter to President Lund in February of 2005, I stated,

> *How depressing it is to know that as we emphasize the serious inconstancies of other faiths, we are to minimize or edit out the superficial issues of our own. For this very reason I have taught my children, investigators and those whom I have baptized that it is prudent to keep some distance between the actions, activities or policies of the Church and the Gospel of Jesus Christ.*

At that time I had not come to the full understanding that the many inconsistencies of the Mormon faith were anything but superficial; they were in fact the very foundation of Mormonism. After a full year of virtually no support from the leadership of the Columbia Maryland Stake, I was naive and trusting enough to think that a member of the First Presidency might be able to help. On January 30, 2006, I wrote a letter to President Thomas S. Monson, then the First Counselor to the Prophet. I included a copy of my Priesthood Authority Line,[20] as President Monson ordained the man who ordained me. A portion of that letter reads:

> *Over the past two years it has become obvious, both when sharing the Gospel and now on a personal level, that a number of subjects found to be in the "anti-Mormon" category, are in fact, True and Accurate accounts of the actual teachings of the Prophets and General Authorities as documented within authorized Church publications. . . . How am I to explain or*

---

[20] See appendix A document number 2b.

No answer came from President Monson, just as no answer would ever come concerning some of the most disturbing elements of Mormonism. These activities and doctrines are gently questioned among friends and families within the church, but there does not exist anywhere in the official curriculum of the church the opportunity to freely ask any slightly probing questions.

When asked to review the exceptional points of the "restored gospel," an active and informed member of the Mormon faith might have us consider a few of the key elements of the only "true church" on the earth today. Keep in mind that the much-loved points of the Mormon Church were received in the exact same manner and with the same authority as the more corrupt elements of the church. Following are the more traditional pillars of Mormonism.

1.   *The need for a living Prophet to lead the Lord's church on the earth.*

2.   *The knowledge that the heavens are indeed still open for God to guide and direct the affairs of His church through that living Prophet.*

3.   *The restoration of the power and authority of the Holy Priesthood.*

4.   *The restoration of the organization of the church, which was under the direction of Christ Himself, with a living Prophet, twelve Apostles, Bishops, Priests, Elders, and Deacons as required.*

5.   *A plan of salvation that provides an equal opportunity to all mankind and answers the basic questions of humanity: Where did I come from? Why am I here? Where am I going?*

6.   *The sure knowledge, through a visit to Joseph Smith Jr., that God the Father, His Son Jesus Christ, and the Holy Sprit are separate and distinct individuals.*

---

[21] See appendix A document number 12.

7. *A restoration of lost Scriptures and modern revelation: the Book of Mormon, the Pearl of Great Price, and the Doctrine and Covenants, which provide a second witness to the mission and testimony of the Lord Jesus Christ of Nazareth.*

8. *A restoration of ancient temple ordinances, which seal throughout eternity family relationships.*

9. *A church organized for the perfection of all mankind, through missionary service, higher education, financial independence, spiritual support, and fellowship.*

10. *Providing a meaningful opportunity to serve the Lord as we serve each other in our homes, in our churches, and in our worldwide communities.*

This collection of largely attractive doctrines of the Mormon Church has come to us through the revelations of the living Prophets and the canonized Scriptures of the restored gospel of Jesus Christ. To a large extent, the doctrines listed here are known to Mormons as examples of the "plain and precious teachings," which were lost from the Bible but restored by the Book of Mormon.

One of the claims made for the Book of Mormon is that it has restored to the world many of the plain and precious teachings which have been taken out of the Bible in its many translations, so that the blind who were not able to see and the deaf who could not understand would have their eyes and their ears opened to the truth which should be revealed.[22]

An essential purpose of each of the Mormon Prophets who have lived on this earth is to continue the restoration of God's church through direct revelations specific to the needs of the people and the will of the Lord. Such revelations are directly reflected through the example of the ten doctrines listed above. For faithful Mormons the indisputable fact remains that through this precise process of direct revelation that introduced what they see as very positive elements of the Mormon Church also

---

[22] Joseph Fielding Smith, Prophet of the Mormon Church, *The Restoration of All Things* (Salt Lake City: Deseret Book Company, 1973), 98.

came the repulsive doctrines of polygamy, polyandry, blood atonement, and lying for the Lord. This, as well as the years of deceit and deception, will be documented from the records of the church itself within the pages of this book. Latter-day Saints have been instructed that polygamy will return and that the practice will sustain them, as they become gods and goddesses of their own worlds.[23]

How, then, does one filter the truly good from the truly bad? Does the Lord actually intend for us to accept and practice the good with the bad? Is there not just a moment of uncertainty, when considering whether these appalling events actually were directed by the Lord Jesus Christ? I find it much more in keeping with the teachings of the Bible and the many testimonies of the Apostles, to conclude that Joseph Smith Jr. was simply a false Prophet. The alternative Mormon view seems to be that the Lord Jesus Christ experienced a massive personality change in about 1830 and came to favor what had earlier been recognized as lying, cheating, immorality, murder, and deception. I think not.

It is critical to understand that at that very moment of hesitation, in that instant of doubt, when one questions whether these teachings are *really* of the Lord, there is found in that moment of clarity the still small voice of the Holy Spirit of God. Does He not testify to the truth that these actions were of deceitful men? It is that simple; it is that straightforward. It does not require complex analysis or a far-reaching debate. What you do with what the Holy Spirit has given you at that moment may in fact be the most important single event of your life. In that moment you are free to balance your family history, your friends, your finances, or even the impending embarrassment before you against the sincerity of your heart or the potential denial of the Holy Spirit. Consider the words of Jesus Christ.

But the Comforter, which is the Holy Ghost, whom the

---

[23] "As man is, God once was; as God is, man may become" Snow, *The Millennial Star* 54:404.

Father will send in my name, he shall teach you all things, and bring all things to your remembrance, whatsoever I have said unto you. (John 14:26)

Wherefore I say unto you, all manner of sin and blasphemy shall be forgiven unto men: but the blasphemy against the Holy Ghost shall not be forgiven unto men." (Matt. 12:31)

Only among the members of the Mormon faith can one find such a high degree of selective acceptance with regard to the known teachings of the men they recognize as authorized representatives of the Lord Jesus Christ. To my knowledge there is no other religion whose adherents are *less* aware of their faith's own true history than that which calls itself the "true church." I know well the talent of selective application of questionable doctrine, for I practiced and taught it for over thirty years. As a spiritual self-defense mechanism, the average Mormon applies a high degree of rationalism. What I have come to call the "Rockwood Doctrine," as outlined in chapter 2, is an excellent example of such rationalization in the face of clear and concise information, and clear and concise Scripture. If such information casts even the slightest shadow of doubt on the actions of the leadership of the church, another explanation must be invented. Yet again I reflect back to the harsh warning of Dallin H. Oaks, who has been sustained by the entire Mormon Church as a Prophet, Seer, and Revelator: "It's wrong to criticize leaders of the Church, even if the criticism is true." [24]

If the attractive and morally sound doctrines of the Mormon Church have come through the revelations of the living Prophets and the canonized Scriptures of the restored gospel, then by equal measure the questionable doctrines also must be respected. I would now like to consider a few of those questionable doctrines, all of which have been formally delivered by Prophets, Seers, and Revelators of the Church of Jesus Christ of Latter-day Saints. These are the formal and official teachings of men who are considered to have been "called by the Lord," sustained and set apart to guide and direct

---

[24] Interview of Dallin H. Oaks, "The Mormons," PBS documentary, 2008.

the affairs of the Lord's church here on this earth.

To a large extent, the questionable doctrines discussed here are known to the Mormons as examples of the "plain and precious teachings" that were lost from the Bible but restored through the Book of Mormon and the revelations of the living Prophets of the church. In introducing and documenting these specific doctrines of questionable origin, I will also explain the impact each has had on my life as they have contributed to my resolution to leave the Mormon Church.

Polyandry, Taking the Wife of Another Man, is Worse Than Polygamy

If this entire book were to be reduced to only one serious and fundamental message, only one clear example of the wicked control through religious deception and deceit, it will be found in this section.

The core motivation for my leaving the Church of Jesus Christ of Latter-day Saints after thirty-two years of association requires very little analysis, only a modest debate, and certainly no complex justification. If what Joseph Smith Jr. did with the wives of so many other men was both authorized and directed by Jesus Christ Himself, then I can publicly state without any reservation whatsoever, "*I want no part of Christianity, and I wish for no relationship with a heavenly Master who would require such action.*" If this is the Christ of the Mormons, they are welcome to Him. And yet, with all praise, glory, and humility, I know that my Redeemer, my Savior, and my Lord is not of such character to appeal to the dark and evil desires men.

Based exclusively on how he deceitfully concealed the practices of polygamy and polyandry from his wives and from his own church, I believe the brief example of the limited practice of polygamy within the Bible was used as the ideal excuse to satisfy the personal desires of Joseph Smith. I further believe that polyandry, the taking of another man's wife, is far worse than polygamy and is utterly and completely disgusting when it is described as a *commandment* from the Lord.

The same God that has thus far dictated me and directed me and strengthened me in this work, gave me this revelation and commandment on celestial and plural marriage, and the same God commanded me to obey it. He said to me that unless I accepted it, and introduced it, and practiced it, I, together with my people would be damned and cut off from this time henceforth. We have got to observe it. It is an eternal principle and was given by way of commandment and not by way of instruction.[25]

When that principle was revealed to the Prophet Joseph Smith, he very naturally shrank, in his feelings, from the responsibilities thereby imposed upon him; foreseeing, as he did in part, the apparently insurmountable difficulties in the way of establishing it, in the face of the popular opinion, the traditions and customs of many generations, the frowns, ridicule, slander, opposition and persecutions of the world. Yes, this man of God, who dared to meet the opposition of the whole world with bold and fearless front, who dared to dispute the religious authority and accumulated learning and wisdom of the age—who dared everything for the truth, and shrank not even from the sacrifice of his own life in testimony of his divine mission, shrank, in his feelings, from the weight of the responsibility of inaugurating and establishing this new innovation upon the established customs of the world. But he did not falter, although it was not until an angel of God, with a drawn sword, stood before him; and commanded that he should enter into the practice of that principle, or he should be utterly destroyed, or rejected, that he moved forward to reveal and establish that doctrine.[26]

It should be established here that within any known version or translation of the Bible, the Lord may have allowed polygamy, but He *never* once authorized the doctrine, and He certainly *never* "commanded" the practice. This is quite different from the Mormon view of polygamy, as Joseph Smith has declared it. The very foundation of the Mormon view of

---

[25] Prophet Joseph Smith, *Contributor* 7, 5:259.

[26] Elder Joseph F. Smith, Delivered in the Tabernacle, Salt Lake City, Sunday morning, July 7, 1878. *Journal of Discourses* 20:29.

polygamy centers on the biblical references to the practice,[27] but the undisputed fact is that of the many hundreds of polygamist wives and concubines, all were taken or given by kings, priests, prophets, or even by their own wives but *never* once by the Lord. Abram took Hagar and Keturah, David took Bathsheba, and Solomon had seven hundred wives and three hundred concubines, but the Lord was *never* a participant or even implicated as taking part in any of it.

Concerning polyandry, the practice of taking another man's wife, it should be noted that of Joseph Smith's first twelve wives, nine were the wives of other men,[28] and the Lord clearly had something to say about that. In the book of Genesis is a graphic example of how the taking of another man's wife is a sin and how the Lord Himself intervened to stop it. The Lord willingly revealed Himself in this situation not to His servant Abraham but to a pagan king named Abimelech in order to prevent the impending sin of polyandry. Abraham had plainly misrepresented his relationship with his wife Sarah, telling the king that she was his sister. With that false information, the king sent for Sarah and had plans to take her that very evening.

> *But God came to Abimelech in a dream by night, and said to him, Behold, thou art but a dead man, for the woman which thou hast taken; for she is a man's wife. ... Then Abimelech called Abraham, and said unto him, What hast thou done unto us? and what have I offended thee, that thou hast brought on me and on my kingdom a great sin? thou hast done deeds unto me that ought not to be done. (Gen. 20:3, 9)*

And yet, even with this example that the taking of another man's wife is a sin that warranted the intervention of God Himself, the Mormon practice of polyandry is defended, justified, and rationalized to this very day. As with the several other clear examples of false Mormon teachings noted in this book, I believe the defense of this practice is obviously anti-

---

[27] Gen. 16:3; 25:1; 1 Sam. 18:27; 19:11-18; 25:39, 43-44; 2 Sam. 3:3-5, 13-14; 5:13, 6:20-23; 12:7-8, 24; 15:16; 16:21-23; 1 Kings 11:3; 1 Chron. 14:3.
[28] Compton, *In Sacred Loneliness: The Plural Wives of Joseph Smith.*

Christian and degrades the very character and dignity of God Himself. And even within the Mormon Scriptures there is evidence that the Lord disapproved of polygamy and polyandry until Joseph Smith contradicted the Lord within the Mormon Doctrine and Covenants.

> *There are some prophetic utterances in the Old Testament, but we get most of our knowledge of Christ from the New Testament and from the Book of Mormon.*[29]

So, with that simple declaration from a General Authority of the Church of Jesus Christ of Latter-day Saints and a member of the First Council of the Seventy, what does the New Testament and the Book of Mormon teach the Latter-day Saint concerning Christ's view of the practices of polygamy and polyandry? Note the following comments from the Apostle Paul, as well as an unambiguous and unyielding proclamation from the Mormon Prophet Jacob.

> *A bishop then must be blameless, the husband of one wife, vigilant, sober, of good behavior, given to hospitality, apt to teach. (1 Tim. 3:2, emphasis added)*

> *Let the deacons be the husbands of one wife, ruling their children and their own houses well. (1 Tim. 3:12, emphasis added)*

> *If any be blameless, the husband of one wife, having faithful children not accused of riot or unruly. (Titus 1:6, emphasis added)*

> *Behold, David and Solomon truly had many wives and concubines, which thing was abominable before me, saith the Lord. (Jacob 2:24, emphasis added)*

I want nothing to do with a church whose members still defend this practice as legitimate and praiseworthy and teach that it will continue in heaven. I have often wondered exactly what type of so-called "Christian" man would willingly give his wife to another and believe the act not only acceptable but also

---

[29] Elder Antoine R. Ivins, Conference Report, April 1939, Afternoon Meeting, 127.

required of the Lord. I have considered the tension that might be present as the shared wife returns from an intimate appointment with the second and more authoritative husband. I have reflected with disgust on just how Joseph Smith would offer such an arrangement to a happily married couple. It should be noted that when Joseph Smith, for a second time, secretly proposed to the wife of his own friend and counselor William Law, she refused his advances and reported the event to her husband. Joseph's obsession with these "plural marriages" set in motion the very events that would split the church and lead to his murder. With the death of Joseph in 1844, Emma Smith herself could no longer even passively support the practice of polygamy or the leadership of Brigham Young. Until her death in April of 1879, she repeatedly and passionately denied any participation by her or Joseph in the practice of plural marriage.

No such thing as polygamy or spiritual wifery was taught, publicly or privately, before my husband's death, that I have now, or ever had any knowledge of.[30]

As a leader in the Reorganized Church of Jesus Christ of Latter-day Saints, Emma Smith sponsored an article of faith that specifically refuted the practice of polygamy. She separated herself from the main body of Mormons and supported her and Joseph's son, Joseph Smith III, as the only authorized Prophet. As a result she and Brigham Young became bitter enemies during an extended legal dispute over the property of the church and assets of the murdered Prophet Joseph. After Emma left the church and married a non-Mormon, Major Lewis C. Bidamon, some of the Utah Mormons further alienated and despised her, with the Prophet Brigham Young reportedly stating in General Conference, *"Emma Smith is one of the damnedest liars I know of on this earth."*[31] Although modern Mormons now consider

---

[30] "Last Testimony of Sister Emma," *The Saints' Herald* 26 (Oct 1879): 289-90.

[31] Brigham Young at the October session of General Conference 1866. The Foundation for Apologetic Information and Research (FAIR), http://en.fairmormon.org/Emma_Smith_and_Brigham_Young. Note: This Web site defending Mormonism was the site Arvada Colorado Stake

Emma Smith a pillar of faith, the early Prophets after Joseph saw her for what she was, an apostate of the church who openly spoke against the priesthood authority of Brigham Young.

My first encounter with the Mormon concept and practice of polyandry came on the ride home from work while listening to a talk on CD. The CD series[32] I was listening to can be found in the homes of millions of Mormon families. The speaker is noted on the church-owned Deseret Book Web site as having *"mined the most reliable historical sources available to tell the stories of the Church Presidents."* One such story, concerning the life of President John Taylor, third Prophet of the Church 1880-1887, caused me to pull completely off the side of the road in total disbelief. I had progressed through the lives of Joseph Smith and Brigham Young when Truman Madsen, speaking in front of a live congregation, told of a short, almost insignificant event. John Taylor was ordained an Apostle in 1838, only two years after he and his wife, Leonora, were baptized. He retuned to his homeland of England and served several very successful missions for the church. In 1844, he was with Joseph Smith Jr., Hyrum Smith, and Willard Richards in the Carthage, Illinois jail, where the Smiths were murdered by an incensed mob. Madsen speaks slowly and deliberately to his audience:

> *Now I haven't yet brought into the same picture a fact that is troubling to many. It's Wilford Woodruff's journal that tells us this: [Joseph Smith "tested"] the Prophet John Taylor [with the same test he] had also done to Heber C. Kimball. He actually asked [Taylor] to let Leonora be sealed to him, Joseph Smith. John Taylor agonized over that. John Taylor, the man with a spine like steel, he came to the Prophet and said, "If the Lord wants Leonora, then the Lord can have her. If you're asking, NO!" (The congregation laughs out loud.)[33]*

President Michael D. Jones used to support his research.

[32] *The Presidents of the Church: Insights into Their Lives and Teachings,* talk by Truman G. Madsen on CD (Salt Lake City: Shadow Mountain, 2004). This set was purchased at church-owned Deseret Book Store.

[33] Ibid., CD-3, Track-4, 1:17 minutes into the track.

The laughter from the congregation sent a chill down my spine. These men and women had just been told that the "Lord" wanted Joseph Smith to take the wife of another man, and they found it amusing. The fact was that Joseph had been successful in his proposals to take the wives of eleven other men, thus representing fully one-third of his thirty-three wives. Even more disgusting, of his first twelve wives nine were the wives of other men, indicating that the practice of polyandry was not just an abnormality. Joseph even married the wife of one of his Apostles, after Joseph had sent him on an overseas mission. Joseph married Marinda Hyde, wife of the charismatic Apostle Orson Hyde, without Hyde's knowledge while he was away on a three-year mission for the church in Jerusalem.

Todd Compton's book, *In Sacred Loneliness* is the most authoritative work on the subject of the plural wives of Joseph Smith. The detailed, firsthand accounts of the pain, humiliation, and torment of the many women forever scarred by both polygamy and polyandry is heartbreaking. His book was recognized on the official Church of Jesus Christ of Latter-day Saints Web site with the following comments.

> *Overall, In Sacred Loneliness is extremely informative. The book features a high level of research, generally good judgment in the use of source materials, and fairly a comprehensive collection of known data pertaining to the wives of Joseph Smith. . . . In Sacred Loneliness was recently honored with the annual best book award from the Mormon History Association. This recognition is deserved because it is the most detailed study of the lifetime experiences of the women sealed to Joseph Smith.* [34]

My first reading of *In Sacred Loneliness* became a pivotal point of research, as I came to understand that the exact same primary sources Mr. Compton had used in his research were those sources used by the church itself to construct the official lesson manuals we had used in our Sunday classes. As these

---

[34] Richard Lloyd Anderson, and Scott H. Faulring, A review of *In Sacred Loneliness: The Plural Wives of Joseph Smith,* by Todd M. Compton. *FARMS Review* 10 (2): 67-104. http://mi.byu.edu/publications/review/?vol=10&num=2&id=290

sources could scarcely be considered anti-Mormon, my spiritual depression became even more overpowering as I contemplated the secret liaisons, private conversations, and intimate acts within what I could only describe as "wife swapping" among the leadership of the Mormon Church. It should be remembered that the doctrine of polygamy remains within the official Scriptures of the Mormon Church, and this eternal principle is clearly a requirement to progress to the highest kingdom in heaven as recorded in the Mormon Doctrine and Covenants, sections 131 and 132. In a very personal and graphically related experience, a Mormon High Priest once told my wife and me, "You do not know for sure that you will be required to share Kathy in the next life." In connection with the specific acts of polyandry by Joseph Smith, I have questioned my local Mormon leadership as to whether the explicit procedure for taking another man's wife was actually a requirement from the Lord Jesus Christ. In August of 2008, I received a letter from Bishop Richard Merkley, which stated his position very clearly.

> *Lee, I know that most of the questions you pose deal directly with the prophet Joseph and things he did, or did not do. My testimony is that Joseph did what he was supposed to do.*[35]

As a striking example of how the knowledge of the truth can change one's view of a seemingly insignificant event, consider the following illustration. When I left the Mormon Church in the winter of 2008, the current study manual was the 586-page *Teachings of Presidents of the Church—Joseph Smith.* Chapter 39 of that manual is titled "Relief Society: Divine Organization of Women." Opposite the chapter heading is a painting depicting the first meeting of that exceptional women's organization, with the caption, *"On March 17, 1842, the Prophet Joseph Smith organized the Female Relief Society of Nauvoo."* The painting depicts approximately sixteen women who, with Emma Smith front row center, seem to be attentively listening to every word of the Prophet, with a variety of expressions ranging from deep admiration to sincere reverence.

---

[35] See letter of August 2008, appendix A document number 24.

After I had learned the facts about both polygamy and polyandry, I further researched the official church history to find that only twenty women were at that first meeting. That idyllic painting of these devoted women assumes a somewhat disturbing feeling when viewed in the light of the following documented facts of that spring day in 1842. As Joseph Smith presided over the meeting of those twenty good sisters in the church, he was married to exactly half of them. Only a few days earlier, on March 9, he had married the mother of a woman he had married only the month before, neither of which his first wife, Emma Smith, had known about. As if to ridicule the very foundation of marriage itself, both the mother and daughter Joseph Smith had married within a month of each other were already married with children.[36] So, among the adoring faces captured in the deceptive image of that day were ten of Joseph Smith's wives, five of whom had other husbands at home tending to their children. In my view of what I believe to be the true gospel of Jesus Christ, polygamy was and is wrong, but polyandry is unmistakably from the Devil.

One of the great blessings I have come to appreciate after my self-inflicted excommunication from the Church of Jesus Christ of Latter-day Saints is that I now know that my wife, my daughters, and my granddaughters will never be subjected to polygamy or polyandry, for it was then, as it is now, a terrible lie. On the other hand, the sad fact of the Mormon faith is that no current member of that church can believe what I have just stated without contradicting Mormon Scriptures and the teachings of the Prophets, Seers, and Revelators of their own church.

Equally disturbing is the long history of sexual mistreatment and exploitation directed toward the sisters of the church, which has been nearly obliterated from the official history of the church. For those who might question my view on this subject,

---

[36] Sylvia Sessions (Lyon), wife to Windsor Lyon, married Joseph Smith on Feb. 8, 1842, and her mother Patty Bartlett (Sessions), wife to David Sessions, married Joseph Smith on March 9, 1842. See Compton, *In Sacred Loneliness: The Plural Wives of Joseph Smith,* 4.

consider the following facts. Brigham Young had a total of 55 wives. At times he married 3, 4, or 5 women in a single day. In 1844 he married 11, and in 1846 he married 19 women. Additionally, at the age of 44, Brigham Young married two 16-year-old girls. At the advanced age of 67, he married the 24-year-old Ann Eliza, whom he noticed during a Sunday morning church service and returned to propose marriage that same evening. Ann Eliza, who feared she would be killed by the Danites,[37] escaped Utah, met President and Mrs. Grant, and lectured across the country for over ten years, exposing the bondage of polygamy. Many Latter-day Saints want to believe that the majority of these polygamist and polyandrous marriages were strictly for spiritual purposes and were not consummated by sexual relations. This appears to be true with regard to the very young and the older wives of Joseph Smith. Those marriages were described in spiritually dynastic terms as guaranteeing the salvation of family groups through marriages to the Prophet. Any rational implication that sex was of no consideration to Joseph Smith, however, is not supported by actual interviews, diaries, and recorded accounts of Smith's wives.[38]

As an accurate expression of the opinions held by some of the leadership of the early church concerning women, one should reflect on the following, the specifics of which have never been retracted by the current leadership of the Mormon Church. Heber C. Kimball served as one of the original twelve Apostles under Joseph Smith, and as the First Counselor to Brigham Young from 1847 to his death in 1868. He gave his fourteen-year-old daughter to Joseph Smith when Smith was thirty-seven, at the same time his own wife, Vilate Murray Kimball, was asked, as a test, to also be a plural wife to Joseph. His personal views on the management of women as a

---

[37] During the early years of the Mormon Church, the Danites operated as a vigilante group and/or secret police force. They were the foundation and core of the militia that was active in the 1838 Mormon War, the 1857 Utah War, and Mountain Meadows Massacre.

[38] Compton, *In Sacred Loneliness: The Plural Wives of Joseph Smith.*

commodity are documented here in instructions to *departing missionaries.*

> *You are sent out as shepherds to gather the sheep together, and remember that they are not your sheep: they belong to Him that sends you. Then do not make a choice of any of those sheep; do not make selections before they are brought home and put into the fold. You understand that. Amen.*[39]

> *Brethren, I want you to understand that it is not to be as it has been heretofore. The brother missionaries have been in the habit of picking out the prettiest women for themselves before they get here, and bringing on the ugly ones for us; hereafter you have to bring them all here before taking any of them, and let us all have a fair shake.*[40]

I do not consider the words, actions, or character of Heber C. Kimball to be in any way, shape, or form inspired by the Lord Jesus Christ. Although he has been revered and honored by millions, I believe him to be no better than Joseph Smith or Brigham Young—simply a religious fraud driven by the most basic of physical desires. I have often reflected on the words chosen by our Stake President, Michael D. Jones, as he made a mockery of our serious appeal to understand what he thought of Joseph Smith. I believe that his words were chosen in a brief unguarded moment of transparency and recognition of precisely what Joseph Smith really was.

> *My petition to the Lord was not whether Joseph was some fallen and conniving con man who stole other men's wives, or a well-meaning, but libidinous prophet who preyed on people's faith; I asked Heavenly Father "where does he stand as prophet of the restoration?"*[41]

---

[39] President Heber C. Kimball, Instructions and Counsel to Departing Missionaries at a Special Conference held in the Tabernacle, Great Salt Lake City, August 28, 1852, *Journal of Discourses* 6:255.

[40] Quoted in Stanley P. Hirshon, *The Lion of the Lord: A Biography of Brigham Young* (New York: Knopf Press, 1969), 129-30.

[41] E-mail to Kathy Baker from Michael D. Jones, President, Arvada Colorado Stake, Church of Jesus Christ of Latter-day Saints, March 31, 2008

The practices of polygamy and polyandry provide one of the clearest examples that the Church of Jesus Christ of Latter-day Saints has been led by corrupt men. It should be remembered that the formal teachings of the Mormon Church are clear that the practice of polygamy is an eternal principle commanded by God and that its practice has only been suspended. Additionally, the actions of those dishonest men unmistakably were motivated by power, greed, and lust. And yet remarkably, they still invoke the loyalty and passionate defense of men like Stake President Michael D. Jones.

As the current leadership of the Mormon faith irrationally struggles to identify any conceivable justification for the sexually motivated actions of Joseph Smith, Brigham Young, John Taylor and so many others, unquestionably the Bible itself provides the most obvious guidance for the true followers of Christ:

"But among you there must not be even a hint of sexual immorality or of any kind of impurity, or of greed, because these are improper for God's holy people." Ephesians 5:3

"But now I am writing you that you must not associate with anyone who calls himself a brother but is sexually immoral..." 1 Corinthians 5:11

"Dear children, do not let anyone lead you astray...He who does what is sinful is of the devil because the devil has been sinning from the beginning." 1John 3:7-8

Blood Atonement in the Modern Mormon Temple

Several times during my journey of discovery through the official history, class manuals, Scriptures, and records of the Mormon Church, I came across doctrines so disturbing that I became emotionally and physically ill. The intensity of these episodes was greatly magnified by my deep embarrassment before the Lord for unknowingly offending Him. What I was

---

(emphasis added). See appendix A document number 25.

learning was the truth about my own church, the truth about the many ordinances, ceremonies, and practices in which my wife and I had personally participated hundreds of times.

I believe that all Mormons share the dishonor and embarrassment of what has been offensive to the Lord, but when they come to *know the truth* of these actions and continue to defend them, ignorance is no longer a shield from accountability. The disturbing issue of blood atonement began for me on the morning of March 10, 1979, at the Washington D.C. temple. That was the day my wife and I were "sealed" to each other for all time and eternity. This required that we first participate in the Temple Endowment ceremony. A portion of the ceremony requires that those who take part in it will not disclose what they have learned under the penalty of death. Before the Temple Endowment ceremony was changed in 1990, the specific portion of the ceremony that required a gruesome penalty was as follows.

> *I, [John], covenant before God, angels and these witnesses that I will never reveal the First Token of the Aaronic Priesthood, with its accompanying name, sign and penalty. Rather than do so, I would suffer my life to be taken.*[42]

At the exact time when the words "suffer my life to be taken" are spoken, the following action was to be completed with the right hand.

> *Placing the thumb under the left ear, the palm of the hand down, and by drawing the thumb quickly across the throat to the right ear, and dropping the hand to the side represents the execution of the Penalty.*[43]

For many years I did not comprehend just how disgusting my actions were, nor did I understand that these actions were in reality a representation of the blood atonement doctrine, as taught by Brigham Young. Even more repulsive was the

---

[42] A portion of the Temple Endowment known as the First Token of the Aaronic Priesthood.

[43] Ibid.

knowledge that these measures were actually forced upon early apostates and sinners in the church. This explanation, of course, was not provided to those of us who participated in the Temple Endowment. Looking back now, it is disturbing just how selectively ignorant the leadership of the church can be. In the fall of 2008, my wife and I attended the Denver Mormon Temple for one of the last times. Although two of my four children had been sealed in this beautiful temple, our last few visits were overshadowed by the unsettling education we had come to acquire by reading the history of the church. On this particular visit, we asked to see the Temple President for a few moments after we had completed the assigned Temple Endowment.

At first, Temple President Dennis K. Brown was very polite and invited us into his office. After some small talk, which centered on what ward we were from and how often we had attended the temple, I asked if I could request his explanation concerning polygamy in the current version of Doctrine and Covenants, section 132. My first question was, "Do we believe that polygamy will be practiced in heaven, and will it return to the earth with the return of the Savior?" His warmth and charm were gone. He said, "Well, we will not know these things until we die." I asked for his consideration of a second issue, to which he stated, "There just is no time this evening." My second question concerned the practice of mimicking, in the temple, the slicing of our own throats. I should have asked that, the more poignant question, first. We were politely but decisively excused from his office.

Although I had always felt uncomfortable making the gesture of slicing my own throat from ear to ear, I did not understand the historical reference, nor did I know at the time the specifics of the teachings of President Brigham Young, or his Second Counselor, President Jedediah M. Grant, or other early leaders of the church. Upon reflection, I have no doubt whatsoever that the intimidation of the temple ceremonies was directed as a warning to all the millions of us who participated in that graphic representation of how a life was to be taken. I equally have no doubt that the author of that graphic scene of butchery there in the temple, in which I participated so many times, was Brigham Young himself and not the Lord Jesus Christ. In fact, as it was pointed out to me by a good Christian Brother, that in John 16:2-4, Jesus Christ Himself warned believers of this very sadistic action, that of taking a life and teaching that it was actually a service to the Lord; *"...in fact, a time is coming when anyone who kills you will think he is offering a service to God. I have told you this, so that when the time comes you will remember that I warned you."*

Given the graphic sermons and specific instructions provided to the early members of the Mormon Church, who firmly believed that the men to whom they were listening were the living Prophets, Seers, and Revelators of God, even murder could be seen as divinely inspired. To this day I believe that one of the clearest testimonies to the depth of both the gruesome attraction and the present-day reverence that has been afforded to the teachings of Brigham Young and others who taught blood atonement is that it remained as an essential element of the Mormon Endowment ceremony until 1990. That translates to nearly 150 years of this gruesome and personally threatening demonstration of what the "Lord" authorized to happen to millions upon millions of Mormons, myself included, should we disclose precisely what I have shared with you. I believe that if my comments, which you now have in your hand, were spoken within the first fifty years of the Utah-based Church of Jesus Christ of Latter-day Saints or if I were a member today of any one of the Texas-based fundamentalist Mormon Churches, my life would be in real danger.

Some members of the Texas-based Fundamental Church of Jesus Christ of Latter-day Saints, as instructed by the founding fathers of the Utah-based Church of Jesus Christ of Latter-day Saints, have performed such "blood atonements," here in the United States well into the 1980s.[44] In a letter to the office of

---

[44] The definitive work on this subject is Jon Krakauer's *Under the Banner of Heaven: A Story of Violent Faith* (New York: Doubleday Books, a Division of Random House, Inc, 2003).

the First Presidency of the Mormon Church in Salt Lake City, with a copy to Stake President Michael D. Jones, I closed yet another request for support that had gone unanswered with a clear reference to such murders.

> *Don't you just miss the good old days when you could dispatch the Danites, and the problem children in the Church would simply "vanish."*[45]

Two of the foremost sadistically cooperative events within Mormon History, the specifics of which I will only briefly address here, are the Mormon Reformation (1856–1858) and its frequent teaching and encouragement of the grotesque practice of blood atonement by the leadership of the Mormon Church. Of the several books written on the Mormon Reformation, one of the best first-hand accounts comes from one of the 55 wives of Brigham Young himself. Ann Eliza Young (1844-1925) documented not only the Mormon Reformation but her personal knowledge of the practice of blood atonement within her book "Wife No. 19, The Life & Ordeals of a Mormon Woman During the 19th Century [46]".

So accepted was the doctrine of blood atonement, which near the turn of the Century, a public debate within the local and national newspapers concerning its origins, played-out between the leadership of the Utah and Reorganized Church in Illinois. The quote below is from the life of the tenth Prophet of the Mormon Church, Joseph Fielding Smith who for 49 years prior was the Official Historian of the Mormon Church. His casual comments specific to blood atonement, as just another doctrinal difference between the two churches as well as the fact that his unedited comments were reprinted for the modern Mormon in 1971, suggest that the doctrine of blood atonement was generally accepted by the Prophet of the Mormon Church as a

---

[45] Letter to President Thomas S. Monson with copy to President Michael D. Jones, May 12, 2008. See appendix A document number 15, page 4.
[46] Wife No. 19 The Life & Ordeals of a Mormon Woman During the 19th Century by Ann Eliza Young, Oakpast Ltd, London, Copyright 2010, ISBN: 978-85706-272-7, Chapter 10, The Blood-Atonement Preached, pages 133-148

valid practice.

"*During this same period the Reorganized Church of Jesus Christ of Latter Day Saints was making rather strenuous efforts to discredit the "Utah" church and to proselyte its members. Joseph Smith, son of the Prophet Joseph Smith, was president of the Reorganites, and his counselors were his son (the Prophet's grandson) Frederick M. Smith and Richard C. Evans. Several doctrinal differences existed between the two churches, including the right to succession in the church presidency, priesthood authority, plural marriage, blood atonement, and rebaptism. The Reorganites claimed that the Prophet's son was the rightful heir to the church presidency, rather that Brigham Young or any other. They also claimed that the Prophet Joseph neither taught nor lived plural marriage, but that this "abominable doctrine" was introduced by Brigham Young; likewise blood atonement and rebaptism. When The Church of Jesus Christ of Latter-day Saints suspended the practice of plural marriage in 1890 the Reorganites considered it a victory for them, and stepped up their missionary efforts in Utah, hoping to win other "concessions" from the Utah church.[47]*"

During the Mormon Reformation itself Brigham Young and his most conservative counselor Jedediah M. Grant preached nearly all of the graphic and obvious references to the practice of blood atonement. During this period of spiritual reformation the "Home Missionaries", the forerunner of today's Home and Visiting Teachers within the Mormon Church, were established to formally question the spiritual devotion of each member of the church. The duty of these Home Missionaries included a collection of very personal and searching questions specific to religious practices, past sins of all descriptions, a general call for public confessions as well as review of one's loyalty to the church. Within the years of this religious reformation nearly

---

[47] The Life of Joseph Fielding Smith, by Joseph Fielding Smith, Jr., and John J. Stewart, Copyright 1971, Deseret Book Company, Salt Lake City, Utah, pages 133 – 134, Chapter 6, On Becoming a Historian and a Defender of the Faith.

95% of the membership of the Mormon Church were rebaptized as a show of commitment to the church generally and specifically to the leadership of Brigham Young.

Although the teaching of blood atonement was primarily directed at the Mormon community, in September of 1857 the passion and devotion to the practice spilled into the non-Mormon world when some 120 unarmed men, women and children were brutally executed at close range by an overwhelming Mormon Militia and a small band of Paiute Indians, each acting under the direction of the leadership of the Church of Jesus Christ of Latter-day Saints in southern Utah. This, the largest slaughter of white immigrants found within the entire history of the American West, is skillfully documented within the book "Blood of the Prophets: Brigham Young and the Massacre at Mountain Meadows"[48]. This religiously motivated coldhearted butchery of entirely innocent men, women and children demonstrates, in my opinion, the very worst of Mormon leadership and Mormon fanatical devotion when left unchecked. So complete was the absolute callousness of the Mormon participants, that apart from the gruesome murders, the expensive treasures of the wagon train were then divided among the murderers themselves to include the very clothing of the dead. And yet, as the final act of defiance and supreme arrogance, the several Mormon families who then took in the only survivors of the massacre, 17 children eight years old and younger, then fraudulently charged the United States Government[49] some $2,000 as a repayment for the "ransom" they claimed they had paid to the Indians to save these children, this too was a Mormon lie against the small Paiute Tribe. One of the most authoritative and exceptionally unbiased documentation of the Massacre is the History Channel video

---

[48] Blood of the Prophets: Brigham Young and the Massacre at Mountain Meadows by Will Bagley, University of Oklahoma Press, Copyright 2002, ISBN: 978-0-8061-3639-4

[49] Blood and Thunder by Hampton Sides, Random House, Inc. New York, Copyright 2007, ISBN: 978-1-4000-3110-8, page 399

presentation of: "Investigating History – Mountain Massacre[50]".

To remove any confusion or distraction that the modern Latter-day Saint might offer concerning the clarity with which the early leadership taught this doctrine of blood atonement, the following is provided as only a sample of the teaching itself. What cannot be reproduced in this book is the fanatically devoted environment under which these teachings were presented. Imagine if you will, that you are in a congregation of fellow Saints who have been persecuted for your faith, and a true Prophet of God is speaking to you, directly to you. Furthermore, as an early Latter-day Saint, you might believe that he has been authorized by Jesus Christ Himself to give you divine instruction that some of the other Saints may need to be killed here on earth to atone for their sins.

But man may commit certain grievous sins—according to his light and knowledge—that will place him beyond the reach of the atoning blood of Christ. If then he would be saved he must make sacrifice of his own life to atone—so far as in his power lies—for that sin, for the blood of Christ alone under certain circumstances will not avail.[51]

I could refer you to plenty of instances where men have been righteously slain, in order to atone for their sins. I have seen scores and hundreds of people for whom there would have been a chance (in the last resurrection there will be) if their lives had been taken and their blood spilled on the ground as a smoking incense to the Almighty, but who are now angels to the devil, until our elder brother Jesus Christ raises them up—conquers death, hell, and the grave. I have known a great many men who have left this Church for whom there is no chance whatever for exaltation, but if their blood had been spilled, it would have been better for them. The wickedness and ignorance of the nations forbid this principle's being in full force, but the time

[50] A&E Television Networks, Copyright 2005, VHS Documentary, Cat. No. AAE44264
[51] Joseph Fielding Smith, *Doctrines of Salvation,* ed. Bruce R. McConkie (Salt Lake City: Bookcraft, 1954-56), 1:134.

will come when the law of God will be in full force.[52]

Then I saw two ruffians, whom I knew to be mobbers and murderers, and they crept into a bed, where one of my wives and children were. I said, "You that call yourselves brethren, tell me, is this the fashion among you?" They said, "O, they are good men, they are gentlemen." With that, I took my large bowie knife, that I used to wear as a bosom pin in Nauvoo, and cut one of their throats from ear to ear, saying, "Go to hell across lots." The other one said, "You dare not serve me so." I instantly sprang at him, seized him by the hair of the head, and, bringing him down, cut his throat, and sent him after his comrade; then told them both, if they would behave themselves they should yet live, but if they did not, I would unjoint their necks. At this I awoke.[53]

All mankind love themselves, and let these principles be known by an individual, and he would be glad to have his blood shed. That would be loving themselves, even unto an eternal exaltation. Will you love your brothers or sisters likewise, when they have committed a sin that cannot be atoned for without the shedding of their blood? Will you love that man or woman well enough to shed their blood? That is what Jesus Christ meant. He never told a man or woman to love their enemies in their wickedness, never.[54]

I say, that there are men and women that I would advise to go to the President immediately, and ask him to appoint a committee to attend to their case; and then let a place be selected, and let that committee shed their blood.[55]

---

[52] Brigham Young, "To Know God Is Eternal Life-God the Father of Our Spirits and Bodies-Things Created Spiritually First-Atonement By the Shedding of Blood," delivered in the Tabernacle, Great Salt Lake City, February 8, 1857. *Journal of Discourses* 26 4:220.

[53] An address delivered by President Brigham Young in the Tabernacle, Great Salt Lake City, March 27, 1853. *Journal of Discourses,* 1:83.

[54] President Brigham Young, Salt Lake Tabernacle, February 1857. *Journal of Discourses* 4:220.

[55] President Jedediah M. Grant, Second Counselor to President Brigham Young, Father to Heber J. Grant, Delivered in the Bowery, Great Salt Lake City, September 21, 1856. *Journal of Discourses* 4:49.

You may think that I am not teaching you Bible doctrine, but what says the apostle Paul? I would ask how many covenant breakers there are in this city and in this kingdom. I believe that there are a great many; and if they are covenant breakers we need a place designated, where we can shed their blood.[56]

We have those amongst us that are full of all manner of abominations, those who need to have their blood shed, for water will not do, their sins are of too deep a dye.[57]

Brethren and sisters, we want you to repent and forsake your sins. And you who have committed sins that cannot be forgiven through baptism, let your blood be shed, and let the smoke ascend, that the incense thereof may come up before God as an atonement for your sins, and that the sinners in Zion may be afraid.[58]

I would ask whether these sermons speak of the Jesus Christ that you have come to know. I would ask if these sermons testify to you that the men who spoke these words and the church that today defends them and recognizes them as "Prophets" are truly representatives of the Lord Jesus Christ. I would ask you if you believe that the atonement of Jesus Christ was for all the sins of man, or are there conditions on this earth that might require another man to slit your throat from ear to ear? At each and every general conference of the Church of Jesus Christ of Latter-day Saints, the membership is asked to sustain the leadership of the church.

This is a great Church. It is indeed the kingdom of God. We have a great man at the head of the Church. He is the revelator, the seer, and the prophet of God in this day. It is a reality that we walk in the presence of a living prophet of God. Let us be willing to accept him as such. And these others, who uphold his

---

[56] Ibid., 50.

[57] Ibid.

[58] Ibid., 51.

How is it that a "Prophet, Seer, and Revelator" of God Himself might give a sermon within the context of a general conference, only to have it be discarded or abandoned by the church or any single member thereof? I fully understand and have witnessed firsthand that this is a matter of personal faith. When I have asked my former Mormon brothers and sisters to explain the apparent disconnect between ordinary Christian values and exclusive Mormon doctrines, I have frequently heard the comment, *"I have faith that whatever the Prophets have said is of the Lord."* The faith they spoke of is exactly the faith I once had, that is, the simple faith that the "Prophets" of the church had not lied to us. Well, they have certainly lied to us, and *now* my faith is confidently placed only in the Lord Jesus Christ and no longer in men who by their own words have dishonored my association with them.

We Do Not Teach That Anymore; It Is In Our Past

One of the more peculiar and nearly cultish activities of my own close friends has been the completely detached and eerily clinical belief that whatever the church leadership has done should not be questioned. This experience was most disturbing to me when it came from lifelong friends whom I knew to be well educated and extremely rational in every other aspect of their lives. I once asked an older, more senior Melchizedek Priesthood friend of mine in Maryland, how it is that we would never give a public or civil official the wide-ranging moral leniency or ethical rationalization we routinely give to our past church leaders. I continued, asking why it is that none of us would think of giving a "pass" to a dishonest political candidate, a police chief, or even a high school principal if moral or ethical issues were clearly established. Is it right or even remotely logical to be more concerned with the character and actions of those who only exercise some minor civil

---

[59] Elder Mark E. Peterson, Conference Report, April 1949, Third Day— Morning Meeting, 145.

authority over us and ignore such concerns when our eternal salvation may be at risk? His answer was firm, "We do not teach that anymore; it is in our past." With just a hint of sarcasm, I reminded my dear friend that the teachings of the many Prophets of the Book of Mormon and the Bible and even the tender teachings of Jesus Christ Himself were in the "past."

Time and again I have been offered the same basic justification when, over the five years of my research, I sincerely asked how some of the more offensive teachings or doctrines could have come from a loving Father in heaven. It was as if the more unusual or distasteful Mormon teachings of the past were somehow exempt from any examination, even from within their own time period. It could not have been that the young women, daughters, and wives of the nineteenth century valued their own chastity, morality, or relationships with their own husbands any less than do the women of today. It could not have been that the derogatory or racial mocking of the black race in the nineteenth century was any less spiteful than it is today. I have been told that those things were in the past and that they are of no concern to us today. As an active Latter-day Saint High Priest in leadership positions, I was reminded that the teachings of the living Mormon Prophet of God are more significant than the actions or teachings of the past Prophets. But oddly enough, all the current church lesson manuals, priesthood study guides, and instruction handbooks are centrally focused on the teachings of the past Prophets. If the formal sermons and counsel from the current Prophet of the day is in fact more significant and relevant, every Latter-day Saint would agree that the primary method to communicate that direction and guidance from the living Prophet is the semiannual general conference held under the direction of the First Presidency of the Church. It would not be an unfamiliar concept to the modern Latter-day Saint that the words of the living Prophet and the General Authorities of the church are to be considered modern-day Scripture.

We meet together frequently as a Church in general conference for the transaction of business and to receive the word of the Lord. We have the ancient Scriptures and we have the modern Scriptures, and scriptures are being made now, as has always been the case when the Lord has had His Church upon the earth, with the living oracles; for when they speak by the inspiration of the Holy Ghost, what they say is scripture.[60]

My simple question has been, what effect do the ravages of time alone have on the validity and application of modern-day Scripture if it is *not* corrected, altered, or dismissed by a subsequent living Prophet of the church? If the formal teachings of the Book of Mormon Prophets do not fade with time, why then would the formal teachings of Joseph Smith, Brigham Young, or any of the modern-day Prophets and Apostles fade with time? I would suggest that these formal, if somewhat peculiar teachings, do not fade with time; they are simply shelved due to current social, political, or legal conditions of the day. I do not believe that even my most dedicated past Latter-day Saint friends and colleagues with whom I have served would ever question the power and authority by which past general conferences of the church were conducted. So then, the individual member and not the church itself is left to struggle with any explanation or justification of which conference teachings are or are not under the guidance and authority of the Holy Spirit of God to qualify as Scripture. At the time, and as a faithful Latter-day Saint, I did not understand the need for personally evaluating and then deciding whether or not a given general conference talk was or was not of the Lord. If these men were called and set apart as Prophets, Seers, and Revelators to communicate the mind and the will of the Lord to the entire church, and if I sustained them as uniquely having the right, power, and authority to accomplish that task through the proper priesthood keys, why would I then question them after the fact? My inexperience and simplicity became painfully obvious once I had actually read some of these peculiar teachings. The need to distance myself from these fanatical teachings, if the church as a whole would not, became

---

[60] Apostle Francis M. Lyman, Conference Report, April 1900, First Day— Morning Session, 7.

exceptionally clear.

As an example of some of the extreme teachings of the Church of Jesus Christ of Latter-day Saints from the official general conference meetings, canonized set of Mormon Scriptures, or official church publications, which in my view have not been given the dignity of any practical rebuttal or complete revision from the Mormon Church and as such do not simply fade away, are the following teachings of the Mormon faith. I believe these teachings should be viewed as active, simply because they have never been corrected by the Mormon Church. Several times in completely different locations good Latter-day Saints have struggled to explain to me the notion, "*We do not teach that anymore; it is in our past.*" It is a concept I have yet to fully comprehend. I have come to see this absurd belief as the indispensable but unofficial Mormon strategy required to put some logical distance between what would obviously be exceptionally anti-Christian doctrine and their own personal beliefs and practices. A Mormon Stake President of ours once told my wife and me that it was his opinion that if a church doctrine or teaching was not repeated or expounded upon within twenty years, it could be dismissed. So inconsistent and ridiculous was his comment that I actually could not formulate a serious response to it, and we simply walked away. He spoke as if each member of the Mormon Church is at liberty to independently decide just how long a particular doctrine or teaching of the church is valid or if it was ever valid at all. What, then, is the point of the membership of the Mormon Church openly sustaining the local and general officers of the church if the official and authorized guidance from those sustained as Prophets, Seers, and Revelators is subject to a self-determining assessment by the same membership? Do they or do they not speak on behalf of the Lord as promised? Over a thousand sermons have been given concerning the safety and protection of "following the Prophet." And yet a number of the teachings listed below have been personally *rejected* by some Latter-day Saints, even though those in authority have presented them to the membership of the Mormon Church in precisely the same authorized manner as the doctrines and teachings they do accept. As an ordained High Priest and a Bishop of the Mormon faith, I repeatedly asked my Latter-day Saint companions how these teachings from the highest leadership in the "only true church on the earth today" could gradually lose the power and authority by which they were first delivered?

Mormon Teaching: The official and authorized words of the Prophets, Seers, and Revelators of the Church of Jesus Christ of Latter-day Saints shall stand as modern-day Scripture.

Official Statement: *"And whatsoever they shall speak when moved upon by the Holy Ghost shall be scripture, shall be the will of the Lord, shall be the mind of the Lord, shall be the word of the Lord, shall be the voice of the Lord, and the power of God unto salvation."*

Reference: Doctrine and Covenants 68:4

Mormon Teaching: That Jesus Christ was in fact a polygamist and that He had several wives and that He fathered children during his ministry on this earth.

Official Statement: *"I discover that some of the Eastern papers represent me as a great blasphemer, because I said, in my lecture on Marriage, at our last Conference, that Jesus Christ was married at Cana of Galilee, that Mary, Martha, and others were his wives, and that he begat children."*

Reference: President Orson Hyde, Quorum of the Twelve Apostles, General Conference, October 1854. *Journal of Discourses* 2:210.

Mormon Teaching: That the atonement of Jesus Christ did not in fact apply to all the sins of men, so that at times through the spilling of the sinner's blood from his or her own neck by authorized Mormon priesthood holders, he or she may be saved.

Official Statement: *"Will you love your brothers or sisters likewise, when they have committed a sin that cannot be atoned for without the shedding of their blood? Will you love that man or woman well enough to shed their blood?"*

Reference: President and Prophet Brigham Young, Salt Lake Tabernacle, February 1857. *Journal of Discourses* 4:220.

Mormon Teaching: That in some cases even an Area Authority of the Mormon Church (Elder J. W. Marriott) can for many years profit significantly from the rental of pornographic films and the sale of alcohol. See Chapter 4 for more details

Official Statement: *"Members of the Church everywhere are urged to not only resist the widespread plague of pornography, but as citizens to become actively and relentlessly engaged in the fight against this insidious enemy of humanity around the world."*

Reference: *Teachings of Presidents of the Church– Spencer W. Kimball* (Salt Lake City: Intellectual Reserve, Inc., 2006), 184.

Mormon Teaching: That the functional practice of honoring the laws of the land, where the Church of Jesus Christ of Latter-day Saints has been established, is dependent on peripheral factors.

Official Statement: *The Mormon Prophet John Taylor "receives word during a visit to California that federal officials have ordered his arrest for practicing polygamy. Returns to Salt Lake City on 27 January. On 1 February, preaches his last*

public sermon and, in hopes of limiting the persecution against the Church by federal authorities, goes into hiding."

Reference: Teachings of the Presidents of the Church—John Taylor, x.

Official Statement: *"We believe in being subject to kings, presidents, rulers, and magistrates, in obeying, honoring, and sustaining the law."*

Reference: Article of Faith Number 12.

Official Statement: *"Let no man break the laws of the land for he that keepeth the laws of God hath no need to break the laws of the land."*

Reference: Doctrine and Covenants 58:21.

Mormon Teaching: That at times "nigger," "darky," or "Sambo" jokes were appropriate in official church conferences or in authorized publications of the church.

Author's Statement: *I will not humiliate the reader by listing the nearly one hundred such jokes, stories, or comments found within the LDS Collectors Library 2005, which documents the formal references noted below. My only observation would be a clear recognition that at no time in the history of the United States have these derogatory terms been used for anything other than slander. I fully recognize that at times the use of these terms has in fact been both widespread and socially acceptable within America. My primary reason for raising the existence of these well-documented examples of bigotry and prejudice by the leadership of the Mormon Church is to question the divine spiritual guidance of the church itself. At a time when other churches were taking great risks in the many abolitionist movements,[61] the Mormons who owned slaves were*

---

[61] Primarily the Quakers, Congregational-Presbyterians, Methodists, and Baptists were the most active churches in a wide range of abolitionist movements that included political, financial, and material aid for the

moving their "property" west with them. If the uninspired leadership of the nation considered both slavery and polygamy evil, how is it that both were accepted as righteous by the Mormons and their God? Furthermore, if God Himself spoke to the Mormon Prophet of His disapproval of the use of racially disparaging remarks in April of 2006,[62] what did God really think of such remarks in the 1850s or 1950s?

References: Elder Heber J. Grant, Quorum of the Twelve Apostles, Conference Report, October 1900, Second Day—Morning Session, 35-36; Apostle Matthias F. Cowley, Quorum of the Twelve Apostles, Conference Report, April 1902, Second Day—Morning Session, 36-37; Elder Reed Smoot, Quorum of the Twelve Apostles, Conference Report, October 1907, Afternoon Session, 55-56; and President Rudger Clawson, Conference Report, October 1920, First Day—Morning Session, 22. Official Mormon Church publications have repeatedly used these derogatory terms have been both the *Contributor* and the *Improvement Era*, well into the 1950s.

I have wondered how the African American members of the Church of Jesus Christ of Latter-day Saints dismiss these teachings, since the church itself has not. In an apparent bid for some self-recognition of the true history of blacks within the Mormon Church, a unique Web site has chronicled some of the historical issues I have captured within question 3 in the questions I raise in chapter 5.[63]

The point of this discussion is not to suggest that the Mormon Church is now infected with a disproportional number

---

transportation and the sustaining of runaway slaves.

[62] "Now I am told that racial slurs and denigrating remarks are sometimes heard among us. I remind you that no man who makes disparaging remarks concerning those of another race can consider himself a true disciple of Christ" (President Gordon B. Hinckley, General Conference, *Ensign* April 2006, 58.)

[63] BlackLDS.org is dedicated to black members of the Mormon Church.

of racists and bigots. However, I do believe that within the early years of the Mormon Church, especially under the leadership of Brigham Young, John Taylor, and many of the General Authorities of the church well into the twentieth century, racial discrimination and bigotry were generally accepted within the Mormon culture. I further believe that as with polygamy, polyandry, and disobeying the laws of the land, the social, spiritual, and emotional damage done by widespread bigotry within the Mormon Church has never been sufficiently acknowledged.

The Power and Authority of the Mormon Priesthood

One of the most sensitive questions for the Latter-day Saint reader, and specifically for those men and women who might have known me or served with me in the Church of Jesus Christ of Latter-day Saints, might be, "Can he or will he *ever* deny the power of the priesthood?" I have both seen this question in the eyes of my children and heard it hidden deep within the superficial comments from those I once considered Mormon friends.

Is it possible that after some thirty consecutive years in leadership positions within the Mormon Church, I did not see and feel the power of the priesthood? Is it even feasible that as a Bishop I never would have known the sweet promptings of the Spirit to help guide and direct my family or my congregation of over 250 souls? These things I can *never* deny or diminish in the least degree. I know well and have often felt the awesome power and authority of His will. I have known the hand of God, through His irresistible Spirit as I was moved to speak words that were not mine and take actions I would never have considered, all for the benefit of others. I know without question, that countless times I have served as the instrument through which powerful blessings, counsel, and comfort have been delivered to many faithful and more humble followers of the Lord than I. But I also know now, without a shadow of a doubt, that none of those inspirational events was a confirmation of any "Mormon priesthood" because I know in my heart that the immoral and unethical behavior of the Mormon Prophets could never maintain or convey to others the authority of the true priesthood of God.

Within the Mormon faith, it would appear that much more importance is placed on the mechanics of the "Priesthood Authority Line"[64] than on the actual worthiness of the individuals within that line. The primary purpose of this document is to record an unbroken line of men holding the "priesthood" from the Lord Jesus Christ, through Peter, James, and John to the modern day. On the surface it might seem to be a spiritually rational and historically sound practice. The unwavering deterrent from its true practicality is that without the divine approval of the Lord, no man receives His authority, with or without the paperwork. The Apostle Paul did not have a "Priesthood Authority Line," and yet he was clearly an authorized representative of the Lord. And yet, the Sanhedrin undoubtedly had the "Priesthood Authority Line" but certainly not the right, power, or authority to represent the Lord. Unfortunately for the Mormon Church, the direct connection between a man's behavior and the authority of the priesthood is well documented. Thus the invention of an illogical "Rockwood Doctrine"[65] type of defense is the only method of bridging the gap between obviously unchristian behavior and the relentless need to pass the priesthood to the next generation. The gap is then filled by an exclusive set of moral standards for the leadership of the church alone.

The only real issue with this strategy is that every now and then someone might actually question the actions of the leadership in comparison to the absolute clarity of standards for the rest of us. Even a young Deacon in the Mormon Church, at age twelve, is instructed to read and understand the roles and

---

[64] The Priesthood Authority Line is issued from the Historical Department of the Church. See appendix A document number 2b for the author's Priesthood Authority Line as an example.

[65] See chapter 2 for a complete explanation of the "Rockwood Doctrine."

responsibilities of the priesthood, along with the requirement he has to honor it with his righteousness, for it can be taken from him.

> *That they may be conferred upon us, it is true; but when we undertake to cover our sins, or to gratify our pride, our vain ambition, or to exercise control or dominion or compulsion upon the souls of the children of men, in any degree of unrighteousness, behold, the heavens withdraw themselves; the Spirit of the Lord is grieved; and when it is withdrawn, Amen to the priesthood or the authority of that man.* (Doctrine and Covenants 121:37)

So, for the "Priesthood Authority Line" to be valid within the Church of Jesus Christ of Latter-day Saints, there is no compromise. For my individual priesthood as a Mormon Bishop to be legitimate, the priesthood power and authority of both Joseph Smith and Brigham Young had to have been legitimate. This then requires that, according to the Mormon Scripture referenced above, these "Prophets" *did not* undertake to cover their sins, or to gratify their pride or their vain ambitions, or to exercise control or dominion upon others in any degree. More significantly, and certainly to the point of the matter, are we to believe that polygamy, polyandry, blood atonement, and lying to the authorities of the United States of America were all done righteously before the Lord and accomplished under His personal direction? What I have come to see and understand more clearly about the "Mormon priesthood" has been one of the key milestones in my journey of discovery. With the utmost sincerity and seriousness I can bear witness, "I once was lost, but now am found, was blind but now I see."[66]

Any person who knowingly calls upon the Lord with a clear and specific understanding of the scandalous foundation of the Mormon faith, and yet takes no action to preserve and protect the character of the Lord, willingly endangers his very

---

[66] A few words from "Amazing Grace," a Christian hymn written by the English poet and clergyman John Newton (1725–1807), and published in 1779.

salvation. I believe that in whatever church we may find ourselves, if our relationship with the Lord was established honestly, we have committed our lives to Him and *not* to the actions, teachings, and judgments of the past prophets, priests, deacons, or pastors of that church. We have come to the Lord based on what we have come to know of Him through the Holy Spirit of truth. Our relationship changes, grows, and develops as we come to know more of His will for us. We come to know Christ through prayer, scripture study, fasting, and putting into practice what we know by His own example of service, sacrifice, and sympathy for others. As we come to know more, or even as we come to know less, our personal behavior and dedication to our Lord and Savior will change.

How is it any different, when we come to know the truth about a man? I was once totally and completely dedicated to the Church of Jesus Christ of Latter-day Saints, based on what I knew of Joseph Smith. When I came to know more about Joseph Smith the man or the Prophet, from his own words, teachings, and actions, my behavior and dedication to him changed. I also came to know the power and authority of the Lord Jesus Christ, and as the seemingly insignificant gap between the lives of these two extremely important men in my life began to widen, a change was required. My baptism into the Mormon Church in 1977 did not come with the condition that I follow the teachings of a man. As with my baptism into a new church, I have not devoted my life to the pastor, the deacons, or the elders but to the Lord. The difference is that I no longer must reshape, rewrite, and reform the teachings of my Savior to justify the actions of a man.

The Book of Mormon—An Inspired, Invented, or Imitated Manuscript?

One of the fundamental elements of my conversion to Mormonism in the late 1970s was a belief that the Book of Mormon was authentically a set of ancient Scriptures that had been lost to the modern world. As I became familiar with both the Dead Sea Scrolls[67] and the Nag Hammadi Library,[68] the elementary concept of lost Scriptures like the Book of Mormon was well established within my personal testimony. In fact, many times, both logically and historically, I defended the general notion of lost Scriptures and specifically the Book of Mormon through precisely those two examples. The world-renowned copper scroll, ancient stone boxes with gold and silver plates, as well as the discovery of thousands of stone and clay tablets all validated the Joseph Smith story that ancient sacred records had in fact been intentionally buried.

Several times during my discussions of the character and integrity of the Prophet Joseph Smith, frustrated Mormons have stated, "*Well, if Joseph did make mistakes in his personal life, that does not change the fact that the Book of Mormon is still true.*" This section will address the shortcomings of that viewpoint with clear examples of how the Book of Mormon itself cannot withstand even a limited review of its errors, inconsistencies, and spiritually ambiguous statements when taken within Mormonism as a whole.

Words cannot describe the hopelessness I felt when I first learned of and then purchased a copy of the book "*View of the Hebrews*", which was first published in 1825. Knowing that the Book of Mormon was published in 1830, I was overwhelmed to learn that the book, *"View of the Hebrews"* was written by a Preacher, the Rev. Ethan Smith of Oliver Cowdery's family in Poultney, Vermont. For those unfamiliar with the Book of Mormon story, Oliver Cowdery was the first scribe of Joseph Smith for the Book of Mormon and it could hardly be coincidental that major elements of the first book "*View of the Hebrews*" would be repeated in the Book of Mormon after

---

[67] Discovered in 1947 by Bedouin children near the village of Qumran, these manuscripts of the Old Testament were at least one thousand years older than any previously discovered biblical manuscripts.

[68] Discovered in 1945, *The Nag Hammadi Library in English* (James M. Robinson, ed. [San Francisco: Harper San Francisco, 1978]) represents the translation of fourth-century Coptic manuscripts of early Christian (Gnostic) writings, many of which claim apostolic authorship.

Oliver began to work for Joseph. Of the many similarities between the two books, several foundational Mormon points of Doctrine, found within the *"View of the Hebrews"* completely shattered my testimony of the Book of Mormon. A few of the religiously essential and uniquely foundational Mormon positions that were first published in the *"View of the Hebrews"*, which are now found in the Book of Mormon are: 1) The origin of the American Indians were from the Israelite Nation, 2) Extensive quotations from the book of Isaiah, 3) Once in America, the sharp division of these migrants from Jerusalem into civilized and uncivilized warring clans, 4) That these clans were of the Ten Lost Tribes, 5) Great wars and extensive military fortifications, 6) The Gospel of Jesus Christ is taught among the American natives, 7) The burial of a "lost book" with "yellow leaves" and much more. So harmful was the rediscovery of this obscure little book that in the 1920's, that the senior Mormon historian of the day, B.H. Roberts, sent a confidential letter to Mormon President, Heber J. Grant and other Church leaders suggesting that a response should be prepared to explain the apparent plagiarism by Joseph Smith as to not damage the faith of the Youth in the Church.

Joseph Smith himself not only knew of the *"View of the Hebrews"* book and its theory that the Native Americans were from the Ten Tribes, he even quoted from it pages within the Mormon Newspaper[69] of his time:

> *"If such may have been the fact, that a part of the Ten Tribes came over to America, in the way we have supposed, leaving the cold regions of Assareth behind them in quest of a milder climate, it would be natural to look for tokens of the presence of Jews of some sort, along countries adjacent to the Atlantic. In order to this, we shall here make an extract from an able work: written exclusively on the subject of the Ten Tribes having come from Asia by the way of Bherings Strait, by the Rev. Ethan Smith. Pultney, Vl."*

---

[69] The Mormons., Times and Seasons, vol. 3, Joseph Smith Jr. (November 1841-October 1842), Vol. 3 No. 15 June 1, 1842, p.814

Whether it was Mormon, Nephi, Alma, or Joseph Smith himself who wrote the Book of Mormon, to remain impartial as to the writer, I will simply refer to the individual as the "author," the person responsible for the work, whoever that may have been. As stated on the first page, the Book of Mormon is *"an account written by the hand of Mormon upon plates, taken from the plates of Nephi, Translated by Joseph Smith, Jun."* From the first book of Nephi, to the last book of Moroni, the total of fifteen separate books constitutes 522 pages of text in the 1980 edition. The details of the translation of the Book of Mormon set the rock-solid foundation for this review. The cornerstone for that foundation is the claim that Joseph Smith, as the stated translator and *not* the presumed author of the Book, had only three translation aids at his disposal: (1) the Urim and Thummim, (2) a seer stone, and (3) the inspiration of the Holy Ghost. At no point in the history of the Church of Jesus Christ of Latter-day Saints have any additions, changes, or corrections been made to this list of the only tools Joseph Smith used to translate the "Reformed Egyptian" engravings from the gold plates into English. Of the hundreds of church statements that affirm only these three translation support aids, consider the following representative examples.

> *Two days after the arrival of Mr. Cowdery (being the 7th of April) I commenced to translate the Book of Mormon, and he began to write for me, which having continued for some time, I inquired of the Lord through the Urim and Thummim.* [70]

> *The perfect agreement between the prediction of Isaiah (chap. xxix) and Mr. Smith's account of the finding and translation of the Book of Mormon is another collateral proof that he was divinely commissioned. Mr. Smith testifies that the plates from which that book was translated were taken out of the ground, from where they were originally deposited by the prophet Moroni; that the box containing them was composed of stone, so constructed as to exclude, in a great degree, the*

---

[70] Smith, *History of The Church of Jesus Christ of Latter-day Saints,* 1:32-33.

moisture of the soil; that with the plates he discovered a Urim and Thummim, through the aid of which he afterward was enabled to translate the book into the English language.[71]

The Seer Stone referred to here was a chocolate-colored, somewhat egg-shaped stone which the Prophet found while digging a well in company with his brother Hyrum, for a Mr. Clark Chase, near Palmyra, N.Y. It possessed the qualities of Urim and Thummim, since by means of it—as described above—as well as by means of the Interpreters found with the Nephite record, Joseph was able to translate the characters engraven on the plates.[72]

My statement was and now is that in translating he put the seer stone in his hat and putting his face in his hat so as to exclude the light and that then the light and characters appeared in the hat together with the interpretation which he uttered and was written by, the scribe and which was tested at the time as stated.[73]

Mr. Smith, though an unlearned man, testifies that he was commanded to translate them, through the inspiration of the Holy Ghost, by the aid of the Urim and Thummim and that the Book of Mormon is that translation.[74]

With the fact firmly established that Joseph Smith did not have any other tools or manuscripts to aid in the "translation" of the Book of Mormon, the following questions will be directed to the "author," whoever that may have been, if not Joseph Smith.

Question 1: If by the gift of the Holy Spirit of God, the authors of the Book of Mormon in *America*, knew exactly what the Apostles in *Jerusalem* were going to write in Greek, six to eight decades before those apostles even knew of Jesus Christ,

---

[71] Milton V. Backman, Jr., *Eyewitness Accounts of the Restoration* (Salt Lake City: Deseret Book Co., 1986), 82-83.

[72] B. H. Roberts, *A Comprehensive History of The Church of Jesus Christ of Latter-day Saints* (Salt Lake City: Deseret News Press, 1930), 1:129.

[73] Backman, *Eyewitness Accounts of the Restoration*, p.232

[74] Ibid., 82-83.

and if those same authors also knew precisely what the *Greek* would be translated into as *English* some 1,600 years later, and if all this was initially recorded in *"Reformed Egyptian engravings,"* why would Joseph Smith then translate each passage as it appears in the King James 1611 version of the Bible, if he *did not* use the Bible to build the Book of Mormon?

Question 2: How is it that the author of 3 Nephi wrote in approximately *AD 34* a book that documents the statements of Jesus some thirty years before those same statements made by Peter were recorded by Luke in approximately *AD 65*?

Question 3: How is it that the author of 3 Nephi records Jesus as paraphrasing Deuteronomy rather than quoting Moses himself, just as Peter did in Acts as recorded by Luke? By the very nature of a paraphrase, it is a one-time and unique reshaping of written or spoken material to reiterate a specific thought using other words, especially in order to make the given concept simpler or shorter. The absolutely precise version of Peter's paraphrasing of Deuteronomy as recorded by Luke in A.D. 65 found within the Book of Mormon, by Nephi (the son of Nephi, who was the son of Helaman) some 30 years *before* it was recorded by Luke on an entirely different continent in an entirely different language is ridiculous. Even more absurd is the Mormon position that Jesus Christ Himself in America quoted this *exact* paraphrased version of Deuteronomy given by Peter, rather than the Book of Deuteronomy itself; and did so even *before* it was written by Luke in what would become the Book of Acts, Chapter 3. Is it not more likely that Joseph Smith, in the 1830's, simply turned to his King James Version of the Bible and selected the exact sentence structure, the precise punctuation and the very unique and specific para-phrased version of Deuteronomy? Although it is the official position of the Church of Jesus Christ of Latter-day Saints that Joseph Smith did not use the King James Version of the Bible to build the Book of Mormon, over a dozen such extraordinary examples of unmistakable plagiarism from the Bible are found within the Book of Mormon.

Question 4: How is it that the author of 3 Nephi incorrectly records Jesus continuing to speak by using the words of Peter as recorded in the book of Acts as if they were the words of Moses in Deuteronomy? (See quotations in question 2.)

Question 5: How is it that verbatim sections of the *New Testament* can be found within the *Book of Mormon* some *eighty years* before the birth of Christ?[75]

---

[75] Alma 5:52 is from Matthew 3:10; 3 Nephi 13:1-23 is from Matthew 6:1-23; Moroni 7:45 is from 1 Corinthians 13:4-7; Moroni 7:48 is from 1 John 3:2; and Moroni 10:8-17 is from 1 Corinthians 12:4-11.

3 Nephi 20:23-26, written in A.D. 34

23 Behold, I am he of whom Moses spake, saying: A prophet shall the Lord your God raise up unto you of your brethren, like unto me; him shall ye hear in all things whatsoever he shall say unto you. And it shall come to pass that every soul who will not hear that prophet shall be cut off from among the people.

24 Verily I say unto you, yea, and all the prophets from Samuel and those that follow after, as many as have spoken, have testified of me.

25 And behold, ye are the children of the prophets; and ye are of the house of Israel; and ye are of the covenant which the Father made with your fathers, saying unto Abraham: And in thy seed shall all the kindreds of the earth be blessed.

26 The Father having raised me up unto you first, and sent me to bless you in turning away every one of you from his iniquities; and this because ye are the children of the covenant—

Acts 3:22-26, written in A.D. 65

22 For Moses truly said unto the fathers, A prophet shall the Lord your God raise up unto you of your brethren, like unto me; him shall ye hear in all things whatsoever he shall say unto you.

23 And it shall come to pass, [that] every soul, which will not hear that prophet, shall be destroyed from among the people.

24 Yea, and all the prophets from Samuel and those that follow after, as many as have spoken, have likewise foretold of these days.

25 Ye are the children of the prophets, and of the covenant which God made with our fathers, saying unto Abraham, And in thy seed shall all the kindreds of the earth be blessed.

26 Unto you first God, having raised up his Son Jesus, sent him to bless you, in turning away every one of you from his iniquities.

3 Nephi 20:23, written in A.D. 34	Acts 3:22-23, written in A.D. 65
23 Behold, I am he of whom Moses spake, saying: A prophet shall the Lord your God raise up unto you of your brethren, like unto me; him shall ye hear in all things whatsoever he shall say unto you. And it shall come to pass that every soul who will not hear that prophet shall be cut off from among the people.	22 For Moses truly said unto the fathers, A prophet shall the Lord your God raise up unto you of your brethren, like unto me; him shall ye hear in all things whatsoever he shall say unto you. 23 And it shall come to pass, [that] every soul, which will not hear that prophet, shall be destroyed from among the people.

Deuteronomy 18:15, 19, written c. 1400 B.C.

15 The LORD thy God will raise up unto thee a Prophet from the midst of thee, of thy brethren, like unto me; unto him ye shall hearken;

19 And it shall come to pass, [that] whosoever will not hearken unto my words which he shall speak in my name, I will require [it] of him.

Question 6: Why does the second chapter of the book of Jacob from the Book of Mormon record a serious contradiction with the equally authoritative set of Mormon Scriptures known as the Doctrine and Covenants? Even within my relatively short association with Mormonism, I have seen changes within the several versions of the Mormon Scriptures I have owned. As an example of these small yet very significant changes, consider the *chapter headings* of Jacob chapter 2, from my slightly different versions of the Book of Mormon.

Printed in 1999 CHAPTER 2 *Jacob denounces the love of riches,* *pride, and unchastity--Men should* *seek riches to help their fellow men--* *Jacob condemns the unauthorized* *practice of plural marriage--The* *Lord delights in the chastity of* *women.*	**Printed in 1976** CHAPTER 2 *Jacob's denunciation of unchastity and* *other sins—Plurality of wives* *forbidden because of iniquity.*

Although *none* of the actual text within Jacob chapter 2 had changed between the two printings of the Book of Mormon, a significant change was made within the chapter heading. In my 1976 copy of the Book of Mormon, Jacob forbids the practice of polygamy; in the 1999 edition, Jacob now condemns only the "unauthorized" practice of polygamy. Yet the major contradiction with the Lord's guidance on the same subject in the Doctrine and Covenants remains constant. I do not question the fact that the Lord can, has, and may in the future, change His guidance to His people. He has both required and then restricted the very same actions at different times. Examples of His will changing for His own purposes at different times would be the requirement and then the restriction of: the law of animal sacrifice, the law of circumcision, and the law of kosher meals. At issue here is not the alteration of the Lord's will but the representation of both condemnation and authorization of the same event by the same participants at the same time. The author of the Book of Mormon clearly records the Lord's severe disapproval of David and Solomon taking many wives, and yet the author of the Doctrine and Covenants clearly records the Lord's personal endorsement and approval of the same act.

Book of Mormon	Doctrine and Covenants
"David and Solomon truly had many wives and concubines, which thing was abominable before me, saith the Lord."(*Jacob 2:24*)	"David also received many wives and concubines, and also Solomon…and in nothing did they sin… David's wives and concubines were given unto him of me."(*Doctrine and Covenants 132:38-39*)

My question is simply this: Did the Lord really intend to both approve and condemn the very same event? Or are the personal actions of the "author" of the Doctrine and Covenants—who began practicing polygamy in 1831 but did not write of it until 1843, while the church did not admit to the practice until 1852 or publish the "commandment" until 1876—truly more enlightening?

The Book of Mormon covers a period of history from about 600 BC to AD 421. At its conclusion, Moroni describes the total destruction of the Nephites at the hands of the wicked Lamanites. The 1981 printing of the Book of Mormon states in the introductory page that the Lamanites are *"the principal ancestors of the American Indians."* Given that statement, I consider it odd that within only a thousand years, the distinctive physical traces unique to the Nephites, Lamanites, Jeredites, and Mulekites had simply vanished. The simultaneous disappearance of these unique animals, plants, human DNA, and technologies is somewhat perplexing by the very diversity of the specific trace elements each should have left on pre-Columbian America. The Book of Mormon speaks of a great multitude of genetically Hebrew descendants and of cattle, horses, swine, goats, elephants, barley, figs, grapes, silk, steel, brass, coins, and chariots. Yet all traces of these are now gone without a hint that they once existed in early America. Even the substantial impact of the wheel was lost to any succeeding cultures or generations within an astonishingly short period of time.

In addition to the major inconsistencies found within the Book of Mormon, the average Latter-day Saint has no comprehension of the questionable history of the Book of Abraham, also canonized Mormon Scripture, found within the Pearl of Great Price. In 1835 Joseph Smith Jr. purchased for $2,400, four Egyptian Mummies (two of which were sold by Emma after his death) and an unknown number of papyrus from a traveling Egyptian Exhibition owned by Mr. Michael Chandler. From that same papyrus came the unlikely Mormon Scriptures now known as the Book of Abraham.

The vast majority of Mormons do not know that according to recently published official information from the Mormon Church itself, the ancient Egyptian papyrus which became both the Book of Abraham and Facsimile Number 1, found within the Pearl of Great Price as Mormon Scripture, has now been formally acknowledged, as just a "common" Egyptian funerary text and "not the original" from the Book of Abraham. And yet, remarkably for over forty years the Mormon Church continues to publish both the same Facsimile of that papyrus, and their associated, but incorrect explanations, as if they were still authentic and from the hand of Abraham himself.

The Mormon story of the Book of Abraham was relatively safe for a number of years as the original Egyptian papyrus, which was thought to be destroyed in the 1871 Great Chicago Fire, were found in 1967 within the archives of the Metropolitan Museum of Art in New York. Professional Egyptologist[76] around the world consider the Book of Abraham to be totally unrelated to the text of the papyri which are portions of common Egyptian funerary text, dating to about the first

---

[76] Publication, Joseph Smith, Jr. As a Translator, An Inquiry Conducted by Rt. Rev. F.S. Spaulding, D.D. Bishop of Utah. Salt Lake City, Utah, Copyright November 1, 1912. Technical validation from: The Book of the Dead, An English Translation of the Chapters, Hymns, Etc., Of The Theban Recension, With Introduction, Notes, Etc., London, Copyright 1901, vol. 1, pp. 50-51

century B.C, and bear no resemblance to the translation given by Joseph Smith.

> *"... these three facsimiles of Egyptian documents in the 'Pearl of Great Price' depict the most common objects in the Mortuary religion of Egypt. Joseph Smith's interpretations of them as part of a unique revelation through Abraham, therefore, very clearly demonstrates that he was totally unacquainted with the significance of these documents and absolutely ignorant of the simplest facts of Egyptian writing and civilization."* Egyptologist Dr. James H. Breasted, of the University of Chicago

> *"It may be safely said that there is not one single word that is true in these explanations"* Dr. W.M. Flinders Petrie of London University – Statement of Authenticity of the Mormon Book of Abraham

> *"It is difficult to deal seriously with Joseph Smith's impudent fraud.... Smith has turned the goddess [Isis in Facsimile No. 3] into a king and Osiris into Abraham."* Dr. A.H. Sayce, Oxford professor of Egyptology

In one of the finest examples of modern Mormon irrational narratives, in which the simultaneous acceptance and then rejection of the same evidence is used, would be concerning the history and authenticity of the Book of Abraham. The Official Mormon Sunday School Manual on this subject in my possession includes the following diametrically opposed illogical statements:

> *"In 1967 portions of the papyri that the Church purchased in 1835 were discovered and presented to the Church. Among the most important and interesting was the original of what became Facsimile 1 in the Pearl of Great Price."* [4]

> *"In 1967 eleven fragments of the Joseph Smith papyri were rediscovered by Doctor Aziz S. Atiya, in the New York Metropolitan Museum of Art. Studies of them have confirmed*

that they are mainly ancient Egyptian funerary texts of the sort commonly buried with royalty and nobility and designed to guide them through their eternal journeyings." [77]

"The papyri which the Church now has in its possession are clearly not all that Joseph Smith had. There is no reason to assume that any of those we now have is the original of the Book of Abraham. In fact, there is good reason to think that we in fact do not have the original." [78]

These questions and many more issues concerning the probability that Joseph Smith invented the Book of Mormon have assumed only a supporting role in my decision to leave the Mormon Church. The real corruption I have seen, the true deceit I have experienced, and the pure evil I have learned from the past and present leadership of the Church of Jesus Christ of Latter-day Saints are more significant than the literary traces of a nineteenth-century fraud. The harvest of what Joseph has planted is my only required evidence: "A good tree cannot bring forth evil fruit, neither can a corrupt tree bring forth good fruit" (Matt. 7:18). I have served with the men who accurately reflect the true nature and character of the Mormon Church, and it is their behavior, remarks, and ethical standards that most clearly demonstrate the iniquitous core of their religion.

In conclusion, I would also state that the testimony of Joseph Smith himself, concerning how he came to learn of the Book of Mormon from an angel of light, is questionable based on both the deceitful and unchristian doctrine that would

---

[77] Church History in the Fulness of Times, The Official Mormon Sunday School Manual, Copyright 1989, 1993 by the Corporation of the President of the Church of Jesus Christ of Latter-day Saints, Salt Lake City, pages 257-258.

[78] On the Official Church site (lds.org) http://www.lds.org/churchhistory/byu/0,15483,3941-1-2086,00.html, > http://farms.byu.edu/ > The Book of Abraham: Divinely Inspired Scripture Review of *By His Own Hand upon Papyrus: A New Look at the Joseph Smith Papyri* by Charles M. Larson, Reviewed By: Michael D. Rhodes Provo, Utah: FARMS, 1992, Pages 120-26 (note first two lines of paragraph 4)

eventually come from his "revelations", as well as this warning from the Scriptures:

"For such men are false apostles, deceitful workmen, masquerading as apostles of Christ. And no wonder, for Satan himself masquerades as an angel of light." 2 Corinthians 11:13-14

"While I was thus in the act of calling upon God, I discovered a light appearing in my room, which continued to increase until the room was lighter than at noonday, when immediately a personage appeared at my bedside, stand in the air, for his feet did not touch the floor." Testimony of the Prophet Joseph Smith, 21, Sep 1823, Introduction to the Book of Mormon

Found within the Official History of the Church of Jesus Christ of Latter-day Saints, is a remarkable example of where Joseph Smith himself was reportedly deceived by a "revelation" from the devil. In 1831, Smith directed through a Seer Stone "revelation" several Elders of the Church to sell the copyright of the Book of Mormon in Toronto, Canada. This desperate financial strategy utterly failed to secure any funds for the Church, and Joseph Smith returned to the Lord to seek an explanation. His answer from the Lord was as follows:

"Some revelations are of God: some revelations are of man: and some revelations are of the devil."[79]

The use of the "Seer Stone" to both translate the Book of Mormon and to receive "revelations" was in itself a peculiar process and may account for both the inconsistencies of the translations and the opportunity for demonic intervention.

"I will now give you a description of the manner in which the Book of Mormon was translated. Joseph Smith would put the seer stone into a hat, and put his face in the hat, drawing it closely around his face to exclude the light; and in the darkness the spiritual light would shine. A piece of something resembling

[79] B. H. Roberts, A Comprehensive History of The Church of Jesus Christ of Latter-day Saints, 6 vols. [Salt Lake City: Deseret News Press, 1930], 1: 162 - 166.

parchment would appear, and under it was the interpretation in English. Brother Joseph would read off the English to Oliver Cowdery, who was his principal scribe, and when it was written down and repeated to Brother Joseph to see if it was correct, then it would disappear, and another character was translated by the gift and power of God."[80]

Two Sets of Scriptures—The Church Hides Polygamy

I want to return now to a subject that is partially covered in chapter 1. The very idea of a decoy set of Scriptures that contradicted what the leadership of the church was actually practicing at the time is morally reprehensible. One of the practical results of my meticulous review and verification of Mormon Church history has been that I now better understand the deceit and dishonesty I have experienced firsthand. I remember well the sinking feeling as I shared with my wife the fact that the 1835 version of the Doctrine and Covenants, section 101, actually denied the practice of polygamy and taught that marriage should be between one man and one woman. Following is the deceptive instruction from Joseph Smith himself during the time when he had at least thirty-three wives, one-third of whom were the wives of other men. What possible motive could he have, other than intentional deception, for issuing such a statement to his fellow church members, to his political critics, and to the government of the United States of America? As an apparent mockery to the stark reality of the practice of polygamy and polyandry by Joseph Smith himself, the church printed the words "BUT ONE WIFE" in all capital letters.

---

[80] Testimonies of Book of Mormon Witnesses, p.12, Encyclopedia of Mormonism, Vol. 1, Book of Mormon Witnesses, Statement from David Whitmer, one of the Three Witnesses to the Book of Mormon, Copyright © 1992 by Macmillan Publishing Company

> *As to the charge of polygamy, I will quote from the Book of Doctrine and Covenants, which is the subscribed faith of the church and is strictly enforced. [Doctrine and Covenants 101:4 says,] "Inasmuch as this church of Christ has been reproached with the crime of fornication and polygamy, we declare that we believe that one man should have BUT ONE WIFE, and one woman but one husband except in case of death when either is at liberty to marry again."* [81]

After recognizing that my wife and I had in reality mimicked the doctrine of blood atonement by acting out the slicing of our own throats in the temple, it seemed that nothing more disgusting than this could be discovered. But fully comprehending the early church leadership's twisted course of deceit and then the publishing of the unbelievable lie of polygamy within their own "Scriptures" marked a new low in my journey of discovery concerning the deception within the Mormon Church. To clearly illustrate the deception found within the official canonized Scriptures of the Church of Jesus Christ of Latter-day Saints, consider the diametrically opposed Scriptures from the same church on the same subject:

It should be clearly understood that in total disregard to the laws of the land or even the words of their own Scriptures, the leadership of the Church of Jesus Christ of Latter-day Saints practiced, taught, and actively concealed the doctrine of polygamy from the 1830s to the 1900s. The church intentionally approved and printed these deceptive Scriptures for many years. The 1876 version of the Doctrine and Covenants, which endorsed the practice of polygamy, remains as official Scripture, even though the practice has been suspended at this time. It should be noted that with whatever set of Scriptures the church published and at whatever time they were circulated, none had *any* influence whatsoever on the actual practice of polygamy. Under the authority of the 1835 version, no polygamy was authorized, and yet it continued to be taught and

---

[81] Joseph Smith Jr., "On Marriage," *Times and Seasons,* vol. 3 (November 1841-October 1842), no. 23 October 1, 1842, p. 939; see also, Joseph Smith Jr., *History of The Church of Jesus Christ of Latter-day Saints,* 2:247.

practiced, as acknowledged by the church. And under the authority of the 1876 version, polygamy was authorized, but only within the three stated conditions, which again were never fully achieved. I have identified only a few Mormon plural marriages wherein all three conditions required by the Mormon "Scripture" were satisfied, namely, that the next wife to be taken must (1) be "a virgin," (2) the first wife must "give her consent," and (3) the new wife be "vowed to no other man, . . . belongeth unto him and to no one else."[82]

1835 Doctrine and Covenants	1876 Doctrine and Covenants
Inasmuch as this church of Christ has been reproached with the crime of fornication and polygamy, we declare that we believe that one man should have but one wife, and one woman but one husband except in case of death when either is at liberty to marry again. (Section 101)	*If any man espouse a virgin, and desire to espouse another, and the first give her consent, and if he espouse the second, and they are virgins, and have vowed to no other man, then is he justified; he cannot commit adultery for they are given unto him.* (Section 132)

Additionally, it should be clearly understood that within the chapter *outline* of section 132, the segment just quoted above appears under the heading, "Laws governing the plurality of wives are set forth." As such, it is most hypocritical that these conditions are found within what should be considered by Mormons as "Scripture." They are further identified as "laws," and still they command no reverence from the leadership of the Mormon Church. The ethical double standards for the early Mormon Church leadership, when compared with the same practices among the current Mormon Church leadership, is most impressive. Chapter 4 of this book documents what I have

---

[82] Doctrine and Covenants 132:61-64, Mormon Scripture as recorded by Joseph Smith himself.

considered to be the dishonest practices of Arvada Colorado Stake President Michael D. Jones; yet in view of the founding fathers of the Mormon faith, I believe his deceitful actions can only be considered third-rate.

When, through church resources[83] I learned that the Doctrine and Covenants I had used as a Mormon Bishop was not even close to the version the early Latter-day Saints used, I was stunned. What, then, was the point of studying for years the history of the church through the Doctrine and Covenants, when this was not the Scriptures the early Saints lived under? I soon came to understand that the primary deception of practicing polygamy and polyandry in the flesh while denying it in print was not the only misleading purpose of the Doctrine and Covenants. The official church history confirms that the first printing of the Doctrine and Covenants used code names for certain people and places. As the practice of concealing the names of the leaders of the church and the location of communal land centered on the functions of the United Order,[84] it is my view that this practice was also a dishonest use of the Mormon "Scriptures." Within the original 1835 edition of the Doctrine and Covenants, Joseph Smith Jr. was known as Enoch, Gazelam, or Baurak Ale, the city of New York was known as Cainhannoch, and the local printing office was known as the Lane-shine-house. The most likely use for such code names concerning the activities of the United Order was to avoid lawsuits, taxes, and any associated liabilities linked with this communal practice. Additionally, one of the many reasons the early leadership of the Mormon faith may have practiced polygamy and polyandry in secret was that the state of Illinois was somewhat ahead of the nation as a whole, in that the state law specifically prohibited bigamy and polygamy,[85] whereas no

---

[83] *LDS Collectors Library 2005.*

[84] The United Order was a short-lived communal system practiced by the Mormons from 1855 to 1858. See Doctrine and Covenants, sections 54, 92, and 104.

[85] Illinois State Law, Section 121, page 198-99: "Bigamy consists in the having of two wives or two husbands at one and the same time, knowing that

federal law was so specific by 1833.

A Mormon History of Anti-American Teachings and Actions

The point of this section is to highlight the several clearly anti-American statements delivered by both past and present leaders of the Church of Jesus Christ of Latter-day Saints. While the early leaders of the Mormon Church may have been the ones to initially voice many of these anti-American statements, these statements have been reprinted and retold again and again in our generation. I must question the motives of the modern leadership and their several associated committees who review the printed curriculum and messages of the church. From the thousands of sermons, lectures, and comments of the past Prophets and General Authorities of the Mormon Church covering a myriad of religious subjects, the modern Mormon is intentionally exposed to a disproportional number of anti-American statements by those who approve the printing, reprinting, and retelling of the supposed persecution against the Mormon saints, not at the hands of the unruly mobs, but at the hands of the United States government.

One of the constant struggles I have had as I have organized my thoughts and the hundreds of references in support of this book is simply where to stop. On each subject I have asked myself two primary questions: How did I not see this as religious deception years ago, and how much information is too much? To strike a balance between the sheer volume of information and the value of my personal experiences within the Church of Jesus Christ of Latter-day Saints, I have attempted to restrict my work to authoritative references and significant events in my life. The subjects of national patriotism and religious hypocrisy certainly require such restrictions.

My lack of formal literary skills may become painfully obvious in this section, as I will ask the reader to take a step

the former husband or wife is still alive."

back and reflect on what exactly is being presented here. Simply stated, the many documented examples of Mormon hypocrisy as it relates to the subject of national patriotism are overwhelming and certainly enlightening as to the real motives of the Mormon faith. I believe that as the Mormon Church attempts to become more conventional and seeks a greater acceptance from the wider Christian community, the fundamental elements of a religious split personality can be detected. It is as if the Mormon Church would like to be viewed as both typically Christian and naturally patriotic. This desired worldwide perception is a formidable challenge for a church with such a politically turbulent past that can be considered only marginally Christian and selectively patriotic. The issue of just how well the doctrine of the Mormon Church intermingles with the generally accepted standards of Christianity is addressed in chapter 1. This section addresses the question and issues of Mormon patriotism in some detail.

As a retired Army officer[86] and a disabled veteran, I have on more than one occasion been extremely offended by the obvious slurs directed toward the United States government by the leadership of the Mormon Church. After spending the better part of my adult life knowing the Mormon leadership's viewpoint of persecution, and in consideration of their earlier attitude of vengeance, it is difficult to accept their claims of patriotism.

Consider the fact that the past generations of Mormon leaders, specifically the grandfathers of those who currently lead the Church of Jesus Christ of Latter-day Saints, each would have taken a Temple Oath of Vengeance against this nation as part of the Mormon Temple Endowment ceremony. The Temple Endowment would have been one of the most significant religious experiences of their lives. It should be clearly understood that this oath of vengeance against the United States of America would have been taken within the

---

[86] See appendix A documents 21 and 22, Certificate of Retirement and The Legion of Merit. I am also a life member of the Disabled American Veterans, Service Connected – Department of Veteran Affairs.

Mormon temple, invoking the most solemn and severe of consequences for failure to live up to it.

> *You and each of you do covenant and promise that you will pray and never cease to pray to Almighty God to avenge the blood of the prophets upon this nation, and that you will teach the same to your children and to your children's children unto the third and fourth generation.*[87]

One of the more poignant examples of the dissociative identity disorder[88] I believe the Mormon Church suffers from can be found within one of the *Teachings of the Presidents of the Church*, a series of study manuals established by the First Presidency and Quorum of the Twelve Apostles. From the manual that features the teachings of Heber J. Grant, Mormon Prophet from November 1918 to May 1945, is one of the most dysfunctional attempts at rational thought I have ever been asked to recite within a Mormon classroom. I remember very well that just the title of the chapter, "Being Loyal Citizens,"[89] was enough to raise questions about the teaching approach our instructor might use that Sunday.

On page 160 of that manual is a collection of statements so hypocritical that they caused me to become uncomfortable to the point that I excused myself from the room and walked around the outside of the church for the remainder of the class. The opening line of this lesson states, "As Latter-day Saints, we have a duty to be law-abiding citizens and to do all we can to help our governments operate according to moral principles." The church's callous and uncompromising history of opposition to the laws of the land indicates that the key words here are,

---

[87] Mormon Temple Oath of Vengeance, 1845 to 1927. Buerger, "The Development of the Mormon Temple Endowment Ceremony," 33-76. See also *U.S. Senate Document 486 (59th Congress, 1st Session).*

[88] Dissociative identity disorder is a psychiatric diagnosis that describes a condition in which a person displays multiple distinct identities or personalities, each with its own pattern of perceiving and interacting with a given situation.

[89] *Teachings of the Presidents of the Church—Heber J. Grant* (Salt Lake City: Church of Jesus Christ of Latter-day Saints, 2002), chapter 17, p. 157.

"according to moral principles." When the Prophet Joseph Smith, a formal candidate for the presidency of the United States in 1844, was practicing and teaching the doctrines of polygamy and polyandry, his "moral principles" certainly were crystal clear to his thirty-three wives, but they were certainly much lower than what the nation deserved.

The modern-day editors of this Mormon study manual, and thus the First Presidency and Quorum of the Twelve Apostles, added a most perplexing section, where the Mormon Prophet quotes Abraham Lincoln concerning reverence for the law:

> *Let reverence for the laws be breathed by every American mother to the lisping babe that prattles on her lap; let it be taught in schools, in seminaries and colleges; let it be written in primers, spelling books and almanacs; let it be preached from the pulpit, proclaimed in legislative halls, and enforced in courts of justice.*[90]

If the broad-spectrum hypocrisy of the Mormons actually quoting Abraham Lincoln about reverence for the *laws* of the United States is somehow lost to the reader, consider the following point. Within the very same speech given by Mr. Lincoln, he warns the nation of a society that disregards the laws of the land and follows furious passions. In my view, it is utterly ridiculous that the Mormon Church would quote Abraham Lincoln on the pretense that the church was in some way an example or the model of citizenship. The simple fact is that Abraham Lincoln pledged to end the "twin relics of barbarism," polygamy and slavery, both supported by the Utah Mormons. Lincoln himself struck powerful blows at each in 1862, when he signed both the Emancipation Proclamation and the first anti-polygamy bill, the Morrill Act. Some would have us believe that Lincoln was a friend of the Mormons, yet the reason the Mormon Church needed to avoid Mr. Lincoln's

---

[90] The quote on page 160 of *Teachings of the Church—Heber J. Grant* comes from President Heber J. Grant, Conference Report, June 1919, Afternoon Session, 138; quoting Abraham Lincoln, "The Perpetuation of Our Political Institutions," Springfield, Illinois, January 27, 1838.

additional comments from that *very same speech* are clearly understandable:

> *I hope I am over wary; but if I am not, there is, even now, something of ill-omen amongst us. I mean the increasing disregard for law which pervades the country; the growing disposition to substitute the wild and furious passions, in lieu of the sober judgment of Courts; and the worse than savage mobs, for the executive ministers of justice.*[91]

It may be prudent at this point, in comparing the reality of American history with the propaganda of a Mormon study manual, to remind the reader that the Mormon Church left the United States in the spring of 1846 for the then Mexican territory in the west to establish "Zion." There they lived under the theocracy of Brigham Young, began their own language and writing system, built a new monetary structure, burned the laws of the United States Congress, and maintained a secret organization[92] to take the lives and property of those who questioned the power of the church. Outrageously, within only months of the Mexican-American War (1846-1848), in which over 13,000 U.S. soldiers died, Brigham Young arrogantly petitioned Congress to approve the new Mormon state of "Deseret," which encompassed approximately one fifth of the United States. The proposed Mormon state was to include all of Utah, most of present-day Nevada and Arizona, and a large part of southern California, including the port of San Diego, as well as over half of Colorado and parts of Wyoming, New Mexico, Oregon, and Idaho.

It should be noted that both Brigham Young and the Mormon Church in general believed that the American Civil War was *"a God-given retribution or punishment for Mormon persecution*[93]*"*. So desperate to leave the nation and separate

---

[91] Lincoln, "The Perpetuation of our Political Institutions."

[92] The Danites were founded by the Latter-day Saints in June of 1838 in Far West, Missouri, and operated as a vigilante group in both Missouri and Utah.

[93] At Sword's Point, Part 1: A Documentary history of the Utah War to 1858 (Kingdom in the West: The Mormons and the American Frontier), Copyright 2008, William P. MacKinnon, University of Oklahoma Press, ISBN 978-0-87062-274-8

themselves from all ties to the United States, that once in the Salt Lake valley the Mormons developed their own language and alphabet (Deseret) as well as an independent monetary system.

To clarify my understanding of the true relationship between Abraham Lincoln and the Mormon leadership of his time, I would like to add a few items from my research and personal experience on the subject.

> *Occasionally [in clearing timber from a field] we would come to a log that had fallen down. It was too hard to split, too wet to burn, and too heavy to move, so we ploughed around it. That's what I intend to do with the Mormons. Tell Brigham Young that if he will let me alone, I will let him alone.*[94]

> *Despite Lincoln's impartiality toward the Saints, many critical opinions about him were voiced publicly by Church leaders before and after his inauguration. When word reached Utah in 1860 that Lincoln had been elected, John D. Lee referred to him as "the Black Republican" (Hubbard, 97). In a Tabernacle address on 10 February 1861, President Brigham Young spoke of the weakness of Lincoln's political position and mockingly called him "King Abraham" (JD, 8:323-324). Again, during April 1861 general conference, President Young explicitly stated that the president was "like a rope of sand, or like a rope made of water. He is as weak as water" (Young, 9:4).*[95]

> *To add insult to local injury, in the presidential election that year [1840] the Saints in Nauvoo crossed out the name of elector Abraham Lincoln (Whig justice of the peace in Fountain Green [Illinois]—not Abraham Lincoln) on several hundred ballots and substituted Democrat James H. Ralston, a Mormon*

---

[94] Attributed to Abraham Lincoln in an 1863 Washington D.C. interview with T. B. H. Stenhouse, who was editor of the *Deseret Tribune* in Salt Lake City. See Utah State History Web site, Bicentennial of the Birth of Abraham Lincoln (1809-2009):
http://history.utah.gov/front_page/abraham_lincoln.html
[95] *Encyclopedia of Latter-Day Saint History, LDS Collectors Library 2005.*

sympathizer.[96]

To ensure that the federal government clearly understood that the issue of polygamy was not the only element of Mormon life that should be of no concern to the current president of the United States, Brigham Young himself rebuked the government concerning the treatment of the slaves in Utah.

Even if we treat our slaves in an oppressive manner, it is still none of their business and they ought not to meddle with it.[97]

So, to reiterate the dramatic difference between the reality of the outside world and the propaganda of the Mormon study manual placed in my hands in 2003 by my priesthood leader, consider this: The Mormon Prophet Heber J. Grant, whose father had freely taken an oath of vengeance against the United States of America, quoted Abraham Lincoln within a lesson entitled, "Being Loyal Citizens." Abraham Lincoln had campaigned forcefully against polygamy and slavery (both practiced by the Mormons), and he was the first of several presidents to sign a federal law against the Mormon Church, which the Mormon Church rejected, disavowed, and ignored. Furthermore, on the same page, Heber J. Grant quotes Joseph Smith from 1835 and declares as Mormon Scripture the following: "We do not believe it just to mingle religious influence with civil government" (Doctrine and Covenants 134:9).

Without question, the Mormon Prophet Heber J. Grant knew that Joseph Smith actually ran for president; so just how is that scandalous activity *not* to be considered mingling influences, as both the polygamist Prophet of the church and president of the United States? Then, as if to mock those who might question this obvious hypocrisy, Heber J. Grant adds, "Please remember that this was published way back in 1835, as the position of the

---

[96] Dennis Rowley, "The Mormon Experience in the Wisconsin Pineries, 1841-1845." *BYU Studies* 32 (1992): 158.

[97] Brigham Young, 1856, *Journal of Discourses* 4:40.

Church and it has never changed."[98]   And finally, Heber J. Grant, the living Prophet of God for the Church of Jesus Christ of Latter-day Saints adds, "When any law is enacted and becomes a constitutional law, no man who spends his money to help men break that law can truthfully say that he is a loyal citizen."[99] This is a rather strange comment from a child of polygamy who came to be the Prophet of a church that battled the United States government for nearly eighty years.

On Sunday, February 27, 2005 at the Washington D.C. Temple Visitor's Center, my wife and I hosted some 45 young single adults from our Columbia Maryland Stake congregation. That evening we listened, along with some 2,000 other visitors, to a Church-sponsored, formal fireside lecture titled "Abraham Lincoln and the Church" presented by fellow Mormon, Dr. Chris Brewer. Several times during his presentation, he clearly stated that *"Abraham Lincoln was a friend of the Church."* I found the statement to be both dishonest and very misleading. In support of my accusation against Dr. Brewer, consider all of the preceding statements from the leadership of the Mormon Church, along with this quote from H. Dean Garrett, professor of church history and doctrine at Brigham Young University.

> *Abraham Lincoln was no friendlier towards the Mormons and, if anything, took more political advantage of attacks against the Saints than did Douglas.*[100]

It is as if the Mormon Church desperately wants to be seen as patriotic with a long history of loyal American citizens, but the facts of their own history cannot support such a view. They take pride in that Mormon history and pride in their Mormon religious independence, but at times, depending on the intended audience, that Mormon independence and perseverance becomes a liability as well. Indeed, the only church ever negatively mentioned within an inaugural address of any

---

[98] *Teachings of the Presidents of the Church—Heber J. Grant*, 160.

[99] Ibid.

[100] H. Dean Garrett, ed., *Regional Studies in Latter-day Saint History: Illinois, LDS Collectors Library 2005*, 374.

president of the United States of America has been the Mormon Church. Consider the following statements of two American presidents, which certainly challenge the patriotism of the church.

> *The Mormon Church not only offends the moral sense of manhood by sanctioning polygamy, but prevents the administration of justice through ordinary instrumentalities of law.*[101]
>
> *...and that polygamy in the Territories, destructive of the family relation and offensive to the moral sense of the civilized world, shall be repressed.*[102]

And yet, it is the behind-the-scenes control and editing of the current Mormon Church manuals that concerns me so deeply. I know well the original and very deliberate speeches, sermons, and Scriptures of Joseph Smith, Brigham Young, John Taylor, and Heber C. Kimball. It is the sanitized statements from the early leadership that are then placed in the Mormon manuals I have in my home that distress me, for this reflects the intentions of the current leadership of the Mormon Church to rework, misrepresent, or hide the true history of the church, which is much easier to conceal than the original ambitions of the early Mormon leaders.

To bridge the gap of over 180 years of anti-American insults, consider the following verbatim statement from Michael D. Jones, President of the Arvada Colorado Stake of the Church of Jesus Christ of Latter-day Saints, issued in November of 2008. His statement is in response to my questioning the true motives of Joseph Smith Jr. to become president of the United States of America.

> *Joseph Smith taught the Gospel of Jesus Christ and restored the practices, covenants, and ordinances of salvation under the direction of the Savior. His political activities were intended to protect the religious freedom of the Saints because the*

---

[101] President James A. Garfield, Inaugural Address, March 4, 1881.
[102] President Grover Cleveland, Inaugural Address, March 4, 1885.

government would do nothing to protect such freedoms.[103]

The "religious freedoms" that Michael D. Jones was speaking of included polygamy and polyandry, as practiced by Joseph Smith, the presidential candidate. Since the United States Congress had enacted several federal laws to restrain the practice of polygamy, I asked President Jones just how the United States could have endured any further the heavy-handed theocracy of Brigham Young. And yet even today, the modern Mormon leader, specifically President Jones in this case, continues to justify and defend actions that were clearly in direct opposition to the Constitution of the United States of America. In what I have come to see as his typically sarcastic and arrogant response, Michael D. Jones provided the following statement:

> *After being driven out of and rejected by the United States and forced to settle a wilderness in the Great Basin, it would have been odd for Brigham Young to send a message to the federal government saying, I have a territory full of people and we cannot govern ourselves, please send one of your wise men to rule over us.*[104]

This comment from President Jones might suggest that Utah was somewhat deficient in wise men, as a wise man might have thought it a good idea to simply follow the laws of the United States of America. The long history of legal issues that the Mormon Church has had with the United States is somewhat confusing, considering that the Mormon Scriptures themselves seem to require its members to respect and follow the laws of the land. Yet this is a very bold statement indeed, when one considers the unquestionable fact that when Joseph Smith wrote the requirements for his church, he himself was in violation of those very laws.

> *We believe in being subject to kings, presidents, rulers, and magistrates, in obeying, honoring, and sustaining the law.*

---

[103] Stake President Michael D. Jones within an undated and unsigned letter in November of 2008.
[104] Ibid.

(Twelfth Article of Faith)

Let no man break the laws of the land for he that keepeth the laws of God hath no need to break the laws of the land.
(Doctrine and Covenants 58:21)

The obvious hypocrisy notwithstanding, the point here is that both the past and present leadership of the Mormon Church have felt, and apparently still feel, that they have been seriously wronged by the government of the United States of America. It is my firm belief that the animosity and bitterness for those perceived wrongs fester even today among a majority of the American-born Latter-day Saints. As evidence for that conclusion, I include here a collection of statements that demonstrate clear resentment towards the government of the United States of America. Additionally, I have found it somewhat bewildering to speak with active Latter-day Saints on the subject, as invariably they do not support the practice of polygamy for themselves, but they are adamant that the government should not have interfered with its practice back in the 1800s.

So as not to belabor the point, I will cite only official Latter-day Saint references critical of the United States government, the majority of which have been printed or reprinted within my lifetime, thus emphasizing that the target audience is Mormons alive today. So just what message are they to learn from these statements?

Background of the Statement: On the cover of the November 2006 issue of the *Ensign,* the official magazine of the Mormon Church, is a superb painting by Carl Heinrich Bloch titled "Christ with Boy." Without the proper investigation, this tender scene might communicate that only love, compassion, and Christian values will be found within the pages of this attractive magazine. This issue is a summary of the 176th Semiannual General Conference of the Church. A formal sermon from the Prophet and President of the Church, Gordon B. Hinckley, begins on page 82. At this point it should be noted that statements of the living Prophet of God during a general conference are to be considered as modern-day Scripture to the Latter-day Saints. With that understanding, consider just what would be the purpose of this slur against the government of the United States of America, made in the fall of 2006:

> *And so it has been with each of the Presidents of the Church. In the face of terrible opposition, they have moved forward with faith. Whether it was crickets destroying their crops. Whether it was drought or late frost. Whether it was persecution by the federal government.*

Comment: As our family watched that general conference on the BYU Channel in our home, I remember cringing at President Hinckley's condescending statement about the federal government. Did he really consider the federal government's efforts in the 1800s to uphold the laws of Congress as "persecution"? These were the very same laws the State of Utah would use to prosecute polygamists during his lifetime, even though the Scriptures he would take to church that Sunday claimed that activity to be a commandment from God. So the living Prophet of the Mormon Church had just instructed me, and the world, that the past Presidents of the Church had bravely faced terrible opposition, including persecution from the federal government. What was the point of that statement in the fall of 2006, if not to indicate that it was a mistake on the part of the Untied States of America to oppose the church?

Background of the Statement: Within the 152-page Mormon booklet titled *Our Heritage: A Brief History of the Church of Jesus Christ of Latter-day Saints* is an excellent example of one of the few times when the screeners of the church may have been asleep at the delete button. Again, the importance of just who the target audience is for these statements printed in 1996 cannot be overstated. These comments certainly were not printed for those Mormons who were hiding the Prophet John Taylor from federal authorities in 1885. This handsome booklet was printed in downtown Salt Lake City for you and me and the new members of the Church of Jesus Christ of Latter-day Saints.

From the 1996 booklet we read the official Mormon statement that echoes the bitterness of 150 years ago. Judging by the current publications, comments, and formal sermons of its leadership, does the Mormon Church still feel that it was wrong for the United States government to enforce the laws of the land? Additionally, I find it very arrogant and condescending that the Mormon Church would continue to publish a document today that suggests that the government had no right to legislate against the practice of polygamy and invade the privacy of their homes. The Mormon argument here is extremely hypocritical in view of the comments the church has made regarding the activities of the Fundamental Church of Jesus Christ of Latter-day Saints in Texas. This booklet essentially takes the position that it was wrong for the United States Congress to pursue the real Mormons in Utah, yet the current opinion of the Mormon church is that polygamists in Texas should be enthusiastically prosecuted.

The following quotes are taken from the 1996 manual. Again, please consider the purpose of the insult on page 97 against many of America's religious and political leaders, who apparently became very angry for no reason.

Persecution Continues

Many of America's religious and political leaders became very angry when they learned that Latter-day Saints living in Utah were encouraging a marriage system that they considered immoral and unchristian. A great political crusade was launched against the Church and its members. The United States Congress passed legislation that curbed the freedom of the latter-day Saints and hurt the Church economically. This legislation ultimately caused officers to arrest and imprison men who had more than one wife and to deny them the right to vote, the right to privacy in their homes, and the enjoyment of other civil liberties. . . . Many Church leaders went into hiding to avoid arrest by federal officers searching for men with more than one wife. [105]

---

[105] *Our Heritage: A Brief History of the Church of Jesus Christ of Latter-*

The Manifesto

As the 1880's drew to a close, the United States government passed additional laws that deprived those who practiced plural marriage of the right to vote and serve on juries and severely restricted the amount of property the Church could own. . . . God, not the United States Congress, brought about the official discontinuance of plural marriage.[106]

Comment: Again, I question the intent of the modern leadership of the Church of Jesus Christ of Latter-day Saints, as they approve, print, and distribute around the world the clear and official observation that the opposition from the United States government was, and is now, to be considered persecution. It is ridiculous beyond all possible description to imagine that within a single authorized publication from the Mormon Church would be a lesson on how to be a loyal citizen, in the very company of openly cynical and negative comments directed at the United States government throughout Mormon history. It is as if the fanatical personality of the Mormon Church has poured onto the pages of its own manuals. They would desperately love to be good Americans, but they equally cannot simply dismiss their revered ancestors who openly spat in the face of the same nation.

Background of the Statement: Within the first few pages of the series *Teachings of the Presidents of the Church*, which are Mormon Church study manuals, is a "Historical Summary" of the life of the Prophet that the particular manual focuses on. The few items below are in chronological order from both the Mormon Prophets John Taylor, who presided over the church from October 1880 to July 1887, and Wilford Woodruff, who presided over the church from July 1887 to September 1898. The point of my inclusion of these relatively minor items is not to review any noteworthy event from the lives of these Mormon Prophets but to clearly demonstrate the negative, pompous, and condescending manner in which these events are recorded for

---

day Saints, 97.
[106] Ibid., 100-101.

the *modern* Latter-day Saint, as these manuals were printed in 2001 and 2004 respectively.

> *In 1882, the United States Congress passes the Edmunds bill, making plural marriage a felony and prohibiting polygamists from voting, holding public office or performing jury duty.*[107]

> *[In 1885 Prophet John Taylor] "receives word during a visit to California that federal officials have ordered his arrest for practicing polygamy. Returns to Salt Lake City on 27 January. On 1 February preaches his last public sermon and, in hopes of limiting the persecution against the Church by federal authorities, goes into hiding.*[108]

> *The United States Congress passes the Edmunds-Tucker Act, another anti-polygamy law, allowing the federal government to confiscate much of the Church's real estate. The act becomes law on March 3, 1887.*[109]

Despite the several laws forbidding polygamy, the practice continued in Utah until about 1906, and the Mormon Prophet John Taylor died in 1887 at the age of 78, while still in hiding from federal authorities as a *felony fugitive on charges of polygamy.* Yet while the Mormon Prophet John Taylor died as a fugitive from the United States government and from the laws of the Congress of the United States, he is still viewed as a martyr for Jesus Christ, as documented in this recently published statement.

> *In significant ways, the conclusion of John Taylor's life paralleled that of his esteemed Prophet as a martyr for the truth; like the Prophet Joseph Smith, John Taylor gave his life for the gospel of Jesus Christ.*[110]

As yet another example that the Church of Jesus Christ of

---

[107] *Teachings of the Presidents of the Church, Wilford Woodruff,* xiii.

[108] *Teachings of the Presidents of the Church, John Taylor,* x.

[109] *Teachings of the Presidents of the Church, Wilford Woodruff,* xiii.

[110] Editor's note in John Taylor, *Witness to the Martyrdom: John Taylor's Personal Account of the Last Days of the Prophet Joseph Smith,* ed. Mark H. Taylor (Salt Lake City: Deseret Book Company, 1999), 147.

Latter-day Saints is torn between its obstinate but honored past and the deep desire to be considered loyal Americans, consider the following two-faced official statement. Under the title "Protecting the Church's Identity," the official newsroom of the Mormon Church issued a press release the morning of June 26, 2008, at the height of the sexual abuse charges involving the Texas polygamous group, the Fundamentalist Church of Jesus Christ of Latter-day Saints. I found three lines particularly hypocritical.

> Once again, as it has done many times, The Church of Jesus Christ of Latter-day Saints reiterates that it has nothing whatsoever to do with any groups practicing polygamy.

> Like all other religions, the FLDS have the right to worship according to the dictates of their conscience, subject to the law.

> Perhaps more than anything else, this effort seeks to highlight the fact that Mormons are much like everyone else.

With some degree of restraint, I have asked myself if the public relations department of the Mormon Church might truly think that there is a confidential, private, and very distinctive Mormon history completely divorced from our American history. The most condescending, hypocritical, and arrogant statement from the press release is without question, "Like all other religions, the FLDS have the right to worship according to the dictates of their conscience, subject to the law." It might just be me, but did the Mormon Church just openly reprimand another religious group *for not following the law when it comes to polygamy?* I have in my home, as millions and millions of current Latter-day Saints do right now, an official study manual from the church that openly celebrates the tenacity and persistence of the Mormon Prophet John Taylor for *disobeying the very same federal law*. If that is not one of the finest examples of bold "in-your-face" hypocrisy, I have never understood the meaning of the word. Again, I quote from that manual:

> *[In 1885 Prophet John Taylor] receives word during a visit to California that federal officials have ordered his arrest for practicing polygamy. Returns to Salt Lake City on 27 January. On 1 February preaches his last public sermon and, in hopes of limiting the persecution against the Church by federal authorities, goes into hiding.*[111]

It is this abundant collection of candidly recorded facts from the Mormon Church itself that causes me to question the true value and seriousness of a Mormon lesson on "Being Loyal Citizens" from the very same set of manuals that document open contempt for the laws of the United States. Many times in the formal worldwide general conferences of the Mormon Church, sarcastic, insulting, or offensive comments have been directed at the people, government, and laws of the United States of America, and for what purpose? Certainly these comments from the highest levels of the leadership of the church and seen as "Scripture" by many have been intended to help the millions and millions of Mormons in "being loyal citizens." Following are a few examples.

> *We believed for years that the law of July 1, 1862, was in direct conflict with the first amendment to the Constitution, which says that "Congress shall make no law respecting an establishment of religion, or prohibiting the free exercise thereof." We rested upon that, and for years continued the practice of plural marriage, believing the law against it to be an unconstitutional one, and that we had the right, under the Constitution, to carry out this principle practically in our lives.*[112]

> *It was not until 1862 that Congress enacted a law forbidding plural marriage. This law the Latter-day Saints conscientiously disregarded, in their observance of a principle*

---

[111] *Teachings of the Presidents of the Church,* John Taylor, x.

[112] President Wilford Woodruff in relation to Plural Marriages, Sixty-first Semi-Annual Conference of the Church of Jesus Christ of Latter-day Saints, October 6th, 1890.

sanctioned by their religion.[113]

> *I rejoice in an individual testimony of the truth of the statements of Joseph Smith, that his name should be had for good and evil in all parts of the world; that the time would come when not only a city, a county and a state should be arrayed against the handful of people called "Mormons," but the day would come when the whole United States of America should be arrayed against them. And the army of the United States was sent against them, and the government of the United States did confiscate all of the property belonging to the Church. Day after day and month after month during the litigation for the return of the Church property I picked up the paper and read, "The United States of America versus the Church of Jesus Christ of Latter-day Saints." And I have laid the paper down and said, "Thank the Lord that the United States have placed the stamp of divinity upon the utterances of the Prophet Joseph Smith."*[114]

Comment: The clear anti-American history of the Church of Jesus Christ of Latter-day Saints is well documented by the church itself. By the time of the Reed Smoot congressional hearings, 1904 to 1907, the veil of secrecy that covered the church's open desire for retribution against the nation was nearly transparent. The animosity and bitterness toward the United States government was so clear that in 1919 the Mormon Prophet Heber J. Grant appointed a special committee to review the content of the temple ordinances, with the charge to remove the Oath of Vengeance and review all church literature for similar references. By 1927 significant action had been taken to remove "all reference to retribution" as reported by Mormon Apostle George F. Richards.

Background of the Statement: Sometimes in the official sermons and publications of the Church of Jesus Christ of Latter-day Saints, it seems the challenge of thinking one way

---

[113] "The Church of Jesus Christ of Latter-day Saints To The World, An Address." Conference Report, April 1907, Afternoon Session, 11.

[114] President Heber J. Grant, Conference Report, The 97th Semi-Annual Conference of the Church of Jesus Christ of Latter-day Saints, held in the Tabernacle, Salt Lake City, Utah, October 3, 1926, 1.

and speaking another way simply becomes too much for the leadership, the authors, and the editors to deal with. I have documented various hypocritical actions and statements from the Mormon Church generally, and from its leadership specifically. Concerning the long history of contempt and disrespect shown by the Mormon Church for the laws of the United States of America, I would like to conclude with one final example and the consideration of two important points.

The first point is that I definitely believe that the contempt for what has been openly perceived and officially taught as "persecution by the federal government"[115] remains only a faintly dormant emotion for the Latter-day Saint. This speculation is based on the fact that literally hundreds of anti-American comments have been repeatedly presented to the population of the Mormon Church under the authority of its own leadership.

The second point, as demonstrated by the comments and publications of the Mormon Church, is that the goal is for this current generation of Latter-day Saints to have some measure of contempt for the United States government. As the concluding example of this assertion, consider the following passages from two of the Mormon Church manuals I used to study the Scriptures with my family for the length of my membership in the Church of Jesus Christ of Latter-day Saints.

The Doctrine and Covenants and Church History, Gospel Doctrine Teacher's Manual,[116] lesson 31, page 182, demonstrates one of the best examples of the Mormon talent for a selective respect for the laws of the United States of America. On a single page, with only a few lines of text between them, the student is given two diametrically opposed concepts of how the practice of plural marriage has been controlled. The first statement is under the heading *"The revelation to practice*

---

[115] President and Prophet Gordon B. Hinckley, 176th Semiannual General Conference, October 1, 2006.

[116] Published by The Church of Jesus Christ of Latter-day Saints, Salt Lake City, 1999.

plural marriage in this dispensation" and explains how the church, not the federal law, managed the practice of polygamy. The second statement under the heading "*The Church's position on plural marriage today*" is from the Prophet Gordon B. Hinckley during the official General Conference of the Church in October of 1998. In stark contrast to the earlier statement, it explains how the federal law and the church now manage the practice of polygamy. Emphasis has been added to each statement, by underlining the key phrases to better illustrate the enormous hypocrisy at work.

> <u>*Church leaders regulated the practice*</u>. *Those entering into it had to be authorized to do so, and the marriages had to be performed through the sealing power of the priesthood.*

> *Not only are those so involved in direct violation of <u>civil law</u>, they are in violation of the law of this Church.*

My question is simply this: How is it that the power and authority of the very same "civil law" referenced by the Mormon Prophet Gordon B. Hinckley in our time had no such power or authority over the Mormon Prophets Joseph Smith, Brigham Young, John Taylor, or Wilford Woodruff in their time? The answer may be found in an equally bold and truly arrogant statement officially approved by the First Presidency and Quorum of the Twelve Apostles in 1981. It is found on page 334 of the *Doctrine and Covenants Student Manual of the Church*,[117] as it describes the power and authority of "the Law of the Priesthood."

> *The truth is here reiterated, that whatever is done in the name of God, according to His law and by His direction, cannot be sin. What human law regards as a crime may, or may not, from the Divine point of view, be a sin.*

Comment: Again, it appears to me that the somewhat schizophrenic publications of the Mormon Church reflect the

---

[117] Published by The Church of Jesus Christ of Latter-day Saints, Salt Lake City, 1981.

desire to maintain a deep loyalty to both the clearly obstinate and anti-American history of the early church and the traditional values of democracy and patriotism. I do not question the individual patriotism of the average Mormon. It is the literary skills of the Mormon leadership, when writing about both the heritage of the church and national patriotism, that I find problematic.

The Fundamental Conclusions of This Chapter

Several times during the writing of this book, and specifically this chapter, I was forced to experience again and again the depressing and disheartening feelings of my personal responsibility. For many years I taught the Mormon version of the gospel of Jesus Christ. I personally helped to bring men, women, and children into the Church of Jesus Christ of Latter-day Saints. And still today I ask myself, how did I not know it was a lie? Upon serious reflection, I can remember the slight but nagging feeling that something was just not right. I recall the early feeling that the Mormon Prophets' sweeping powers and blanket release from any personal responsibilities was something more than just ethically and morally convenient for them. And I can never forget the first time my heart was pierced with the disgusting and nauseating suggestion that Jesus Christ Himself was the author of the practice of secretly having sex with another man's wife or slitting the throat of another Mormon.

If there were but one conclusion for this chapter, it would be my earlier stated observation that the truth matters—it really does. Some members of the Church of Jesus Christ of Latter-day Saints may be able to turn away from these facts, considering me and my book to be simply "anti-Mormon," and return to a pleasant family life behind the veil of self-inflected ignorance. What is lost at that moment in time is any real potential to come to a full knowledge of the true personality and character of the Lord Jesus Christ, for the Jesus Christ seen through the formal teachings of the Mormon Prophets is

Himself deceitful, vindictive, and oppressive to women everywhere. With such a poor example (this Mormon adaptation of Christ) at the head of the Church of Jesus Christ of Latter-day Saints, it is completely understandable that a man ordained as a Prophet, Seer, and Revelator in that church, Apostle Heber C. Kimball, would offer the thirty-seven-year old Prophet Joseph Smith his fourteen-year-old daughter as a wife and then state for himself regarding marriage, "I think no more of taking another wife than I do of buying a cow."[118]

In this chapter are several key subjects that played significant roles in my education with regard to the true nature and foundation of the Mormon Church. And as suggested by the title, "Read, Study, Ponder, and Pray: The Trauma of Learning the Truth," it was a shock coming to terms with the fact that the *current* leadership of the Mormon Church supports, defends, and will excommunicate those who question the actions of any Mormon leader. This then brings the well-documented and repulsive actions of the early church leadership to the feet of my generation of Mormons. I am not so naïve as to discount the fact that many of the early leaders of the Mormon Church knew precisely the moral direction of the faith and still had no issue with sharing their wives and daughters with each other. And I have no doubt whatsoever that the very same base desires are hidden just below the surface of the majority of the male leaders of the current Church of Jesus Christ of Latter-day Saints. I have formed this conclusion based on remarks made to me within closed-door leadership meetings and on the printed comments of the current leadership of the church claiming the United States Congress has "persecuted" the church and limited the freedom of religion.

It should be understood that my comments about the patriotism of the leadership of the Church of Jesus Christ of Latter-day Saints does not reflect poorly on the general membership of the church. What I have presented here is what

---

[118] Irving Wallace, *The Twenty-Seventh Wife* (New York: Simon and Schuster, 1961), 101.

I consider to be the deliberate use of anti-American propaganda to influence the opinions of the current membership of the Mormon Church. I believe that the leadership of the church would like to firmly establish within the minds of all members of the Mormon faith that while the law should be respected and "enforced in courts of justice," this does not apply to the "revelations of a Mormon Prophet," which are apparently above the law.

In closing, the personal challenge of this chapter remains as constant as does the challenge of the entire book, especially for a Mormon. If you think that what I have documented here as my true-life experiences are only opinions, assumptions, or lies, then dismiss the few hours you may have spent with me as a waste of time. But if at some point in your reading you privately thought, "I didn't know that" or "Can that be true?" then you may have an issue with either the teachings of the Mormon Church or exactly who you *think* Jesus Christ really is. Indeed, He cannot be both the creator of polygamy, polyandry, blood atonement, and the many perversions of His own Scriptures and still be the one to whom the world has looked for mercy, grace, compassion, and forgiveness from the very sins the early Mormons considered a central part of their "restored gospel." In this the Mormons are without question correct in their bold declaration to the world that the Church of Jesus Christ of Latter-day Saints is either the *only* true church on the earth or the *greatest* religious fraud known to mankind.[119]

Having been through this myself, I would respectfully suggest that some serious and devoted time of personal reflection is now required. It is now of absolutely no significance whatsoever that you might think of me as an impostor or fraud. What matters now is that you have been given information and a witness that you most likely did not

---

[119] "But if Joseph Smith was not called of God, then this cause that we have espoused, and these proclamations that we make, are the greatest imposition and fraud that have been promulgated in the name of religion in the course of the history of the world" (Elder Bruce R. McConkie, Conference Report, October 1962, First Day—Morning Meeting, 9).

have yesterday. And so it is with all of us who claim to be followers of the Lord Jesus Christ, you can dismiss, disprove, or embrace what you have learned here. With any of these three choices, I believe that your personal relationship with Jesus Christ will change, possibly very significantly and probably forever.

CHAPTER FOUR

Leadership of the Church: A Lower

Standard of Conduct

I have never asked them to withhold their support in **any way. Why would I counsel them about the questions in such a manner?**

Michael D. Jones, President, Arvada Colorado Stake,

Church of Jesus Christ of Latter-day Saints[120]

What a thing it is for a man to be accused of committing adultery, and of having seven wives, when I can only find one.

Joseph Smith Jr., *History of the Church*, 6:411

No man has a good enough memory to make a successful liar.

Abraham Lincoln, 16th President of the United States

Michael D. Jones—Mormon Stake President

I believe that neither Joseph Smith Jr. nor Stake President Michael D. Jones was a devoted student of the speeches or letters of our Sixteenth President, who as noted above, said, "No man has a good enough memory to make a successful liar." However, it is clear to me that the leaders of the Church of Jesus Christ of Latter-day Saints are both superbly talented and faithful students of the doctrine of "lying for the Lord."

---

[120] Note that the comment underlined for emphasis by Michael D. Jones himself is a lie.

I was first introduced to the subject of "lying for the Lord" through a packet of Internet information given to me by Mormon Stake President Michael D. Jones himself, who became the Arvada Colorado Stake President on May 20, 2007 as reported by the official LDS Church News.[121] What I did not comprehend at the time was the relative significance of the Presiding High Priest of the Church of Jesus Christ of Latter-day Saints handing to me in church a collection of unauthorized articles and statements concerning the Mormon view of lying for the Lord. The unofficial information he provided was in response to a collection of well-documented questions I had distributed among the local and national leadership of the church.

The critical difference between President Jones and myself was that each of my questions[122] were based exclusively on Mormon Scripture, Mormon history, Mormon doctrine, and the authorized teachings of Mormon Prophets and Apostles. Each of my questions had been supported by numerous church references and footnotes from official sources. In contrast, President Jones provided me with an assortment of comments, which, it seems now, do not at all represent the policies or position of the church. Why, then, would he give them to me? This would begin a series of actions by the senior representative of the Church of Jesus Christ of Latter-day Saints in my area, namely, President Jones, which demonstrate a strategy of dual standards of conduct and character. The higher standard he would of course apply to my life and excommunicate me for failing to meet his expectations; the lower standard would be reserved for his behavior, documents, and lies.

---

[121] See http://www.ldschurchnews.com/articles/50706/New-stake-presidents. html

[122] Lee B. Baker, "A Formal Request for Spiritual Support and Assistance," December 2007. See introductory letter sent to over sixty members of the church, appendix A document number 18. The questions were basically the same as the Lorin M. Lund questions found in chapter 5.

Just a few months later, President Jones, my brother in the church, my spiritual advisor, and the senior representative of the Church of Jesus Christ of Latter-day Saints in our area, would formally charge me with what *he* was guilty of—"teaching unauthorized doctrine"—and then he would lie about it. Fortunately, I was able to record his lie and his arrogance on audiotape, right in his office. Even with his well-documented character issues, I would still consider him a fairly typical example of the senior-level leadership within the Mormon Church.

As I stated in the introduction of this book, I have often wondered how so much wickedness could have been so effortlessly accomplished by the leadership of the Mormon Church, when within the Mormon Scriptures stood the very standard of conduct for all of us to read. It was not obvious to me at that time that an entirely separate and much lower standard is reserved for the leadership of the Church of Jesus Christ of Latter-day Saints. I was excommunicated for simply asking questions about the Mormon Church, yet its leadership apparently can take the wives of other men without any violation of integrity, honesty, or morality.

> *That they may be conferred upon us, it is true; but when we undertake to cover our sins, or to gratify our pride, our vain ambition, or to exercise control or dominion or compulsion upon the souls of the children of men, in any degree of unrighteousness, behold, the heavens withdraw themselves; the Spirit of the Lord is grieved; and when it is withdrawn, Amen to the priesthood or the authority of that man. (Doctrine and Covenants 121:37)*

What follows is a condensed but accurate account of the sinister development and arrangement of events that culminated in my excommunication from the church. I should state now that at the time it was spiritually demoralizing for me to watch these disturbing and calculated procedures unfold. Since then, I have come to believe with all my heart that those events were a direct intervention from the Lord Himself. The subsequent proceedings and their consequences in my life were an answer to my prayers, which delivered me from the Mormon Church, its deceptive doctrine, and embarrassing history.

This chapter will document numerous examples of the hypocrisy and double standards openly employed by the leadership of the Mormons throughout the history of the church. I will first address the local leadership of the church in both Maryland and Colorado and specifically how their hypocrisy and double standards have affected my life. I will then address the long-term consequences of the lies, deceptions, and depravities of the national leadership of the church, both past and present.

In my frustration and disappointment I wrote several letters directly to the headquarters of the church seeking support. Now years later, and with a much more informed reflection on the events in my life, it was naïve of me to think that as an ordained Mormon Bishop I might receive some guidance from President Thomas S. Monson. I sent letters to him expressing my concerns in January 2006, July 2007, and March 2008 and a final letter with an audiotape of my Stake President caught in a lie in May 2008. Not a single letter was ever answered, but I do remember an extraordinary day that graphically highlighted one of the great hypocrisies of the church. For years, both in Maryland and in Colorado, the local leadership of the church told me that only one man could truly answer my questions, and that would be the Prophet himself. I tried that without any success. Not only did I send letters to the headquarters of the church, but each and every packet of questions I mailed to fellow members and friends (over sixty in total) I also sent to Salt Lake. On Sunday April 13, 2008, it was as if the senior church officers were tired of me. Brother Michael Feil, Second Counselor in the Bishopric of our congregation, the Standley Lake Ward of the Arvada Colorado Stake, stood at the beginning of our worship service and read a letter from the First Presidency of the Church. The letter (I asked for a copy but was refused) stated that letters and phone calls concerning doctrine of the church should not be sent to Salt Lake. Such issues, the letter continued, should be addressed by the local authorities of the church, Bishops and Stake Presidents, who are called and set apart and have the blessing of the spirit of discernment to assist members.

While this is an excellent policy in theory, I found it to be thoroughly lacking in practice, as it will be documented here. As a precursor to the superficial and hypocritical support I was about to receive during the most significant spiritual and emotional event of my life, consider a twenty-four-hour period in late April of 2008. In an e-mail, President Michael D. Jones had implied that I had insulted the reputation of Joseph Smith. Although I was perfectly capable of the act, his accusation was in fact a lie. To his credit, on April 24 he sent a heartfelt letter of apology, stating, "I take full responsibility for my actions and your subsequent pain."[123] His affectionate and straightforward ownership of responsibility was exceptionally short-lived, for the next day, April 25, he sent an equally heartfelt letter in which he claimed that he never asked the other church leaders to "withhold their support in any way."[124] He continued with, "Why would I counsel them about the questions in such a manner?" President Jones did not know at that time that I had recorded his admission to the very act within his own office a few days earlier or that the other church leaders would tell me of his e-mail and instructions to withhold their individual support. I suspect that the two well-written and genuinely heartfelt letters addressed to me were more for his priesthood superiors in Salt Lake City than for me.

It should be noted that several registered letters were sent to each of the local Mormon Leaders referenced within this book, as well as a full copy of the manuscript for their review and comment for accuracy and completeness. And yet, in the classic Mormon leadership style of "disregard the problem and it will go away", each registered letter was refused and returned unopened. But this was to be expected, for what specific events could truthfully and effectively be refuted when the very

---

[123] See appendix A document number 4.

[124] See appendix A document number 5.

foundation of this book is in fact the words, actions and the teachings of deception from the Mormon Leadership themselves both past and present?

Deceit and Deception on a Personal Level

The complete set of the many letters, e-mails, and recordings are provided within appendix A and the footnotes of this book. In this section I will select the relevant sections of the several communications necessary to substantiate my claims of deceit and deception. The depth of despair on the part of my wife and me is hard to accurately communicate, as the total indifference and apathy we were exposed to was demoralizing and emotionally crushing. What we had been told was the most important aspect of our life, our membership in the church and our temple marriage, was unraveling, and our priesthood leadership's advice was to simply let the questions go as if the truth was not a fundamental requirement for our recovery. The first subject of this review will be the actions of Arvada Colorado Stake President Michael D. Jones concerning the issue of my questions about the church and his dishonesty, which resulted in my excommunication. To better illustrate the deception of President Jones, I will use a series of comments relevant to his actions placed in chronological order.

In December of 2007 I distributed among the leadership of the church a packet of questions titled, "A Formal Request for Spiritual Support and Assistance—December 2007." The packet included a four-page letter of introduction, which detailed why I (as an active High Priest in the Mormon Church) was seeking answers to these critical questions.[125]

***

Letter and Packet of Questions, from Lee Baker to the leadership of the church, dated December 2007. Quote is from the cover letter included with the packet.

---

[125] See appendix A document number 11.

In the past five years the most discouraging and frustrating aspect of my life has been, without question, my relationship with my own Church. Specifically, it has become painfully clear that, during the most important spiritual challenge in my life, the level of genuine concern is debatable at best, while the amount of actual support is simply depressing.

Comment: This packet of serious questions eventually was sent to over sixty senior church members in leadership positions, including authorities in Salt Lake City; only one unsigned and undated response was ever received.

***

Letter to Lee Baker from Bishop Richard Merkley, dated January 2008:[126]

I received your packet last month (December 2007) that details the various questions about the history of the church that you have been researching. At the request of our Stake President, Michael Jones, I will not be responding to your individual questions with independent answers.

Comment: The comment in this letter left me with the impression that Bishop Merkley had been given instructions from Stake President Michael D. Jones not to answer my questions. This is a fact that he [Michael D. Jones] openly denied on both the 23rd and 25th of April 2008.

***

E-mail to Kathy Baker from Michael D. Jones, President, Arvada Colorado Stake, Church of Jesus Christ of Latter-day Saints, March 31, 2008.[127]

Let me share with you again my own personal journey through the questions posed regarding Joseph Smith. My petition to the Lord was not whether Joseph

---

[126] See appendix A document number 23.

[127] See appendix A document number 25.

was some fallen and conniving con man who stole other men's wives, or a well-meaning, but libidinous prophet who preyed on people's faith; I asked Heavenly Father "where does he stand as prophet of the restoration?"

The answer I received, as I shared with you and your husband, was that I saw in my mind's eye, Joseph Smith, standing in the heavens, glorious and exalted. There was a beauty and grandeur that I can only poorly express. I saw those who came in judgment of him, and when they entered his presence, they shrank in horror and shame receiving for themselves a full view of the man and of themselves. Now, I don't know whether Joseph misapplied the law of eternal marriage, or if he broke the commandments for his own selfishness (though I believe that he did not), or if his unrighteous actions caused others to stumble and fall. I only know how the Lord regards him today, and for the eternities to come . . . and for me, it is enough and to spare. Having this knowledge, the other questions are meaningless to me. My grateful testimony is that Joseph Smith is a prophet of God.

Comment: For the record: Only Michael D. Jones has ever used the phrase "Joseph was some fallen and conniving con man who stole other men's wives, or a well-meaning, but libidinous prophet who preyed on people's faith." Although I did not say it, I do very much agree with the description provided by President Jones.

***

Recorded Conversation with Michael D. Jones in his church office on the evening of April 23, 2008.

Bro. Lee Baker: Could I ask you a second question?

President Michael D. Jones: Yes.

Bro. Lee Baker: Do you feel, President, that you had the right, authority, or power to pull the priesthood . . . umm . . . support that I had asked for in December, and I had asked Bishop Merkley a year ago, sixteen months ago? Do you feel, when you sent that e-mail that stopped the boys, and said that you would take care of it . . . do you believe that you had the authority to do that?

President Michael D. Jones: Yes.

Bro. Lee Baker: Do you think that was the right thing to do?

President Michael D. Jones: Yes.

Bro. Lee Baker: And you said, you told them that you would take care of it?

President Michael D. Jones: Yep.

Bro. Lee Baker: And has it been taken care of?

Comment: These recorded statements from President Jones in his own office gave me the impression that he did in fact communicate to the group of church leaders (whom I had asked for help), informing them that they did not need to address my questions. This he stated without hesitation, despite the fact that just two days after this conversation he would sign a letter, arrogantly declaring precisely the *opposite* and then provide that very *lie* to church headquarters.

***

Letter to Brother and Sister Baker from Michael D. Jones, President, Arvada Colorado Stake, Church of Jesus Christ of Latter-day Saints, April 25, 2008.[128] (Note: President Jones *himself* underlined the lie to give more emphasis, as *if* it were a true statement.)

> <u>I have never asked them to withhold their support in any way.</u> Why would I counsel them about the questions in such a manner?

Comment: The statements noted previously from Bishop Merkley in January 2008[129] and from President Jones himself on

---

[128] See appendix A document number 5.

[129] See appendix A document number 23.

both April 23 and May 10 (see below) clearly indicate that President Jones lied. Additionally, the only line of this two-page letter that President Jones underlined for emphasis is in fact the lie itself with the extra enhancement of arrogance added by his words "in any way." Michael's arrogance is astounding but completely understandable in that I believe these letters were to be forwarded to church headquarters in Salt Lake City. Michael D. Jones, as the Stake President, was the single individual with the power to excommunicate me. Yet while he considered himself both an impartial judge and an authorized representative of the Lord Jesus Christ, his deliberate deceitfulness in these matters is reprehensible and is a testimony of his dishonesty on behalf of the Mormon Church. On July 27, 2008, President Jones personally informed me, in his office at the stake center, that The First Presidency of the Church in Salt Lake City had received my letter of May 12, 2008 (which had reported his lie and included the audiotape of April 23, 2008, which corroborated my report of his deception). He said at that time that they (The First Presidency) wished to inform me, through him (President Jones), that they had "no comment."

***

E-mail to Lee Baker from Michael D. Jones, May 10, 2008.

Please understand this distinction—it would never be appropriate to withhold the love and regard for the Baker family. That they should be obligated to answer the questions was something I didn't feel was appropriate.

Comment: The reference to "they" in this e-mail is to the leadership of the church to whom I had provided a copy of my questions, asking for their support. Those additional individuals were: Bishop Richard Merkley, Bishop DeVon Doman, and High Priest Group Leader Rod Tarullo. All confirmed that they received instructions from President Jones. Again, he clearly stated that he did influence them not to provide me with the support I had asked for, and then he lied about it. Yet this was the same fair and impartial man who would be in charge of my excommunication.

***

Letter to Lee Baker from Scott Gagon, High Priest and Director of Public Affairs, Arvada Colorado Stake, dated July 29, 2008.

> While I do have a few thoughts about some of the issues you raised, my overwhelming impression is that none of these issues are significant to our personal salvation and well being nor do they raise any question in my mind about the validity or truthfulness of the gospel. They are, as it were, mere fleas of irritation on a dog's back, so to speak, in the eternal sense of what is really important.

Comment: It is my opinion that the casual dismissal of my questions noted here as "mere fleas of irritation on a dog's back" is very typical, in that, regardless of how important they may be to the individual affected, in the view of the leadership they are of no concern.

***

E-mail to Lee Baker from Michael D. Jones, November 12, 2008.

> Effective immediately, and until further notice, you are not welcome in our Church meetings. If you disregard this request, your name and information will be sent to all appropriate leadership. They will be instructed to dial 911 and report you as a trespasser.

Comment: As President Jones had neither made arrangements for me to receive the weekly sacrament outside of the church meetings, nor had I ever been found unworthy to take the sacrament by any council, committee, or procedure, I did attend church services that next Sunday, with my wife, quietly in the fourth row from the back of the church. At the direction of President Jones, his First Counselor, David T. Paulsen, called the police. My wife and I left the church without incident immediately after the meeting. As no disturbance was noted that day or any other day of my thirty-two years as a member and leader of the church, I question the common sense of anyone who would see my presence as a threat of imminent danger, yet armed officers from the Jefferson County Sheriff's Department were called in to satisfy the temper tantrum of the senior representative of the Mormon Church, who had both lied to me and personally frustrated any fair procedure on my behalf.

***

Letter of notification regarding disciplinary action for Lee B. Baker, undated letter from Michael D. Jones received December 2, 2008.[130]

> You are invited to attend this disciplinary council to give your response and, if you wish, to provide witnesses and other evidence in your behalf.

> This council will be held at 7:15 am on December 7, 2008 in the high council room.

Comment: On December 5, a few days after the offer documented in this letter, which is in accordance with church policy permitting both witnesses and other evidence on my behalf, President Jones, who lied to and about me, totally and permanently removed that vital opportunity from my defense and made a mockery of what little fairness and integrity is normally associated with Mormon church disciplinary councils.

***

E-mail to Lee Baker from Michael D. Jones, December 5, 2008.

> You have asked Brother Tarullo and Brother Merkley to participate. Brother Tarullo is scheduled to be out of town. While I haven't spoken to him, would you like to have him provide written answers? If so, send me the questions, and I will ask him to respond.

Comment: Yet again, in accordance with church policy, this e-mail acknowledges the right to present both witnesses and

---

[130] See appendix A document number 6.

other evidence in my behalf. Within just a few hours of this e-mail, however, President Jones totally and permanently removed that vital opportunity from my defense.

***

E-mail from Lee Baker to Michael D. Jones, December 5, 2008.

> Attached are the questions Rod said, in December of last year, that he would "do his best" with. I would like him to complete that offer.

Comment: In preparation for my defense as both offered by President Jones and required by church policy, and further reiterated in his e-mail of December 5 (see above), I provided President Jones a copy of my questions to High Priest Group Leader Rod Tarullo. These questions were then and remain the core issue of my perceived apostasy within the church. They were therefore extremely relevant to my defense and imperative to the procedure of the Mormon Church disciplinary council.

***

E-mail to Lee Baker from Michael D. Jones, December 5, 2008.

> That isn't an appropriate request. Neither Brother Tarullo, nor Bishop Merkley will be asked to attend or participate. The purpose of this council is to examine if your behavior constitutes apostasy, and not to examine the questions.

Comment: With the removal of any impartiality, as noted by this e-mail, my already limited rights to a fair trial were completely removed two days prior to the disciplinary council. It should be clearly noted that at this time my senior priesthood advisor, President Michael D. Jones, was the *most active opponent* to my receiving answers to serious questions concerning the church, and within forty-eight hours he alone would be the senior priesthood authority organizing and establishing procedures for my disciplinary council, conducting the hearing, and then giving the final judgment. I asked him how fair that could be, considering his earlier involvement. No answer was given.

***

Letter of excommunication to Lee Baker from Michael D. Jones, December 10, 2008.[131]

> As a result of the disciplinary council held on December 7, 2008, you are excommunicated for conduct contrary to the laws of the Church of Jesus Christ of Latter-day Saints. . . .
>
> You have the right to appeal. Should you desire to do so, you have 30 days in which to provide such notice to me in writing, specifying the alleged errors or unfairness in the procedure or decision.
>
> Sincerely,
>
> Michael D. Jones
>
> Arvada Colorado Stake President

Comment: In the letter of excommunication I was offered the right to appeal. I did so the next day.

***

Letter of Appeal from Lee Baker to Michael D. Jones, December 15, 2008.[132]

> I do not appeal the judgment or findings of the procedure, only the specificity of the charge "for conduct contrary to the laws of the Church".
>
> On the grounds of fairness noted both in your letter and as stipulated during the Disciplinary Council of 7 December 2008, I request a detailed written list of my conduct which was found to be contrary to the specific laws of the Church which were violated.

---

[131] See appendix A document number 7.

[132] See appendix A document number 8.

What I have provided in written form to both members and non-members of the Church has been well documented as truthful.

Comment: With the offer[133] to provide witnesses and other evidence in my behalf removed from me,[134] I was not given the opportunity to demonstrate the validity and the truthfulness of my questions, comments, or actions.

***

Letter of clarification on excommunication to Lee Baker from Michael D. Jones, December 27, 2008.[135]

On December 7, 2008, you were excommunicated as a member of the church for being in apostasy, which is contrary to the laws and order of the church. You have asked for clarification as to what laws were broken, and what were the specific actions that led to the decision of the council.

What follows is a brief summary of the information that was considered at your disciplinary council. . . .

You persisted in teaching as Church doctrine information that is not Church doctrine after you had been corrected by me and your bishop.

Example: You distributed packets of statements which contained information that is not Church doctrine on multiple occasions, in various forms and to broad audiences despite warnings and your personal commitment to stop doing so.

On the basis of these actions, you were excommunicated from the Church.

---

[133] See appendix A document number 6.

[134] E-mail from President Jones, December 5, 2008. In that e-mail, President Jones wrote, "Neither Brother Tarullo, nor Bishop Merkley will be asked to attend or participate."

[135] See appendix A document number 9.

Comment: As if the prejudiced procedures of the formal disciplinary council of December 7 were not enough, in this letter of clarification of my alleged offenses against the church, President Michael D. Jones describes exactly what he, not I, had done. Although I have clearly documented that he openly lied on several occasions, of particular offense to me is the accusation that I both taught and distributed unauthorized information about the church. At the time of my request for support from my fellow members of the church, I had no calling, no position of authority, and certainly no teaching responsibilities; I only asked questions. In stark contrast to my general membership, the Stake President was both the Presiding High Priest and the senior priesthood advisor and religious teacher for the several thousand church members in his jurisdiction. From the very first days of his advice, direction, and counsel to me, he was in every imaginable capacity known within the church as a teacher, advisor, and mentor. *In April of 2008, within the walls of the church during Sunday school, President Jones personally gave me, a packet of statements containing information that was **not** church doctrine.*[136] To refresh the reader's memory of precisely why I was excommunicated please note: "You [Lee B. Baker] distributed packets of statements which contained information that is not Church doctrine."[137]

Do as I Say, Not as I Do

The next few paragraphs will highlight the outlandish statements and information found in the packet President Michael D. Jones provided as an answer to my questions. I have wondered why he could not have addressed my questions from an official position of the church or from his own vast knowledge of the church. As a reminder, please review the selected pages from the packet of information I provided the

---

[136] See appendix A document number 10.

[137] See appendix A document number 9.

leadership,[138] and compare my use of valid Mormon doctrine with detailed and supporting research to the bizarre and unauthorized Internet packet from President Jones, who was the only true teacher and authorized representative of the church in this situation.[139] I believe that President Jones did not fully understand the limit of his authority, nor did he fully comprehend the guidance below given to all members of the church:

> *We have no authority to interfere with individual opinions; but neither you nor I have any right to teach a principle or doctrine as a tenet of the Church unless it has been sanctioned by the Church or the authorities.*[140]

Several sections of the unauthorized packet President Jones gave me in April of 2008 centered on the practice of lying with the proper motivations. Specifically noted here are two sections: (1) "Lying About Polygamy during the Nauvoo Era," and (2) "Lying About Polygamy in Utah, Prior to 1890."

Offensive to any respectable person, and more specifically insulting to the Jewish community, is the comparison between lying to a Nazi SS officer in helping the Jews to avoid the Holocaust and lying to the United States government, local officials, or other Mormons about the practice of polygamy. I was stunned and completely repulsed by the comparison of the systematic torture and mass murder of six million men, women, and children in contrast to the "break up of polygamous

---

[138] Baker, "A Formal Request for Spiritual Support and Assistance, December 2007." See original set of questions in chapter 5 and the introductory letter sent to over sixty members of the church in appendix A document number 11.

[139] The packet of information provided by the Presiding High Priest of the Mormon Church in Arvada, Colorado was: "Polygamy, Prophets, and Prevarication: Frequently and Rarely Asked Questions about the Initiation, Practice, and Cessation of Plural Marriage in The Church of Jesus Christ of Latter-day Saints," by Gregory L. Smith, from The Foundation for Apologetic Information & Research, http://www.fairlds.org. See cover page along with pages 11 and 16 in appendix A document number 10.

[140] Elder James E. Talmage, Conference Report, Semi-Annual Sunday School Conference, October 1902, 97.

families, and the abandonment of wives without support." At the time I did not know if President Michael D. Jones was supremely arrogant or just simply ignorant of the facts. In December of 2008, when I learned that he would charge me with what he, as the senior representative of the Church of Jesus Christ of Latter-day Saints, had done, namely, "distributing packets of statements which contained information that is not Church doctrine," I was certain that he was both tremendously arrogant and completely ignorant. Following, is the specific statement, which President Jones provided to me:

> *Do you save your family and the Jews you are hiding, or do you tell the Nazis the truth? Do you break up polygamous families, abandon wives without support, or tell the whole truth?*[141]

To place in context the practice of "lying for the Lord" and to better understand President Jones's relative ease with its application, I believe the following obvious lie from Joseph Smith Jr., found within the official history of the Mormon Church, is revealing.

> *What a thing it is for a man to be accused of committing adultery, and of having seven wives, when I can only find one.*[142]

When Joseph Smith Jr. made this false statement, he was in fact married to thirty-three women, many of whom his first wife, Emma Hale Smith, did not know about.[143] Symptomatic of the audacity of the church leadership is the fact that this clear and bold lie from Joseph Smith Jr. himself has remained in print as part of the official history of the church for well over one hundred years.

As I have suggested several times in this book, one of the more depressing aspects of my journey of personal discovery and the research it has required is that the hypocrisy found

---

[141] "Polygamy, Prophets, and Prevarication," 16.

[142] *History of the Church,* 6:411. (Public speech by Joseph Smith to the citizens of Nauvoo, Ill. May 1844.)

[143] Compton, *In Sacred Loneliness: The Plural Wives of Joseph Smith.*

within the teachings of Mormonism is overwhelming. It is as if any given subject can either be supported or refuted by the very same authorities. I have not yet had a conversation with an active Latter-day Saint who would defend Joseph Smith's comment about being accused of having seven wives when he can only find one. All acknowledge it as a lie. And yet a simple search on the Mormon Church's Web site (lds.org) for talks, sermons, or lessons like Elder Marion G. Romney's talk "Don't Lie. Tell the Truth," returns over two thousand similar lessons that would make one think that honesty is truly valued among the leadership of the Mormon Church.

An Assessment of My Excommunication

The morning of Sunday, December 7, 2008, was cold but crystal clear as my wife and I arrived at the Arvada Colorado Stake Center for the last time in our lives. I had commented to her that it was bittersweet that in this very building we had been married and began our life together. Although my wife and I were sealed in the Washington D.C. temple on March 10, 1979, our civil wedding was on a very hot and humid Saturday, July 10, 1976, within the very building I would soon terminate my thirty-two-year association with the Church of Jesus Christ of Latter-day Saints. I told my lovely wife, who had stood by me throughout this incredible ordeal, that I was equally as certain about the appropriateness of my forced excommunication as I was about the day we began our life together within the walls of this same building. She too would ask to have her membership from the Mormon Church revoked.

After a short wait, we were invited into the High Council room, which was adjacent to the office of the Stake President, Michael D. Jones. Although we had not yet spoken, I remember the overwhelming feeling when President Jones and I glanced at each other that within an hour the deed would be done and that we both knew this was merely a required formality. At the head of the highly polished, elongated table sat President Jones with his two counselors, David T. Paulsen and Daren B. Forbes. At the opposite end of the table, I sat center with my wife to my left and our Bishop on my right. I will not identify our good Bishop, the only member of the church who truly respected our right to ask these questions of our church, as he will certainly be ostracized. Flanked on each side of the table were the current members of the Arvada Stake High Council, six on one side and six on the other. Although one of the twelve was a substitute due to the unavailability of a standing member, the significance of the number of the High Council is to represent the twelve Apostles of Jesus Christ. Although I recognize the number twelve, that ends any similarity I can find.

President Jones offered a short prayer, and then he outlined the charge: "We are here to consider the possibility of your disfellowshipment or excommunication as a state of apostasy may exist." I directed my initial statements toward the entire group, less the one substitute member of the High Council, by asking if they had each received the set of my formal questions[144] addressed to "Dear Fellow Brother or Sister" and a copy of my Open and Public Testimony.[145] They had each received the documents. Then I asked why they had not offered any assistance, any comments, or any direction specific to my questions or my stated testimony. The room was silent. I then told them that over the past two months, sixty-five copies of those exact documents were sent to my past associates within the church. I told them that from all of those copies, sent throughout the country to my closest friends in the church, my past Counselors, Bishops, even the man who had baptized me,[146] as well as dozens of local, area, and general leaders of the church, only one sarcastic and condescending response was returned.

The fact that I had known who would be called to judge

---

[144] The full set of questions are found in chapter 5. For the two-page introduction sent to all members of the High Council, see appendix A document number 18.

[145] A copy of my Open and Public Testimony was sent to all members of the High Council. See appendix A document number 16.

[146] Gary D. Bergquist of Saint George, Utah, baptized the author on Thursday, February 17, 1977.

me gave me the opportunity to seek support from them with those letters, while I was still an ordained Bishop, a High Priest within the very same Quorum as each of them. I was at that time a member in good standing with no reason whatsoever for them to hesitate or to come to the aid of a fellow brother, yet they did nothing. I asked President Jones, "What have I ever said, what have I ever written or sent to others that was a lie?" Again, the room was silent. President Jones continued with two false accusations. "You have given this information to a member of your ward who is a new member of the church," he charged. My Bishop confirmed that this was a false statement, as he had been asked to interview the man in question. Then Jones stated, "You have had legal action taken against you in Maryland by a member whom you have attacked there." Again this was a false statement. No such action has ever been brought to my attention.

The "attack" President Jones was referring to was an e-mail I had sent to the employers and coworkers of the several leaders who would either not speak with me concerning my questions or had callously stated, "Yes, I believe everything the Prophets have taught is true." In those cases, I simply shared a collection of the most outlandish but true beliefs and teachings of the Mormon Church, as if they were non-controversial and could be accepted by any true Christian. This e-mail[147] was sent to demonstrate that the teachings and doctrines of the Mormon Church, which I was told were relatively acceptable, were in fact very difficult to explain to non-Mormons and extremely embarrassing as a statement of one's faith. As my "brethren" in my own church would not or could not answer my questions, the thought came to me that this e-mail to their coworkers might spark some interest in the same questions. The fact that each of these bizarre and offensive teachings or doctrines of the church can be validated through official church records and documents proved frustrating if not enlightening to my fellow brethren.

---

[147] This e-mail included the list of what the author considered false teachings. See page 2 of appendix A document number 16.

Of the charge of harassment through these e-mails, I was not guilty. As I asked the esteemed group assembled there, "How can the truth be harassment?" and "How can the truth be offensive?" Although the information I had listed was extremely unpleasant, it was without question accurate, precise, and truthful. It had proven that what the leadership had told me for years was perfectly acceptable was in fact ludicrous and spiritually insulting. President Jones added to my reprimand the fact that after I sent these e-mails, the employers of these men conducted several investigations. This was exactly the intent of the e-mails, which I had sent to the several corporate headquarters, government offices, and business associates of these men, who told me that they had no issues with the collection of bizarre Mormon doctrine. Again, I asked, "Was what I sent a lie?" Once more there was no response. What I had sent were several facts about the church that these men had told me were true, yet I knew they could not confess the same thing to their employers, coworkers, or neighbors.

As documented earlier, at my excommunication I was not provided the opportunity to address witnesses; and when I began to reference the many church manuals, letters, or Scripture references I had brought for my defense, President Jones put up one hand and said, "We are not here to debate Church doctrine; we are here to review *your* actions." With that statement, I immediately began to recall in my mind a nauseating panorama of what I had learned over the past five years. In an instant, I saw Joseph sneaking off with young girls behind Emma's back. I saw the contorted and uncompromising face of Brigham teaching publicly how to slice the neck of an apostate. In comparison to the many despicable, disgusting and un-Christian events I had come to know through the official documents of the church, I then momentarily considered not only what I had actually done, but also exactly what the men before me in this room and the church itself had accused me of: "You acted in clear, open, and deliberate public opposition to the Church and its leaders."[148] It was true, utterly and

---

[148] Official letter of reasons for excommunication. See appendix A

completely true. With what I had learned about the Church of Jesus Christ of Latter-day Saints, its leadership, deception, and dishonesty, I had openly and deliberately opposed the church and its leaders, and I should have proudly accepted that charge as a statement of fact much earlier!

Then, in an instant, it was over, and I knew there was no point in discussing in any great detail the facts or the truth about the church with men who could only follow policy, procedure, and the process outlined by President Jones. Unexpectedly, I became very calm and I had a sure witness from the Holy Spirit of God that it was time to separate myself from these men and the church they represented. They clearly demonstrated that they, like their leadership, had a lower standard of conduct for themselves and an even lower standard of reverence for the Lord. In a flash I remembered an earlier conversation I had with President Jones, with my wife at my side. He asked, "What is it that you really want?" I told him, "I want to know the *truth*. And if the truth, when found, is inconsistent and/or insulting to what I 'believe' to be the teachings of Christ, then I must leave the [Mormon] Church."

It took some time for me to pack up the ridiculous amount of documentation I had naively brought to defend my findings about the teachings of the church. As we left the room, I knew I would never again be called on to share in the enormous spiritual humiliation of defending untrue doctrine or to continue to worship the Lord from behind the shadows of wicked men.

There is no question that I have become a better person, a better father, and a better husband as a direct result of what I have learned from my many years as a faithful Mormon. What I would ask my Mormon friends to do is precisely what I have done. Trust in the Lord, and then nurture and cherish the promptings of the Holy Spirit of God, who will testify that wickedness is never righteousness. I consider the offensive actions and appalling teachings of the Mormon Prophets *not* to be from the Lord, and I trust the Holy Spirit to testify that to

document number 9.

you. I have been told that the leadership of the Mormon Church routinely functions on a much higher spiritual level than does the average Latter-day Saint. From the very core of my soul, I know that statement to be untrue and very condescending. I have known spiritual giants, who might be considered just average members of the Mormon Church, who are truly humble and spiritually superior to any of the senior leadership I have known.

Not for a moment do I believe that we need to function on a higher spiritual level in order to know for certain that it is simply wrong to take another man's wife and then lie about it. How close to the mind and the will of the Lord Himself must one be to know it is extremely wicked to slice the neck of a fellow Latter-day Saint? I believe that those within the Mormon Church today who may be nearest to the true will of the Lord and are most familiar with the sweet promptings of the Holy Spirit of God can be found teaching the children in the nursery or junior Sunday school class or within the young women's organizations. Can any Mormon leader look into the eyes of these dear sisters and brothers and describe the details of how polygamy, polyandry, and blood atonement were practiced? Can they tell them that all this was *really* of the Lord and that those practices will be coming back? I suggest that those "average" members have absolutely no spiritual equal within the national leadership of the Mormon Church and certainly not within the Arvada Colorado Stake Presidency of the Church of Jesus Christ of Latter-day Saints.

Diametrically Opposed Statements and Actions

In addition to simply "lying for the Lord," a common strategy among the leaders of the church has been to provide diametrically opposed statements specific to a given (normally controversial) subject. The obvious benefit of this strategy is that any number of official statements can then be used to defend or reject a given position as the need arises. Following are but a few examples with the associated references.

Diametrically Opposed Statements by the Church on the Identical Subject

OFFICIAL POSITION OR TEACHING	ALTERNATE POSITION OR TEACHING
"We do not believe it just to mingle religious influence with civil government." (Doctrine and Covenants 134:9) "Please remember that this was published way back in 1835, as the position of the Church, and it has never changed." (*Teachings of the Presidents of the Church, Heber J. Grant,* 160)	"While apostasy festered in Nauvoo in late 1843, the Prophet Joseph Smith was busy politically." (*Church History in the Fulness of Times,* 269) *Note:* Few Mormons are aware that the Prophet Joseph Smith Jr. ran for the presidency of the United States, as the Commander and Lieutenant General of the Nauvoo Legion.
"When any law is enacted and becomes constitutional law, no man who spends his money to help men break that law can truthfully say that he is a loyal citizen." (*Teachings of the Presidents of the Church, Heber J. Grant,* 160)	"1882 – United States Congress passes the Edmunds bill, making plural marriage a felony and prohibiting polygamists from voting, holding public office, or performing jury duty." (*Teachings of the Presidents of the Church, John Taylor,* x)

"Throughout the paper (*Nauvoo Expositor*) they accused Joseph Smith of teaching vicious principles, practicing whoredoms, advocating *so-called spiritual wifery,* grasping for *political power.*" June 1844

(Church History in the Fulness of Times, 275, emphases added)

It would appear that the

Nauvoo Expositor was **right**.

Section Notes, Doctrine and Covenants, Section 132: "*Revelation given through Joseph Smith the Prophet, at Nauvoo, Illinois, recorded July 12, 1843, relating to the new and everlasting covenants, including the eternity of the marriage covenant, as also **plurality of wives**. HC 5: 501-507. Although the revelation was recorded in 1843, it is evident from the historical records that the doctrines and principles involved in this revelation had been known by the Prophet since **1831**.*"
(Emphases added)

"The brethren unanimously sustained a motion to propose their own ticket with Joseph Smith as their *candidate for president*."

(Church History in the Fulness of Times, 269, emphasis added)

"We must not treat lightly the counsel from the President of the Church." (*Teachings of the Presidents of the Church, Wilford Woodruff*, 201) *Note:* A search of conference addresses and lessons within church publications on the theme of "Follow the Prophet" number near 100 and would be pointless to list here.	*"Do not, brethren, put your trust in a man though he be a Bishop, an Apostle, or President;* if you do, they will fail you at some time or place; they will do wrong or seem to, and your support be gone; but if we lean on God, He never will fail us." (Cannon, *Gospel Truth: Discourses and Writings of President George Q. Cannon,* 249, emphases added)
"There has been no end to opposition. There are misinterpretations and misrepresentation of us and of our history, some of it mean-spirited and certainly_*contrary to the teachings of Jesus Christ and His gospel.*" (President Boyd K. Packer, "A Defense and a Refuge," General Conference Addresses. *Ensign.* November 2006, 87, emphasis added)	"I would certainly agree with President Packer that a significant portion of the history of the church is very *'contrary to the teachings of Jesus Christ and His gospel.'"* (Statement from the author after reading the address by Boyd K. Packer.)

A few examples of what I consider to be some very revealing and spiritually enlightening comments from Stake President Michael D. Jones are found in an eleven-page letter[149] he wrote to my wife and me. This undated and unsigned letter communicates what I believe to be his most sincere views concerning our set of questions.[150] In addition to his dishonesty,

---

[149] Stake President Michael D. Jones in an undated and unsigned letter in November 2008.

[150] The Lorin M. Lund Questions represent the fundamental questions to be asked of a Mormon. See chapter 5 for the complete questions and all

I consider his statements to demonstrate the fundamental control he presumed to have over me, as at the time of the letter he was my priesthood superior with the authority to take disciplinary action toward me.

To place in context his formal written counseling to me, an opening paragraph contains the following statement, to which I have *not* added any emphasis:

> *Latter-day prophets have taught the fundamental truth,* **what we know is more important than what we do not know.**

This comment from President Jones is somewhat reminiscent of the noteworthy statement concerning the value of the *truth*, from a senior Apostle of the Mormon Church: "Not everything that's true is useful [that is] useful to say or to publish."[151]

In keeping with the general theme of providing me with only discouraging and unauthorized comments, President Jones issued the following warning and stipulation. Again, I have *not* added any emphasis.

> *I can offer my personal opinions* <u>*with the understanding that I do not speak for the Church*</u>*. It is not within my responsibility as a Stake President or church member to speak for the Church and I do not have authority to do so, except within the limited scope of my stewardship in the Arvada Stake.* <u>*Specifically, you are not authorized to represent to anyone that the answers I attempt to share are representative of the positions of the Church.*</u>*"*

In a way, I understand and feel the frustration of President Jones, as I too was left alone many times to attempt to answer hard questions from members and non-members alike that the church itself would not or could not address. This strategy places the general membership in the awkward position of inventing answers that could never represent any official

---

references and footnotes taken from authorized publications of the Church of Jesus Christ of Latter-day Saints.

[151] Interview of Dallin H. Oaks, "The Mormons," PBS documentary, 2008.

position of the church. Given that handicap, it is no wonder President Jones would prefer that I not share his answers with you. And yet, I am compelled to remind the reader that his comments are in fact not the position of the Church of Jesus Christ of Latter-day Saints itself. His comments are truly only his position, and he is the senior Mormon High Priest and President of the Arvada Colorado Stake of the Church of Jesus Christ of Latter-day Saints, responsible for the spiritual direction of thousands and thousands of souls. It is truly a shame that the Mormon Church cannot formally address these issues.

Although President Jones judged me, a common theme within his formal guidance to me was not to judge others. I do not question his authority to judge me, only his ability to judge fairly, reasonably, or consistently. Among most Latter-day Saints, the concept of judging or providing any critical review of one's religious superiors is intolerable. The requirement to avoid such "evil speaking of the Lord's anointed" is a condition that each Latter-day Saint who attends the temple is directed to take under a sacred oath.[152] With that instruction, no transgressions or questionable actions by the church leadership are to be questioned by the general membership. Such an extensive immunity shields both the past and present leadership of the church.

J.W. Marriott Jr.—Area Authority Seventy and Billionaire

J. W. "Bill" Marriott is both a billionaire and an Area Authority Seventy[153] within the senior leadership of the Church

---

[152] A portion of the Law of the Gospel as taken from the Mormon Temple Endowment ceremony.

[153] An area is the largest geographic division of the church. The First Presidency assigns the Presidency of the Seventy to directly supervise selected areas of the church under the direction of the Quorum of the Twelve Apostles. In other areas of the church, the First Presidency assigns Area Presidencies to preside. An Area Presidency consists of a president, who is usually assigned from the First or Second Quorum of the Seventy, and two

of Jesus Christ of Latter-day Saints. I came to know something of Elder Marriott during a formal church disciplinary council[154] meeting under the direction of Clarence E. Johnson, President of the Columbia Maryland Stake of the Mormon Church. As an active High Priest and the High Priest Group Leader of the Columbia 2nd Ward, I was asked to serve as a substitute member of the High Council, since a standing member of that priesthood body was not available. The High Council, in support of the Stake Presidency, conducts disciplinary actions on behalf of the church. There in the High Council room, where such meetings are routinely held, hung a picture of Elder Marriott with President Johnson. I sent challenging letters to both Elder Marriott[155] and President Johnson[156] concerning this picture hanging in a room where average men of the church have been formally disciplined for the use of pornography. The photograph acts almost as a visual mockery of the event of discipline itself, for it pictures a senior leader of the church who actually profits from the sale of pornography within thousands of his hotel rooms. I believe that President Johnson was so proud of that photograph with Elder Marriott, the billionaire, at his side that there was no spiritual, logical, or emotional event that could ever make my point of hypocrisy any more obvious. In September 2005, I did not know that Elder J. W. Marriott Jr. was in fact an Area Authority for the church, nor did I know of what specific stake of the church he was a member. I then

---

counselors, who may be assigned from any Quorum of the Seventy. Area Presidencies serve under the direction of the First Presidency, the Quorum of the Twelve, and the Presidency of the Seventy. See http://www.lds.org.

[154] Bishops and branch presidents and stake, mission, and district presidents have a responsibility to help members overcome transgression through repentance. The most serious transgressions, such as serious violations of civil law, spouse abuse, child abuse, adultery, fornication, rape, and incest, often require formal church discipline. Formal church discipline may include restriction of church membership privileges or loss of church membership. See http://www.lds.org.

[155] Letter to J. W. Marriott Jr. dated August 30, 2005. See appendix A document number 28b.

[156] Letter to Stake President Johnson, dated December 2005. See appendix A document number 30.

completely humiliated myself by acting with all the prudish and childish virtue of a Sunday school boy by sending a letter to church headquarters in Salt Lake, outlining how very wrong it was that Marriott could profit from pornography.[157] I can only imagine the absurdity and pure comedy shared among the several administrative assistants who might have read my letter, knowing what I did not, that Elder J. W. Marriott Jr. was in fact an Area Authority and thus superior to *any* Stake President.

In September of 2006, Mr. Roger W. Conner, Marriott VP for Communications, sent me a letter in which he stated, "The adult movies provide the revenue to pay for the good movies and our owners refuse to change the formula as the economic impact to their hotels would be substantial."[158] I later came to understand that a large number of Christian organizations, including Focus on the Family, had for many years criticized Marriott for "*peddling porn.*" I had no idea that the opposition to this noted Mormon leader had been so well documented and widely published that Pat Trueman, an attorney with the Alliance Defense Fund, had once said publicly that in his view, "the material offered by Marriott could be prosecuted."[159] In the summer of 2007, the Morality in Media organization published a very poignant open letter to Elder Marriott asking him to "Get Rid of the Porn."

I knew that the double standard of the Mormon Church was well understood by my coworkers when, on Monday morning, June 12, 2006, someone placed a copy of the *Washington Post* in the center of my desk, with the front page of the business section facing up. Just to the right of an illustration of a large glass of alcohol was a picture of Mormon Elder J. W. Marriott under the headline "More Than A Place to Grab A Quick Drink." In the article by Michael S. Rosenwald, *Washington*

---

[157] Letter to Marriott's Stake President dated September 26, 2005. See appendix A document number 28a.

[158] Letter to Lee Baker dated September 23, 2005. See appendix A document number 29.

[159] "Marriott Criticized for Peddling Porn." Citizenlink.com Staff Reports, September 6, 2007.

Post staff writer, were a few comments from Elder Marriott himself that were, in my opinion, disgusting. "I've got a company to run and I need to take care of customers," Marriott said. "I live my faith to the very best of my ability but I don't try to impose my beliefs on the customer." "I just do the best I can to live by the rules of my faith," he said. "But it doesn't matter to me that we are sitting here at a bar where they are selling liquor because 90 percent of the people that come in here want to drink." I found his remarkable powers of perception that a full 90 percent of people who come to a bar *want* to drink very impressive. I can only assume, given the bar example, that when those customers retire from the bar to their hotel room and order an adult movie, they must *want* to see naked women. And as Elder Marriott himself said, "I need to take care of customers." It makes me sick to think that this very senior leader of the Church of Jesus Christ of Latter-day Saints once had the audacity to be interviewed by the official magazine of the Mormon Church, where he actually declared that *no* business deal is worth a man's reputation.

> *For himself, Brother Marriott says the idea of dishonesty in business is abhorrent to him. "No business deal is worth your reputation, your honor. Life is too short."[160]*

When I knew I was being considered a candidate for excommunication for asking questions about the church, I asked my local Mormon priesthood authority if he could explain the behavior of Elder Marriott, as it would appear that the sales, distribution, and profiting from liquor and pornography was not widely known as a generally accepted Mormon activity. Once more, I was put in my place by President Jones, as Elder Marriott must have been given some special exemption of accountability for such activity.

> *Once again, I am concerned over your willingness to enter the hearts of others and render judgments upon them and I counsel you strongly to cease doing so. Further, it is not your*

---

[160] "J. Willard Marriott, Jr., "A Time to Every Purpose." *Ensign,* October 1982, 26.

place or my place to counsel his [J. W. Marriott's] priesthood leaders as to what they should or should not do. Neither you nor I are called to do so? Their accountability is to the President of the Church and the Lord.[161]

I later found that during Mitt Romney's presidential campaign CBN News even challenged Candidate Romney's relationship with the Marriott hotel chain and its sale of hardcore pornography. David Brody, a senior national correspondent, questioned Romney's platform of "family values" since the governor had spent nearly ten years on the board of directors of Marriott during some the most publicly vocal debates on the Marriott pornography issue. Additionally, it is somewhat hypocritical for Mitt Romney to say during his presidential campaign that polygamy is "bizarre" and "awful" when the practice is both a significant part of his family heritage and the formal teaching of his own church. I wonder if that is truly what Mitt Romney, the Mormon High Priest, really believes, or was that Mitt Romney the candidate speaking? In January 2010 Mr. Romney was asked on Fox News if being a Mormon would be a political liability? While Elder Marriott is not required to answer to the public, Mr. Romney must be much more responsive, though his answer is still somewhat intangible.

> *I frankly think for most Americans they don't judge a candidate by what church they go to. They judge the candidate by the things they believe, their positions on issues, their capabilities, their skills.* (Emphasis added)

After hearing that Mitt really thinks it is important to know what the candidates *"believe,"* the puzzling question for me is, what exactly is it, then, that Mr. Romney or Elder Marriott presently know or *believe* about their own church? It seems that they are both somewhat out of step with the teachings and values of the leadership of the church.

---

[161] President Michael D. Jones in an undated and unsigned letter in November 2008.

Lorin M. Lund—Mormon Stake Presidency

As my formal representative to the Stake Presidency for issues concerning my responsibilities as the Columbia 2nd Ward High Priest Group Leader, President Lorin M. Lund in many ways was the catalyst for both my journey of discovery and my excommunication from the Church of Jesus Christ of Latter-day Saints; for that I am very grateful. I believe that his arrogance and position of leadership kept him distant from the real world of dealing with significant spiritual issues. Although he has never communicated one piece of information concerning any of my questions, he once told me, "There is an answer for everything."

Several times in the fall of 2005, President Lund enthusiastically pledged to help me find meaningful answers for both my coworkers and the youth of the church for whom I had responsibility. I foolishly believed that his promise would produce some, <u>any</u> response, as I knew he considered himself to be a truly authorized representative of the Lord Jesus Christ and by association, a worthy representative of His true church on the earth today. Upon reflection now, I do in fact consider Lorin Lund to be a near perfect and most worthy representative of the Mormon Church, in that they both say one thing and do another. Although it was completely worthless, his nearly convincing statement was, as always, delivered with great admiration, dignity, and composure:

> *I continue to be interested in understanding the answers to the questions and will continue to pursue them. As I find answers I'll gladly share them.*[162]

After nearly a year of several heartfelt apologies, each without even a single word addressing my specific questions about the church, I realized that much like the method Rodney J. Tarullo would demonstrate some years later, Lorin Lund was simply occupying an administrative position in a complex social

---

[162] Letter to Lee Baker dated September 29, 2005. See appendix A document number 27.

organization, not actually fulfilling a sacred spiritual calling of service and support for the Lord Jesus Christ. And as such, to borrow a phrase from Steven T. Rockwood, "In that context it all makes sense to me."

Richard D. Merkley—Mormon Bishop

My wife and I moved back to Colorado from the Washington D.C. area the third week of September 2006. After we had settled into the area, we spoke candidly with our Bishop, Richard D. Merkley during our tithing settlement[163] meeting in December of that year. With my wife at my side, I provided Bishop Merkley with a short summary of the previous year's struggles concerning the several questions I had about the history of the church. I handed him a small packet of only three or four questions with a minimal amount of reference material for his consideration. The meeting was very friendly, and I was hopeful that he would be able to provide some guidance in the coming months. We immediately became active in the ward that winter. My wife was called to a teaching position in the primary organization,[164] and I was called as a Sunday school teacher for the young adults.

Since the questions I had provided to Bishop Merkley were extremely important to me, I occasionally asked him if he had found the time to review the packet. His answers were always polite but never positive. When I asked in February, April, June, and July if he had found the time to review the

---

[163] "*Declaration of tithing status.* It is an eternal principle that we are accountable for what we have been given by God: our time, talents, and means. We know that we shall be "judged out of those things which [are] written in the books, according to [our] works" (Rev. 20:12; see also 3 Ne. 27:26). At the end of the year, the bishop or branch president is asked to indicate on the records of the Church the tithing status of each member in his unit. It is our privilege to exercise our accountability by declaring for him our own tithing status." (Kenneth L. DuVall, "The Significance of Tithing Settlement." lds.org).

[164] The purpose of primary is to teach children the gospel of Jesus Christ and help them learn to live it. See lds.org.

information, he said no but also said he would work on it. Finally, in late August he called me into his office and stated, "Brother Baker, I see a weight on Sister Baker's shoulders." Knowing that he had *not* talked with my wife, I encouraged him to speak with her about any issues or concerns that he might be "inspired" to. But after over thirty years in the church, and knowing well the imperative phrases and the several implications of them, I knew at once his message was for me to back off the questions for the sake of my wife. Within a few weeks, my wife spoke with Bishop Merkley. With tears in her eyes, she informed him that *if* he truly saw a weight on her shoulders, it was the burden *he* had placed there by avoiding our needs for nearly nine months. She told him how she had been fasting and praying for him to help us with these very serious questions about the church. He did nothing and never even attempted to discuss any of our questions.

In October of 2007, after he had been released as our Bishop, I asked Richard D. Merkley in the parking lot of the church, "Man to man, High Priest to High Priest, tell me why, for almost a year, you did not help us with the questions we gave you." He began to cry and said, "The Spirit of God told me not to talk to you about those questions." I was shocked and traumatized to think that after eleven months of repeatedly asking for his help, he was not even man enough to tell us that he either would not or could not help. After I told my wife of his insensitive comments, she began to cry. Amid her tears and erratic weeping, she asked why, after so many days of thoughtful prayers, diligent fasting, and temple visits on behalf of our leaders, they would not help us. It was the most distraught and fragile I had ever seen her in over thirty years. With that event as the primary motivator, I organized the questions into a more formal packet and included the research I had completed as footnotes and references. I gave Richard and others a copy of that packet in December of that year. This led to the deceit and deception of our Stake President, Michael D. Jones, as recorded earlier in this chapter.

I consider Bishop Richard D. Merkley a particularly sad and

pathetic figure within this tragedy of errors, in that he might have known what to do better, but he lacked any real knowledge of church history to bolster his waning integrity to act. Like so many of the leaders in the Church of Jesus Christ of Latter-day Saints, he was woefully ill equipped and ill supported to handle the real challenges of his life or to support those who might ask for the same.

Rodney J. Tarullo—Mormon High Priest Group Leader

Of all the Mormon High Priests, Bishops, and church leaders of every description we dealt with during this five-year ordeal, Rodney J. Tarullo as our personal home teacher and High Priest Group Leader has been, in our estimation, the most callous, ruthless, and arrogant individual ever to claim to be an authorized representative of the Lord Jesus Christ. He is the ultimate showman, knowing precisely what face to wear for which occasion and for which audience. I have never known anyone who so carefully and strategically selects his words and performs his duties. I have no doubt whatsoever that those in any professional position *above* him will never become aware of his truly "distinctive" character traits that those of us *below* him have come to see.

My point is not to publicly criticize Rod but to highlight the fact that like the other Mormon leaders from whom we had formally asked for some degree of spiritual support, Rod Tarullo also insincerely promised his attention to our questions. The difference here was that Rod was our personal home teacher and my High Priest Group Leader, which placed him exclusively in a unique leadership position to provide direct and focused support to a fellow member of the church. Additionally, when I handed Rod Tarullo the packet of questions about the church, I shook his hand and said, "These questions represent the most significant spiritual event of my life." He smiled and promised to do whatever he could. I was not prepared for "whatever" to become "nothing" at all.

At our last meeting with Rod Tarullo in our Bishop's office, I watched what I have come to consider the most despicable and shameful exhibit of manhood I have ever witnessed. My wife had asked to meet with Rod in the company of the Bishop to ask why he [Rod] had never attempted to help us. As she wept, he would only point to the Bishop and say, "He [the Bishop] holds the keys; ask him." At times, a slightly sinister smile and a shallow nod was the only acknowledgment he provided that he heard any of my wife's tender and heartfelt comments.

Since that time I have come to see Rod Tarullo as a great ally to my cause. For all the years of my research and my passionate efforts to describe to the investigator of Mormonism the many pitfalls and deceptions that may await them, a short visit with Rod Tarullo would save them a great deal of effort.

The Fundamental Conclusions of This Chapter

This chapter has reviewed the several distressing but essentially enlightening dealings I have had with the leadership of the Church of Jesus Christ of Latter-day Saints. I have intentionally used the actual names and positions of these men, not to specifically ridicule or humiliate them, but to establish what I believe is a consistent pattern of denial, deception, and abandonment that is a strategy among the leadership of the Mormon Church. I have provided these examples with the belief that this pattern of deceptive behavior from the leadership of the Mormon Church will be repeated against anyone who takes a similar course of action.

From my own experiences, I believe that the leadership of the Mormon Church at all levels actively employs, supports, and sustains a double standard of moral and ethical behavior. This they do specifically to protect what they see as the good name of the church. It is this overly protective policy of shielding the leadership that sadly causes morally strong and intellectually sound men and women of the Mormon Church to act irrationally and supremely out of character as they faithfully defend actions they would never consider acceptable for themselves.

CHAPTER FIVE

Questions to Ask a Latter-day Saint

Within the general membership of the Mormon Church are some of the most devoted, kindhearted, and generous people found in any church in existence today. They are without question faithful and dedicated to the leadership of the church, and they frequently regard compassionate service as a foundational characteristic of their faith. As a member of the Mormon Church for over thirty years, I feel qualified to make such statements concerning the general membership. I served as a High Priest, a Bishop, and a youth leader in several different congregations (wards) in numerous locations around the world.[1] I have included my Priesthood Line of Authority[2] and my Bishop's Certificate[3] to show that I speak the truth from my heart in these matters.

During my service in the Mormon Church, my wife and I have had the opportunity to provide spiritual support and guidance in a family setting for a group of many young single adults (ages 18 to 30). Our association with this group represents some of the finest times we ever spent in the service of the church. A significant portion of our responsibilities to these young adults on behalf of the church was to teach church doctrine and history as appropriate. The group included a wide variety of outstanding young people from equally diverse spiritual, social, and economic backgrounds. In any given year, we served young adults who were investigators of the church and new members of the church, as well as those born into the church, along with several returned or active missionaries within the church.

---

[1] See appendix A document number 17.

[2] See appendix A document number 2b.

[3] See appendix A document number 1.

We held informal services in our home once a week on Monday as a family home evening program.[4] Once a month we opened the lesson time to any questions those in attendance might have about almost any subject. The foundation of some of the questions that follow in this chapter came from that young single adult group. When difficult questions were presented from this group, my wife and I turned to our senior church leadership for guidance.

On several occasions President Lorin M. Lund of the Columbia Maryland Stake, our priesthood advisor, assured us that he would help answer these questions. He did not. Rather than help us, he asked, "Where did you get such a question?" or made other hollow statements with an attitude of dismissal and disapproval. These basic questions are provided here for you to consider and research and, if you feel so impressed, to share with your Mormon friends and family.

Knowing the Truth Will Improve Your Testimony of Jesus Christ

If you ask any or all of these clear and simple questions of your Mormon friends, coworkers, and relatives, or even of the Mormon missionaries themselves, you will not get a clear answer. They will know that these are not typical "anti-Mormon" questions, because they come from the perspective of a lifelong member of the church who has had access to both the church doctrine and temple ceremonies required to authenticate the actual teachings.

With that, I have asked myself many times, "Can knowing the truth actually challenge or improve my testimony of Jesus Christ?" As the Scriptures and the example of our Lord and Savior teach us, the answer is certainly yes; it can and it will.

---

[4] Church leaders have instructed members to set aside Monday night as "family home evening." This is a time for families to study the gospel together and to do other activities that strengthen the family spiritually, create family memories, and increase unity and love. See lds.org.

The truth will only bring us closer to Him and more into conformity with His true message. At the same time, the truth will expose other teachings or doctrines that are not in harmony with His teachings as counterfeit. These seven questions center on only the most obviously corrupt Mormon doctrines, which are also the most offensive to the character and temperament of the Lord.

As you ask these few specifically focused questions, consider this: Is it possible that any other doctrines, reportedly of Christian origin, would ever require such stonewalling, such apprehension, or personal cross-examination of your motives to simply know the truth?

Any typical follower of Jesus Christ would not hesitate to decisively and clearly clarify the doctrines of salvation, the atonement, faith, grace, or compassion if asked to do so. Yet when a member of the Mormon faith is asked to clarify the doctrines of polygamy, blood atonement, personal exaltation (to become a God), or the apparent inconsistencies of both the teachings and character of the Mormon Prophets, the response is only vague comments, personal assumptions, and individual apprehension, all clearly known to be the accepted companions of fabrications, not facts.

As a member of the Columbia Maryland Stake Presidency and a Mormon High Priest, Lorin M. Lund, my spiritual advisor at the time, never attempted to answer any of these questions. That is why his name is within the title of these questions, so that he might forever be remembered as someone whom I view as the unsurpassed example of an arrogant Mormon hypocrite.

As you will find, these questions are extremely well documented, and I have used only approved Mormon Church Scriptures, Mormon doctrine, Mormon manuals, and the authorized history of the Mormon Church. A careful study of these questions by any member of the Mormon faith will provoke a struggle with the obvious difference between the teachings of Jesus Christ Himself and that of the Mormon Prophets. That struggle and those sincere feelings of disbelief are the tender promptings of the Holy Spirit, testifying that although the outer shell of Mormonism is attractive, the core of this church, as established by Joseph Smith, was founded on deception and immorality.

A Bizarre and Hypocritical Conversation

One of the most peculiar, and somewhat disturbing, experiences I have had with several of my former Latter-day Saint friends has been a conversation about the practices of polygamy and polyandry. Without exception, everyone I have ever spoken to has cringed when faced with the details of polygamy and polyandry, but none would actually denounce the practice by the Mormon Prophets. Considering that at the time of these conversations I was still an active Mormon High Priest and an ordained Bishop, each of these conversations can be seen as a clinical study in self-justified deception, denial, and personal hypocrisy of the highest degree.

The ethical curiosity here is that when faced with how these "plural marriages" were concealed from both the husbands and the wives of many of the partners, the modern Latter-day Saint displays personal rejection of the practice and yet a general acceptance of the principle at the same time. After many years of spiritual programming, the initial Mormon desire is to have total and unwavering faith that whatever the Prophets did was of God, regardless of how personally repulsive it might appear to be. Often these conversations have included a collection of small moral "life rafts" to give some measure of respect and modesty to the explicit discussions. Most frequently, I have heard the justification, "I don't know if I could have done that" or "That would really have tested my faith." I have taken each of these statements to be honest examples of good men and women personally separating themselves from the immoral actions they are now compelled to defend.

I believe the stark difference between how the average Latter-day Saint almost involuntarily is required to defend the practices of polygamy and polyandry and how the Mormon leadership fanatically redirects any serious questions exposes the true wickedness of the practice itself. I have asked several senior Mormon leaders to place for me into some spiritual context the practices of polygamy and polyandry of the nineteenth and twentieth centuries within any framework of the core teachings of Jesus Christ. Without fail this issue is turned back to me in the form of condescending or accusatory statements such as, "Why would you even ask about such a thing?" or "Why would you continue to research such a subject as this?" I remember well a conversation with Stake President Michael D. Jones, when he shook his head and asked me, "Why would you spend time studying such a thing?" I believe the strategy is to make the one asking about polygamy or polyandry somehow feel dirty or humiliated just for raising the issue. I asked President Jones then, as I now ask *all* members of the Church of Jesus Christ of Latter-day Saints, "Is it more offensive to the Lord for a man to simply question the practices of polygamy and polyandry or to actually and secretly take another man's wife in Christ's holy name?" This was not just ordinary adultery; this was intentional adultery hidden behind the power, authority, and majesty of the Lord Jesus Christ.

To recreate this bizarre and disingenuous conversation, I would encourage you to respectfully and sincerely ask a Latter-day Saint to share his or her own feelings on the subject of polygamy, much less polyandry. For me, it was almost painful to watch the internal struggle of my friends as they honestly communicated the fact that they would never take part in such a practice, but by virtue of their faith, they were compelled to defend it on behalf of the leadership of the church. It was rather surreal to know that these good men would not willingly give their wives to another, yet they would not—or maybe they *could* not—denounce the very same practice by someone they follow as their spiritual leader. It was very discouraging to witness the abandonment of someone's own integrity in order to defend what he or she *knew* to be wrong. What these people may not have fully comprehended is that the high price of defending someone else's immorality is a reduction of their own relationship with the Lord. Again, for Mormonism to be true, it is the Lord Himself, *not* Joseph Smith or Brigham Young, who must view women as a commodity to be shared in secret among the early leadership of the Church of Jesus Christ of Latter-day Saints. It has been both disheartening and enlightening at the same time to witness very good men and women justify the very bad behavior of others, in the holy name of the Lord Jesus Christ.

The Lorin M. Lund Questions

Question 1

Did Joseph Smith follow the law of the gospel governing the plurality of wives as recorded in the Mormon Scriptures?

How is it that in the Book of Mormon, Jacob, chapter 2, the polygamy of David and Solomon are specifically called "abominable before me, saith the Lord," yet in the Mormon Doctrine and Covenants, section 132, it is recorded: "I, the Lord justified my servants Abraham, Isaac, and Jacob, as also Moses, David and Solomon, my servants, as touching the principle and doctrine of their having many wives and concubines"?

Why did the 1835 publication of the Doctrine and Covenants, section 101 (canonized Scripture of the Church of Jesus Christ of Latter-day Saints), teach in total opposition to the practice of polygamy from 1835 to 1876 during the very height of the actual practice of polygamy and polyandry? That section states:

> *Inasmuch as this Church of Christ has been reproached with the crime of fornication and polygamy, we declare that we believe that one man should have one wife, and one woman but one husband, except in case of death, when either is at liberty to marry again.*

Why would the church then publish Doctrine and Covenants section 132 in the 1876 edition and right up to the present time, when the introduction to that section plainly states: "*Although the revelation was recorded in 1843, it is evident from the historical records that the doctrines and principles involved in this revelation had been known by the Prophet since 1831*"? It would appear to the reader that the church had a doctrinal statement for the general population of the church and the United States government that denounced the practice during the very time it was in fact expanding the practice from polygamy into polyandry (the act of sharing wives among the leadership). Was this practice of publishing a second set of

Scriptures, which was *not* followed by Joseph Smith Jr., under the direction of Jesus Christ Himself or merely for the personal benefit of "The Mormon Prophet"? Doctrine and Covenants 132:1 states,

> *Verily, thus saith the Lord unto you my servant Joseph, that inasmuch as you have inquired of my hand to know and understand wherein I, the Lord, justified my servants Abraham, Isaac, and Jacob, as also Moses, David and Solomon, my servants, as touching the principle and doctrine of their having many wives and concubines.*

In apparent violation of the "Laws governing the plurality of wives,"[5] Joseph Smith took anywhere from eight[6] to eleven[7] wives of other men as his own, claiming it was a direct commandment from the Lord Jesus Christ.[8]

As clearly recorded by Joseph Smith in Doctrine and Covenants 132:61-64, the Lord set three conditions (laws) that are required for a member of the priesthood who desires to take other wives: The woman must (1) be "a virgin," (2) the first wife must "give her consent," and (3) the new wife be "vowed to no other man . . . [belonging] unto him and to no one else." Joseph Smith "tested" many men in the church by reporting that the Lord had selected their wives and that they were to be shared with him.[9] Examples are Heber C. Kimball, Hiram

---

[5] Doctrine and Covenants 132:61-64 (see section heading).

[6] Anderson, and Faulring, A review of *In Sacred Loneliness: The Plural Wives of Joseph Smith,* by Todd M. Compton. *FARMS Review* 10 (2): 67-104.

[7] Compton, *In Sacred Loneliness: The Plural Wives of Joseph Smith,* 4-9.

[8] As noted earlier, the two major splits within the Church of Jesus Christ of Latter-day Saints were in 1844 and 1890, and both divisions centered on the doctrine of polygamy. The first division came when a large number of the Saints would not *start* participating in polygamy, and the second division came when a large number would not *stop* participating in polygamy. Additionally, the church's history indicates that the first printing of Doctrine and Covenants section 132 was in the year 1876, but the heading of this section documents that the revelation was recorded in 1843 but known (practiced) by the Prophet in 1831.

[9] *The Presidents of the Church: Insights into Their Lives and Teachings,* talk

Kimball, Orson Pratt, John Taylor, and William Law. In eleven other circumstances, Joseph Smith did not simply test but clearly *took* the wives of men, such as the Apostle Orson Hyde, whose wife, Marinda, he took when Hyde was on his mission to Jerusalem. Then when Joseph was publicly questioned about the practice in May of 1844, he clearly lied.

> *What a thing it is for a man to be accused of committing adultery, and having seven wives, when I can only find one.*[10]

In addition to numerous other men's wives, Joseph took two sets of sisters, a mother and her daughter, several teenagers, and two fourteen-year-old girls as wives when he was thirty-seven; one of them was the daughter of Heber C. Kimball. It should also be noted that Joseph did not tell his first wife, Emma, of over half of his thirty-three plural marriages and that she threatened to leave him because of it.[11]

Were the private actions of the Prophet Joseph Smith Jr. as they relate to the practice and teachings of polygamy and polyandry (taking another man's wife) under the solemn direction and commandment of the Lord Jesus Christ Himself?

After fully understanding the immoral details of polygamous and polyandrous marriages, consider these arrogant statements by the Prophets, Seers, and Revelators of the Church of Jesus Christ of Latter-day Saints.

> *All these principles that I have treated upon, pertaining to eternal marriage, the very moment that they are admitted to be true, it brings in plurality of marriage, and if plurality of marriage is not true or in other words, if a man has no divine right to marry two wives or more in this world, then marriage for eternity is not true, and your faith is all vain, and all the sealing ordinances and powers, pertaining to marriages for eternity are vain, worthless, good for nothing; for as sure as one is true the*

---

by Truman G. Madsen on CD.

[10] *History of the Church*, 6:411. (Public speech by Joseph Smith to the citizens of Nauvoo, Ill. May 1844.)

[11] Compton, *In Sacred Loneliness: The Plural Wives of Joseph Smith*, 4-9.

other also must be true. Amen.[12]

The members of the Church are reminded that the practice of polygamous or plural marriage is not the only law whose suspension has been authorized by the Lord. . . . The law of the United Order has likewise been suspended, to be re-established in the due time of the Lord.[13]

The only men who become Gods, even the Sons of God, are those who enter into polygamy. Others attain unto a glory and may even be permitted to come into the presence of the Father and the Son; but they cannot reign as kings in glory, because they had blessings offered unto them, and they refused to accept them.[14]

I think no more of taking another wife than I do of buying a cow.[15]

Question 2

How is the general membership of the church or the public at large to decide which officially recorded and authoritatively published teachings of the Prophets and General Authorities is or is not to be considered Scripture?

How is it that within the Book of Mormon teachings of the Prophets Alma, Lehi, Nephi, Mormon, and King Benjamin are unquestionably Scripture, but the teachings of the modern-day Prophets such as Brigham Young, John Taylor, Spencer W. Kimball, or Thomas S. Monson are at times not to be considered Scripture?

---

[12] Apostle Orson Pratt, Tabernacle Salt Lake, July 18, 1880, *Journal of Discourses* 21:286.

[13] President Heber J. Grant, *Messages of the First Presidency of the Church of Jesus Christ of Latter-day Saints,* 6:327.

[14] President Brigham Young, Salt Lake City, August 19, 1866, *Journal of Discourses* 11:269.

[15] Apostle Heber C. Kimball, quoted in Irving Wallace, *The Twenty-Seventh Wife,* 101.

The official church Web site, lds.org, states that Scripture is "a sacred writing or book; the word of God as revealed to His inspired prophets." Doctrine and Covenants 68:4 says of the Mormon Prophets,

> *And whatsoever they shall speak when moved upon by the Holy Ghost shall be scripture, shall be the will of the Lord, shall be the mind of the Lord, shall be the word of the Lord, shall be the voice of the Lord, and the power of God unto salvation.*

Consequently, the following are examples of modern Mormon Scripture:

> *I remind you that no man who makes disparaging remarks concerning those of another race can consider himself a true disciple of Christ.*[16]

> *You see some classes of the human family that are black, uncouth, uncomely, disagreeable and low in their habits, wild, and seemingly deprived of nearly all the blessings of the intelligence that is generally bestowed upon mankind.*[17]

> *Shall I tell you the law of God in regard to the African race? If the white man who belongs to the chosen seed mixes his blood with the seed of Cain, the penalty, under the law of God, is death on the spot. This will always be so.*[18]

> *I discover that some of the Eastern papers represent me as a great blasphemer, because I said, in my lecture on Marriage, at our last Conference, that Jesus Christ was married at Cana of Galilee, that Mary, Martha, and others were his wives, and that he begat children.*[19]

> *Will you love your brothers or sisters likewise, when they*

---

[16] President Gordon B. Hinckley, General Conference, April 2006, *Ensign*, 58.

[17] President Brigham Young, General Conference, October 1859, *Journal of Discourses* 7:291.

[18] President Brigham Young, Salt Lake Tabernacle, March 1863, *Journal of Discourses* 10:110.

[19] President Orson Hyde, General Conference, October 1854, *Journal of Discourses* 2:210.

have committed a sin that cannot be atoned for without the shedding of their blood? Will you love that man or woman well enough to shed their blood?[20]

Who can tell us of the inhabitants of this little planet that shines of an evening, called the moon? . . . So it is with regard to the inhabitants of the sun. Do you think it is inhabited? I rather think it is. Do you think there is any life there? No question of it; it was not made in vain. It was made to give light to those who dwell upon it.[21]

When the Virgin Mary conceived the child Jesus, the Father had begotten him in his own likeness. He was not begotten by the Holy Ghost. And who is the Father? He is the first of the human family; and when he took a tabernacle, it was begotten by his Father in heaven, after the same manner as the tabernacles of Cain, Abel, and the rest of the sons and daughters of Adam and Eve; from the fruits of the earth, the first earthly tabernacles were originated by the Father, and so on in succession. I could tell you much more about this; but were I to tell you the whole truth, blasphemy would be nothing to it, in the estimation of the superstitious and over-righteous of mankind.[22]

The birth of the Savior was as natural as are the births of our children; it was the result of natural action. He partook of flesh and blood—was begotten of his Father, as we were of our fathers.[23]

The April 1852 General Conference address (Scripture) from President Young clearly states that God the Father had intercourse with Mary.

---

[20] President Brigham Young, Salt Lake Tabernacle, February 1857, *Journal of Discourses* 4:220.

[21] President Brigham Young, Salt Lake Tabernacle, July 1870, *Journal of Discourses* 14:272.

[22] President Brigham Young, General Conference, April 9, 1852, *Journal of Discourses* 1:51.

[23] President Brigham Young, Salt Lake City, July 8, 1860, *Journal of Discourses* 8:115.

Almost all of Brigham Young's sermons were recorded in the *Journal of Discourses,* which was issued and published under the signature of the First Presidency of the Church (Brigham Young, Heber C. Kimball, and Willard Richards). And President Brigham Young himself stated, "I have never yet preached a sermon and sent it out to the children of men, that they may not call Scripture."[24] Official publications of the Church of Jesus Christ of Latter-day Saints continue to cite the *Journal of Discourses* as authoritative.[25]

Question 3

Did Brigham Young alone instigate the restriction against blacks holding the priesthood based on his personal prejudice, or was it a legitimate commandment from the Lord Jesus Christ, which Joseph Smith preferred neither to follow nor to record?

If he did not in fact conduct the ordinance himself, then the Prophet Joseph Smith Jr. unquestionably knew that Elijah Able and other black men had been ordained to the priesthood. Additionally, he never spoke or wrote of any doctrine or policy specific to restricting blacks from the priesthood.

Although Brigham Young denied the request for any Temple Endowments for Brother and Sister Able, then living in Salt Lake, Elijah Able remained a Seventy[26] and in 1883 was called to serve his final mission in Canada. He died on his return to Salt Lake in 1884, but President Young himself never revoked his priesthood.

As documented within the records of the church, black men were ordained to the priesthood prior to the administration of Brigham Young.

---

[24] President Brigham Young, 1870, *Journal of Discourses*, 3:95.

[25] See the documentation in chapter 1 under the heading "Teachings of the Past Prophets and the Value of a Living Prophet."

[26] The calling or office of a Seventy is a position within the Mormon Church normally associated with missionary responsibilities.

Becoming a convert to "Mormonism" he [Elijah Able] was baptized in September of 1832, by Ezekiel Roberts.[27]

March 3, 1836

Elijah Able, a Negro, is ordained an elder and receives his patriarchal blessing from Joseph Smith, Sr.[28]

The entry for March 3, 1836 is of particular value as it appears within *A Joseph Smith Chronology*, which documents the key events in the life of the Prophet and uses his writings and journal as the primary source. It is apparent that Joseph himself ordained Elijah Able. If not, it clearly records that Joseph was fully aware of the ordination and found it noteworthy.

As appears from certificates, he (Elijah Able) was ordained an Elder March 3, 1836, and a Seventy April 4, 1841.[29]

In 1883, as a member of the Third Quorum of Seventy, he (Elijah Able) left Salt Lake City on a mission to Canada, during which he also performed missionary labors in the United States.[30]

Question 4

In view of the overwhelming and clear requirement for all members of the Mormon faith to avoid any association with porn-

---

[27] Andrew Jenson, *LDS Biographical Encyclopedia* (Salt Lake City: Western Epics, 1971), 3:577. See also BlackLDS.org, a Web site dedicated to black members of the church.

[28] J. Christopher Conkling, *A Joseph Smith Chronology* (Salt Lake City: Deseret Book Company, 1979), 87. The introduction states, "What are the important events in the life of Joseph Smith, the man through whom the gospel of Jesus Christ was restored in these latter days? What was his day-to-day life like? *A Joseph Smith Chronology* draws from the Prophet's own writings as well as the writings of his contemporaries and of later historians to present, in a sequential, chronological format, the major events as well as the everyday happenings in Joseph Smith's life and work."

[29] Ibid.

[30] Ibid.

ography, how can an Area Authority[31] of the Church of Jesus Christ of Latter-day Saints, one who sits in judgment of others' moral and ethical conduct in church disciplinary actions, profit significantly from pornography and still be allowed to continue to hold the priesthood and represent the church and the Lord Jesus Christ Himself?

For years Elder J. W. Marriott has been challenged by numerous business and Christian organizations to suspend the rental of hard-core pornography in his hotels.[32] Without question Elder Marriott has profited significantly from the in-room rentals of these pornographic films, as well as the sale of alcohol for many years. His behavior is not only out of harmony with basic Christian values; it is a mockery of the moral standards that are required of the typical Mormon that may be your neighbor.

Members of the Church everywhere are urged to not only resist the widespread plague of pornography, but as citizens to become actively and relentlessly engaged in the fight against this insidious enemy of humanity around the world.[33]

In direct violation of the General Handbook of Instructions

---

[31] An Area Authority of the Church of Jesus Christ of Latter-day Saints is a senior priesthood leadership position that is called to assist a member of the Quorum of the Twelve Apostles with a specific geographic area of the world.

[32] The official church Web site quotes, "Pornography is any material depicting or describing the human body or sexual conduct in a way that arouses sexual feelings. It is distributed through many media, including magazines, books, television, movies, music, and the Internet. It is as harmful to the spirit as tobacco, alcohol, and drugs are to the body. Using pornographic material in any way is a violation of a commandment of God: "Thou shalt not . . . commit adultery . . . nor do anything like unto it" (D&C 59:6). It can lead to other serious sins. Members of the Church should avoid pornography in any form and should oppose its production, distribution, and use" ("Pornography," *True to the Faith* (2004): 117-18. See lds.org.

[33] *Teachings of the Presidents of the Church – Spencer W. Kimball* (Salt Lake City: Intellectual Reserve, Inc., 2006), 184.

– see: pornography, dissemination of, and in view of abundant counsel such as: Elder Dallin H. Oaks, General Conference, 3 April 2005, "For many years our Church leaders have warned us against the dangers of images and words intended to arouse sexual desires. Now the corrupting influence of pornography, produced and disseminated for commercial gain, is sweeping over our society like an avalanche of evil.[34]

On both business and personal travel, I have found it confusing that on the top of the nightstand that holds the Book of Mormon, is an "entertainment" guide, which includes in-room Pornography.[35]

As a High Priest and member of the Church of Jesus Christ of Latter-day Saints, let me say that you are wrong to continue profiting from the sale and distribution of Pornography.[36]

It is my earnest hope, however, that even after so many years of ignoring complaints about the sale of pornography in your hotels, you will yet do the right thing for your family, church and nation.[37]

Some anti-pornography groups are demanding answers as to how much presidential candidate Mitt Romney knew about the Marriott hotel chain's profits of pornography sales during his nearly ten years on the Board of Directors in the 1990's.[38]

For himself, Brother Marriott says the idea of dishonesty in business is abhorrent to him. "No business deal is worth your reputation, your honor. Life is too short."[39]

---

[34] Letter to Elder Marriott, Elder Marriott's Stake President, and the Office of the Presiding Bishopric, Salt Lake City, from Lee Baker, September 26, 2005. See appendix A document number 28a.

[35] Letter to Elder Marriott, Elder Marriott's Stake President, and the Office of the Presiding Bishopric, Salt Lake City, from Lee Baker, August 30, 2005. See appendix A document number 28b.

[36] Ibid.

[37] Robert Peters, President of Morality in Media, News Release, New York, July 23, 2007.

[38] David Brody, CBN News Senior National Correspondent, reported July 3, 2007. http://firstread.msnbc.msn.com/archive/2007/07/03/255163.aspx.

[39] "J. Willard Marriott, Jr., A Time to Every Purpose," *Ensign,* October

He swore off alcohol as a young man and he dislikes noisy places, but if a visit to Studio 54 or any other bar will give him a little more insight into what customers want, save him a table. "I just do the best I can to live by the rules of my faith," he said. "But it doesn't matter to me that we are sitting here at the bar where they are selling liquor because 90 percent of the people that come in here want a drink."[40]

It is especially disturbing that the high moral and ethical standards of the "Lord's Church" do not apply to the leadership of the church, and, in fact, Mormons are told that this specific contradiction should never be questioned.[41] As documented throughout this book, such hypocrisy was commonplace in the early years of the Mormon Church. In my view Elder Marriott and the business that bears his name stand as a modern-day example of the same.

Question 5

With a seventy-year history of active opposition to the laws of the United States of America, how is the current member of the Mormon faith to reconcile the history of the church with the Twelfth Article of Faith as well as the commandment given in Doctrine and Covenants 58:21?

Additionally, in view of the Declaration of Independence, the Constitution of the United States, and specifically the First Amendment, as well as the hundreds of documents from the Founding Fathers concerning the evils of monarchies and theocracies, under what possible conditions would the people of the United States and the existing laws of the democracy ever support a theocracy as proposed by Joseph Smith and then fully

---

1982, 26.

[40] Michael S. Rosenwald, "More Than a Place to Grab a Quick Drink." *Washington Post*, June 12, 2006.

[41] Dallin H. Oaks, Apostle and member of the Quorum of the Twelve, stated, "It's wrong to criticize leaders of the church, even if the criticism is true" ("The Mormons," PBS documentary, 2008).

practiced by Brigham Young?

Totally indifferent to the Twelfth Article of Faith, Doctrine and Covenants 58:21, and numerous talks by the Prophets and General Authorities supporting the law, early church officers clearly and consistently disobeyed the laws of the Untied States of America, in total and complete disagreement with their own words and Scriptures.

> *We believe in being subject to kings, presidents, rulers, and magistrates, in obeying, honoring, and sustaining the law. (Mormon Twelfth Article of Faith)*

> *Let no man break the laws of the land for he that keepeth the laws of God hath no need to break the laws of the land. (Doctrine and Covenants 58:21)*

In Nauvoo, as Prophet of the Church, Joseph Smith Jr. was also the mayor of the city, chief magistrate of the city, lieutenant general of the Nauvoo Legion, chief editor of the city newspaper, leader of the United Order, Master Mason of the five Masonic Lodges in Nauvoo, the Prophet, Priest, and King in the kingdom of God on the earth, ruler over Israel, a practicing polygamist, and a candidate for the presidency of the United States of America in 1844.

With Brigham Young as both the Prophet of the Church and the governor of the territory, Utah (Deseret to the Mormons) became a working theocracy in which church and state functions were totally indistinguishable. Members were expected to revere the direction of the Prophet Brigham Young over the laws of Congress. In what I have found to be a Mormon trademark of leadership, the laws of the land take a distant second place to the laws of the Lord, as viewed by the Mormon Prophets, yet at every turn the modern Mormon will have us believe that they have always been good Americans. In fact, within the current publications of the Mormon Church can be found several clearly provocative statements intended to inform the modern Mormon that the United States government has been oppressive and that that opinion should be carried within the heart of every Mormon today.

When Joseph Smith campaigned for president of the United States of America in 1844, he was a practicing polygamist, he was actively sharing the wives of other men, he was a three-star general in the Illinois State Militia, and he was teaching of a worldwide theocracy with himself as the Prophet of God. His presidential committee openly stated that God had called Joseph Smith "to be a Prophet, Seer and Revelator to my Church and Kingdom; and to be a King and Ruler over Israel."[42] But when newspapers, politicians, and churches throughout the United States all rejected the idea that Joseph Smith was even remotely qualified to be president, the Mormons considered this to be coordinated religious persecution.

As a perfect example that even the modern Mormon may feel that the United States government has been repressive toward the church in general and against Joseph Smith specifically, consider the following informative statement from Michael D. Jones, President of the Arvada Colorado Stake of the Church of Jesus Christ of Latter-day Saints, issued in 2008.

> *Joseph Smith taught the Gospel of Jesus Christ and restored the practices, covenants, and ordinances of salvation under the direction of the Savior. His political activities were intended to protect the religious freedom of the Saints because the government would do nothing to protect such freedoms.*[43]

The following chart highlights the fact that the Mormon Church has always understood the laws of the Untied States of America but has chosen to openly disobey a number of those laws. Presented on the left are the laws of the United States, and on the right, in opposition or disobedience to those laws, are the actions or teachings of the Mormon Prophets. I have included these points of contention, not to document the past adversarial history between the Mormon Church and the government of the United States, but to show that the current generation of Latter-day Saint leadership finds it necessary to

---

[42] D. Michael Quinn, "The Council of Fifty and Its Members, 1844 To 1945." *BYU Studies*, vol. 20 (1979-1980), Number 2, Winter 1980, 186.

[43] In an undated and unsigned letter in November of 2008.

educate modern Latter-day Saints everywhere, that the United States was wrong for actions it took against the Mormon Church, even though the church was acting in defiance of the nation's laws and its own "Scriptures."

LAWS OF THE UNITED STATES	ACTIONS OR TEACHINGS OF THE PROPHETS
President Abraham Lincoln, vowing to end the "relics of barbarism" (slavery and polygamy, both of which were supported and practiced by the Church of Jesus Christ of Latter-day Saints), struck powerful blows at each in 1862, when he issued the Emancipation Proclamation and signed into law the very first anti-polygamy bill, the Morrill Act.	". . . but we do not believe it right to interfere with bond-servants, neither preach the gospel to, nor baptize them contrary to the will and wish of the masters . . . such interference we believe to be unlawful and unjust, and dangerous to the peace of every government allowing human beings to be held in servitude." (Joseph Smith Jr., Doctrine and Covenants 134:12, 1835, Kirtland, Ohio) **Note**: Almost in mockery to the first part of this Scripture—"We believe it just to preach the gospel to the nations of the earth and warn the righteous to save themselves from the corruption of the world"—the second part clearly states that the *only* group of humans on the planet who are *not* to receive the gospel of the Lord Jesus Christ are slaves. "...and even if we treat our

slaves in an oppressive manner, it is still none of their business and they ought not to meddle with it." (Brigham Young, 1856, *Journal of Discourses* 4:40)

"Will the present struggle free the slave? No; but they are now wasting away the black race by the thousands. . . . Ham must be the servant of servants until the curse is removed. Can you destroy the decrees of the Almighty? You cannot. Yet our Christian brethren think that they are going to overthrow the sentence of the Almighty upon the seed of Ham. They cannot do that, though they may kill them by thousands and tens of thousands." (Brigham Young, October General Conference of the Church, 1863, *Journal of Discourses* 10:250)

United States Congress: The Morrill Anti-Bigamy Act, which was signed into law on July 8, 1862 by President Abraham Lincoln, banned plural marriage.

United States Congress: The Poland Act of 1874 sought to eliminate the nearly total control of the Mormon Church over Utah's justice

"Many of America's religious and political leaders became very angry when they learned that Latter-day Saints living in Utah were encouraging a marriage system that they considered immoral and unchristian. A great political crusade was launched against the Church and its members. The United States Congress passed legislation that curbed

system.

the freedom of the Latter-day Saints and hurt the Church economically. This legislation ultimately caused officers to arrest and imprison men who had more than one wife and to deny them the right to vote, the right to privacy in their homes, and the enjoyment of other civil liberties." (*Our Heritage: A Brief History of the Church of Jesus Christ of Latter-day Saints,* 97)

Note: These comments, under the heading of "Persecution Continues," are designed to communicate just that: "persecution" of the church. This is a strange way of viewing it, since it was the members of the church who were not following the "laws of the land." Even more disturbing is that the comments used in this 1996 publication—specifically, "legislation that curbed the freedom of the Latter-day Saints" and "deny them the right to vote, the right to privacy in their homes, and the enjoyment of other civil liberties"—stand in stark contrast to the current position of the church condemning the fundamentalists in Texas who practice the "marriage system" that the church *defends* in the booklet *Our Heritage*.

United States Congress: The Edmunds Act signed into law on March 23, 1882 declared polygamy a felony.	"The United States Congress passes the Edmunds Act, making plural marriage a felony and prohibiting polygamists from voting, holding public office or performing jury duty." *(Teachings of the Presidents of the Church –Wilford Woodruff,* xiii) **Note**: Despite the law forbidding polygamy, the practice continued in Utah. President John Taylor "receives word during a visit to California that federal officials have ordered his arrest for practicing polygamy. Returns to Salt Lake City on 27 January. On 1 February, preaches his last public sermon and, in hopes of limiting the persecution against the Church by federal authorities, goes into hiding." *(Teachings of the Presidents of the Church –John Taylor,* x) **Note**: At the age of seventy-eight, after living on the run from federal authorities for over two years, the living Prophet of the Church of Jesus Christ of Latter-day Saints dies as a fugitive from the laws of the United States of America, in the home of Thomas

	Roueche in Kaysville, Utah.
	Note: The statements above are accurate and clearly demonstrate that the church did not follow either the Twelfth Article of Faith or Doctrine and Covenants 58:21, which are considered Scripture from the Lord. Both these Scriptures are carved in large stones in Temple Square to suggest to the uninformed visitor that these standards from the Lord have had some consistency with the members of the church, yet it seems they must have been suspended for a period of time.
	Twelfth Article of Faith: "We believe in being subject to kings, presidents, rulers, and magistrates, in obeying, honoring, and sustaining the law." Doctrine and Covenants 58:21: "Let no man break the laws of the land for he that keepeth the laws of God hath no need to break the laws of the land."
United States Congress: The Edmunds-Tucker Act of 1887, signed into law on February 19, prohibited polygamy, dissolved the corporation of the church, and	"The United States Congress passes the Edmunds-Tucker Act, another anti-polygamy law, allowing the federal government to con-fiscate much of the Church's

directed the confiscation of church properties, including the temple.

real estate. The act becomes law on March 3, 1887." *(Teachings of the Presidents of the Church – Wilford Woodruff,* xiii)

Note: Again, this statement is accurate and demonstrates that at that time the church did not follow either the Twelfth Article of Faith or Doctrine and Covenants 58:21, which are now considered Scripture.

The addition of the word *another* indicates to the modern reader that this should be considered federal harassment or persecution, as referenced and emphasized by President Gordon B. Hinckley at the October 2006 General Conference of the Church of Jesus Christ of Latter-day Saints: "And so it has been with each of the Presidents of the Church. In the face of terrible opposition, they have moved forward with faith. Whether it was persecution by the federal government..." (*Ensign,* November 2006, 83).

Again, it is the modern reader (you and me) and the current membership of the church who are being taught that it was the federal government that was wrong in its actions against the church.

Question 6

After a complete review of this section, do you believe that the leadership of the church, in an effort to obscure the truth, has ever used "carefully crafted messages"?

In the Sunday afternoon session of the October 2007 General Conference of the Church of Jesus Christ of Latter-day Saints, Elder Richard G. Scott delivered an address on the importance of truth. Near the beginning of his sermon, which was titled, "Truth: The Foundation of Correct Decisions," he stated, "On a given subject we can receive multiple strongly delivered, carefully crafted messages with solutions. But often two of the solutions can be diametrically opposed. No wonder some are confused and are not sure how to make the right decisions."[44] After coming to know the true history of the Mormon Church from the very records of the church itself, I consider the address from Elder Richard G. Scott as the finest example of Mormon misinformation, insincerity, and hypocrisy for the purpose of concealing, weakening, and forever altering the truth.

Following are two preeminent examples of the Mormon effort to obscure the truth through "carefully crafted messages," as Elder Scott has warned us about. It is as if the Mormon Church believes that they alone are the keepers of American history—that no one else is recording the deeds of their prophets and pioneers. These two examples of Mormon deception lend themselves well to an initial conversation or pointed question for the modern Latter-day Saint to consider.

Subject: Mountain Meadows Massacre

Mormon Statement: "He, Brigham Young, and other leaders preached with fiery rhetoric against the enemy they perceived in the approaching army and sought the alliance of

---

[44] Scott, "Truth: The Foundation of Correct Decisions," *Ensign*, November 2007, 91.

Indians in resisting the troops."[45]

Truth: The above statement from the September 2007 *Ensign* concerning the Mountain Meadows Massacre is a carefully crafted message to the *current members of the church*. It clearly suggests to the modern reader that those who might have heard Brigham Young and the other leaders of the time of this crisis lecture on the subject of "the enemy" should have considered such preaching from the living Prophet of God and governor of the territory as only "fiery rhetoric." The point of this carefully crafted message is to place the responsibility directly on the congregation to fully understand and appreciate that whatever was preached by the Prophet of God concerning the "enemy" was in fact nothing more than "fiery rhetoric." This, of course, absolves the Prophet of any responsibility for the massacre, even if his message was "strongly delivered," as Elder Scott has warned us.

Amazingly, an official publication of the church suggests that the preaching (Scripture by his own account) of a past Prophet of the church was in fact nothing more than *"fiery rhetoric."* Indeed, the Mormon Church members of Brigham Young's day were responsible for "filtering" the Prophet's messages, somehow sorting out mere rhetoric from divine Scripture.[46]

Do you believe that this crime was either directed or influenced by the leadership of the church at the time, or should the good Latter-day Saints of the time have known that Brigham Young was speaking only "fiery rhetoric"?

Background: The September 2007 *Ensign* article on the Mountain Meadows Massacre ends with two photographs of smiling descendants of the victims who are now members of the church, along with statements that give the impression that the

---

[45] Richard E. Turley Jr., "The Mountain Meadows Massacre," *Ensign*, September 2007, 16.

[46] See chapter 3 under "Spiritual Loyalty—to My Church or My God?" for more on the Mountain Meadows Massacre and Brigham Young's culpability in it.

church is working with the descendants toward reconciliation. The fact is that after 150 years some of the descendants might even be Jewish by now, and those in the photograph pictured in the *Ensign* in no way represent the official Mountain Meadows Monument Foundation (who are direct descendants) and have a great deal of contempt for the bureaucracy of the church.

Mormon Statement: "The Mountain Meadows Massacre has continued to cause pain and controversy for 150 years. During the past two decades, descendants and other relatives of the emigrants and the perpetrators have at times worked together to memorialize the victims. These efforts have had the support of President Gordon B. Hinckley, officials of the state of Utah, and other institutions and individuals."[47]

The key phrase in this carefully crafted message is *"These efforts have had the support of President Gordon B. Hinckley."* It may be true that only the "efforts" have been supported, but the reality of the situation is that the church constantly has been at odds with the victim's descendants.[48]

- In June of 2007 the church again rejected the request by the descendants to have federal rather than state stewardship of the Mountain Meadows mass gravesite.

- President Hinckley told the group (through Elder Marlin Jensen of the Church History Department), "It would not be in the best interests of the Church to allow federal stewardship in the meadows." [49]

- Phil Bolinger of the Mountain Meadows Massacre Foundation said in an interview: "It's not right for the people who had complicity to the killings to be

---

[47] Turley, "The Mountain Meadows Massacre," 21.

[48] Jennifer Dobner and the official Mountain Meadows Monument Foundation, Inc., "Mormon church, foundation at odds over Mountain Meadows Monument." Associated Press Newswire, June 18, 2007. See 1857massacre.com.

[49] Ibid.

the grave owner." [50]

- Mr. Bolinger asked Elder Jensen: "How do you think the Kennedy family would feel if the Lee Harvey Oswald family had control of the Kennedy tomb?" [51]

- On the Web site of the Mountain Meadows Massacre Foundation is the formal petition to the United States Congress to place the custody and care of the site into appropriate stewardship.

- Additionally, this group, whom the church would have you believe they are working with toward reconciliation, makes a single formal statement to the church: "There will never be closure on Mountain Meadows until the graves are in hands other than an organization involved in the massacre." [52]

Subject: The Doctrine of Polygamy

Background: The number of carefully crafted messages specific to the doctrine of polygamy ranges in the hundreds. I will select only a few to make the point required here.

Mormon Statement: "Part of the difficulty, of course, was the natural aversion Americans held against 'polygamy.' This new system appeared to threaten the strongly entrenched tradition of monogamy and the solidarity of the family structure." [53]

The "*new system*" did more than just appear to threaten the tradition of monogamy and the solidarity of the family structure; it was against the law. In addition to the half-dozen federal Laws in opposition to the "new system," the Mormon Church is the only religious organization in the history of the

---

[50] Ibid.

[51] Ibid.

[52] Ibid.

[53] *Church History in the Fulness of Times*, 256.

- 235 -

United States to be mentioned by name during a Presidential Inaugural Address to the world.

Presidential Statement: "The Mormon Church not only offends the moral sense of manhood by sanctioning polygamy, but prevents the administration of justice through ordinary instrumentalities of law."[54]

Presidential Statement: "Polygamy in the Territories, destructive of the family relation and offensive to the moral sense of the civilized world, shall be repressed."[55]

In my view, the Mormon Church has employed a number of "carefully crafted messages." Again, I quote Elder Richard G. Scott, who stated, "On a given subject we can receive multiple strongly delivered, carefully crafted messages with solutions. But often two of the solutions can be diametrically opposed. No wonder some are confused and are not sure how to make the right decisions." How and why should that statement *not* be applied to the Mormon Church itself? How can the members of that church find specific guidance when so many "diametrically opposed" statements have come directly from the church leadership?[56] Which confusing or diametrically opposed statements should the members of the church or the public at large consider as valid, legitimate, or official from the leadership of the Church of Jesus Christ of Latter-day Saints?

Question 7

In view of the Joseph Smith Translation of Genesis 17:11-12, what is the appropriate age at which the covenant of circumcision was to be administered?

Without question, the purpose of the Joseph Smith Translation (JST) of the Bible is to correct, through inspired

---

54 President James A. Garfield, Inaugural Address of March 4, 1881.

55 President Grover Cleveland, Inaugural Address of March 4, 1885.

56 See the chart "Diametrically Opposed Statements and Actions" in chapter 4.

revelation, the several mistakes of the editors and translators of the Bible throughout the centuries and to bring forth the true and accurate Scripture. The central point of this question is to demonstrate that even when faced with clear biblical guidance, the Mormon Scriptures have been manufactured to represent an illogical and irrational view of the will of God. The Mormon Scriptures have testified to the world that the Lord Himself required polygamy and polyandry, and here Moses and the entire nation of Israel got circumcision wrong for nearly four thousand years.

Joseph Smith corrected the age requirement of the covenant of circumcision with Abraham from eight days old to eight years old.

Genesis 17:11-12 is the first time the Lord outlines the details and age requirements for the covenant of circumcision,[57] which is the sign of the Abrahamic covenant. The objective of the Joseph Smith Translation is exclusively to correct, edit, or change various Scriptures from the years of the mistranslations and edits of scribes over the centuries to bring them back to the original meaning and purpose of the Lord. The Joseph Smith Translation of this critical Scripture clearly "corrects" the age for circumcision from eight days old to eight years old.[58] At no other place within the Old or New Testament is the age of circumcision described as anything but eight days old.

If the Joseph Smith Translation of the age at which the covenant of circumcision was to be administered is correct at eight years old, then clearly Abraham, Isaac, Jacob, Moses,

---

[57] Genesis 17:11-12 in the KJV, LDS Holy Bible: "And ye shall circumcise the flesh of your foreskin; and it shall be a token of the covenant betwixt me and you. And he that is eight days old shall be circumcised among you, every man child in your generations, he that is born in the house, or bought with money of any stranger, which is not of thy seed."

[58] Joseph Smith Translation: Genesis 17:11, KJV, LDS Holy Bible: "And I will establish a covenant of circumcision with thee, and it shall be my covenant between me and thee, and thy seed after thee, in their generations; that thou mayest know for ever that children are not accountable before me until they are eight years old."

Joshua, Samuel, David, Elijah, Isaiah, Jeremiah, Malachi, and even the Lord Jesus Christ Himself, as well as millions of faithful Jews, were in the wrong. Additionally, if the covenant of circumcision were recorded and subsequently executed incorrectly, then the Lord did not correct this oversight through the two thousand years between Abraham and Himself.

In English, the semicolon indicates a close relationship between independent clauses. Thus, "that thou mayest know for ever that children are not accountable before me until they are eight years old" has been clearly and decisively linked to the first clause and primary subject of the verse, which is circumcision. Additionally, this pattern of a semicolon followed by the descriptive phrase "that thou mayest know" is present nearly twenty other times within the Mormon Scriptures.

Following are some examples of the exact use of the semicolon within the exact same sentence structure in the Joseph Smith Translation.

> *And he said, Tomorrow. And he said, Be it according to thy word; that thou mayest know that there is none like unto the Lord our God. (Exod. 8:10 JST)*

> *For I will at this time send all my plagues upon thine heart, and upon thy servants, and upon thy people; that thou mayest know that there is none like me in all the earth. (Exod. 9:14 JST)*

> *And Moses said unto him, As soon as I am gone out of the city, I will spread abroad my hands unto the Lord; and the thunder shall cease, neither shall there be any more hail; that thou mayest know how that the earth is the Lord's. (Exod. 9:14 JST)*

> *And that thou mayest tell in the ears of thy son, and of thy son's son, what things I have wrought in Egypt, and my signs which I have done among them; that ye may know how that I am the Lord. (Exod. 10:2 JST)*

Yet, look at how this clear link is conveniently ignored in order to avoid the obvious truth. In consideration of the straightforward and simple question above (According to the

Joseph Smith Translation, what is the age of circumcision?), Stake President Michael D. Jones of the Arvada Colorado Stake, brought his considerable lifetime Mormon experience and exceptional spiritual skills to bear on this question and provided the following answer.

> Answer: Eight days and sometimes later. For more information see the Bible Dictionary. The age of accountability is not the same thing as the covenant of circumcision. Genesis 17:11-12 (JST) does not say the age of circumcision is eight years old.

I then asked President Jones, what exactly then was the point of the Joseph Smith version? What was so critical that he needed to change in Genesis? What did he correct if *not* the age from eight days to eight years? He obviously was irritated but remained silent. I would suspect that if you decide to have a conversation with a Mormon about any of these questions, particularly with a Mormon in a leadership position, you too might be provided equally deceptive answers.

***

Here is the great dichotomy I now see within the Mormon Church. How can the average members be so gracious, so kindhearted, and so apparently Christian, while the foundation of their church is so clearly established on religious deception and corruption? I believe the answer can be found in how the Mormon psyche isolates and then manages any negative information about the church. I have known a few Mormon men who fundamentally enjoy the immoral element of the church, specifically the doctrines of polygamy and polyandry. But the majority of the Mormons I have known have successfully segregated or rejected outright any facts related to the true history and doctrines of the church if they do not fit their personal view of the church. I do believe the majority of the Mormon Church shares a common core set of values, but outside of the basic beliefs, millions upon millions of Mormons are left to build a personal understanding concerning the subjects of the questions addressed in this book. I have found contradictory views from many active Latter-day Saints on the subjects essential to this book. There is simply no clear and uniform answer to such questions as these: What actually constitutes modern-day Scripture? Are the sermons of the Prophets or General Authorities during general conference advice or Scripture? Do the moral and ethical standards of the church apply to all members of the church equally?

The ability of the average Latter-day Saint to operate within the general boundaries of Mormonism is of little concern to the leadership of the church until a specific doctrine or practice is questioned. Only when the average Mormon feels the need to come to terms with a given subject is he or she confronted with the harsh reality of the formal, authorized, or accepted position of the church. Such a confrontation is needed, however, and I believe it is best brought about through asking simple, honest, and straightforward questions.

While still an active Bishop and High Priest in the Mormon Church, I personally requested of a dozen men I considered friends and brothers in the gospel of Jesus Christ some measure of assistance or guidance to help me through the excruciating ordeal of confronting some foundational questions about our church. Not a one of them had the integrity to step forward. Chief among these pathetic hypocrites and fair-weather friends was the very man who baptized me into the Mormon Church,[59] former Bishops, and several past counselors and companions with whom I once taught the Mormon gospel. In my view these several men and those specifically named within this book have accurately demonstrated that the depth of the corruption and dishonesty within the Mormon Church continues unabated. In fact, I view the silence of these individuals as one of the foundational testimonies that what I have presented here is true. For if it were all lies, what would or could stop any of these men from defending their faith? To me, the very lives they now lead in silence is a mockery of what I perceived them to be.

---

[59] Gary D. Bergquist of Saint George, Utah, baptized the author on Thursday, February 17, 1977.

They each must know now that they have freely chosen to insult the character of the Lord Jesus Christ so that the immoral actions of the Mormon Prophets might somehow fit within the "restored gospel."

The Fundamental Conclusions of This Chapter

The seven core questions presented in this chapter constituted the very foundation of my examination of the Church of Jesus Christ of Latter-day Saints. I have shared these questions with family, friends, and long-term associates within the Mormon Church. Without fail, the first reaction of those I have questioned has been to defend Joseph Smith Jr., the founding Prophet of the Mormon Church. Often the mechanical and somewhat mandatory defense of Joseph Smith has come without even the basic knowledge of the specific accusation or suggested offense. Instinctively, the modern Latter-day Saint knows that if the character or moral fiber of Joseph Smith is proven to be ethically fragile, an enormous weakness is assumed by the church itself. And the church cannot stand on its own if Joseph Smith was either a false or fallen prophet.

I have tested several of my former Latter-day Saint friends, when I was still an active and respected Mormon Bishop. I found the capacity for both the irrational and fanatical defense of Joseph Smith to be practically cultish in intensity and dedication. Several well-educated individuals I have spoken to simply reverted to childlike statements when faced with factual events or teachings of their church that they admittedly had never even heard of.

In view of the documented facts presented throughout this book, it may be more productive to demonstrating the level of irrational indoctrination to ask the Latter-day Saint to focus on some questions that will instinctively be answered in the affirmative. Among fellow Mormons and within the walls of the Mormon classrooms, chapels, or temples, none of the following questions would seem inappropriate. And yet, external to those environments one cannot help but anticipate some measure of criticism because the spirit of truth is unrestricted. The point of this demonstration is both to provide an option to the more detailed seven questions noted earlier and to reveal to the follower of Mormonism that at some point he or she must recognize that Jesus Christ Himself must be considerably reduced in moral character in order to support the teachings of some of the Mormon Prophets. As I too have been asked similar questions, I have organized these subjects so that, from the standpoint of an active Latter-day Saint who is in total harmony with the teachings of the Prophets and the formal doctrine of the church, a simple "yes" is all that is required.

- Do you believe that Joseph Smith Jr. restored the fullness of the gospel of Jesus Christ to the earth?

- Do you believe that both the Book of Mormon and the Doctrine and Covenants are to be considered authorized Scripture from God?

- Do you believe that the living Prophet of God today is Thomas S. Monson and that he is authorized, as were all of the Latter-day Prophets, to give guidance and direction to the church as modern-day Scripture during both the general conferences of the church and through other approved methods of communication?

- Do you believe that for a time, the Lord Jesus Christ authorized the doctrine and practice of polygamy as recorded within the Doctrine and Covenants?

- Do you believe in the Twelfth Article of Faith, which reads, "We believe in being subject to kings, presidents, rulers, and magistrates, in obeying, honoring, and sustaining the law"?

- Do you believe in the values of truth, honesty, and integrity?

- Do you believe that moral, ethical, and virtuous standards of the Church of Jesus Christ of Latter-day Saints apply to all members of the church?

What these straightforward questions do not immediately

reveal is that each one is but a carefully disguised distraction from the actual practices, teachings, and doctrines of the Mormon Church. While the average Latter-day Saint may be able to answer each of the questions above with confidence and resolve, that may well be due to a lack of knowledge or sincere ignorance of the facts. Within the reality of Mormonism, however, the following, more compelling, statements also must be true.

- The gospel of Jesus Christ that Joseph Smith Jr. "restored" included polygamy, polyandry, blood atonement, and lying for the Lord.

- If the Doctrine and Covenants are authorized Scripture from God, then Joseph Smith Jr. and Brigham Young clearly did *not* follow its commandments with regard to polygamy and the need for the additional wives to be virgins, not another man's wife, and for the first wife to give her permission.

- If sermons from the Prophets during general conferences are to be considered *Scripture*, then Christ was a polygamist and had children, blood atonement is a valid doctrine, the sun and the moon have inhabitants, blacks are here to represent Satan, and God the Father had sex with Mary to conceive Jesus.

- If polygamy and polyandry were commanded by Jesus Christ Himself, then He alone *approved* the taking of another man's wife to have sexual relations with her.

- If the Twelfth Article of Faith is a true standard of the church, then church leaders violated that article by *breaking* many federal laws of the United States.

- If you believe in the values of truth, honesty, and integrity, you are not holding your *church leaders* to those same standards.

- If you believe in the high moral, ethical, and virtuous standards of the church, you are ignoring those same standards when an Area Authority of the church is *profiting* from the sale of pornography.

I believe the deception and disloyalty I have experienced from the leaders of the Church of Jesus Christ of Latter-day Saints is representative of the majority of the leadership of the Mormon Church and not simply an abnormality driven by my specific questions. Additionally, I view the several key individuals noted in this book to be outstanding examples of the arrogance, conceit, and self-righteousness one should expect when asking similar questions. In my estimation, they have superbly replicated the precise egotism and pride of the early Mormon leaders when serious moral issues were first raised concerning Joseph Smith or the Mormon faith.

A few of the more peculiar thoughts of the modern Mormon church leaders I have dealt with, I believe, accurately represent their unconditional devotion to Joseph Smith and their superficial interest in any questions remotely critical of the church.

Guidance from My Most Senior Mormon Priesthood Local Stake Leader:

> *I asked Heavenly Father "where does he [Joseph] stand as prophet of the restoration?" The answer I received, as I shared with you and your husband, was that I saw in my mind's eye Joseph Smith, standing in the heavens, glorious and exalted. There was a beauty and grandeur that I can only poorly express. I saw those who came in judgment of him, and when they entered his presence, they shrank in horror and shame receiving for themselves a full view of the man and of themselves. . . . Having this knowledge, the other questions are meaningless to me. My grateful testimony is that Joseph Smith is a prophet of God.*[60]

---

[60] E-mail to Kathy Baker from Michael D. Jones, President, Arvada Colorado Stake, Church of Jesus Christ of Latter-day Saints, March 31, 2008. See appendix A document number 25. These comments came from the senior Mormon leader who had the power and authority to excommunicate me. Although he considered himself fair and impartial, he would lie to and about me, while deceitfully influencing others and manipulating church pretrial procedures.

Guidance from My Own Bishop, as My Spiritual Advisor:

Lee, I know that most of the questions you pose deal directly with the prophet Joseph and things he did, or did not do. My testimony is that Joseph did what he was supposed to do. My faith is in Jesus Christ. He is the one who called Joseph Smith to accomplish the work that was done. He could have called someone else, but he didn't. That's good enough for me. I'm certainly not in a position to second-guess the Savior, and I don't believe anyone else is either. I place my faith in Jesus Christ. And He has placed Joseph Smith among the noble and great ones—and therefore, I accept all that Joseph Smith did in completing the mission he was called to accomplish. That is where Joseph Smith stands in the eternities. Because of that, the questions that you pose are not a concern to me—and I hope, that you can trust in Christ to point where they will not be a concern to you. Our safety comes when we place our trust in Jesus Christ—and those He has chosen. He chose Joseph Smith, and placed him among the noble and great ones following his death. That's good enough for me." [61]

Guidance from My Priesthood Leader in Dealing with the Youth of the Church:

My delay in finding authoritative answers to the questions you sent results from two factors: several unexpected family events on top of a known very busy period and the fact that the questions are interesting to me but I don't feel an urgency to resolve them immediately. . . . Hopefully this provides sufficient explanation of my actions to demonstrate that my intentions and actions have all been forthright, open, and without malice or deceptive intent. I continue to be interested in understanding the answer to the questions and will continue to purse them. As I

---

[61] Letter to Lee Baker from Bishop Richard D. Merkley, August 2008. See appendix A document number 24. It should be remembered that according to Mormonism, Joseph Smith wrote the Mormon Scriptures, which state that Joseph Smith should take additional wives and that Joseph Smith should not be criticized for what he does (Doctrine and Covenants 132:60). On another occasion, when asked why he had not addressed my questions, Bishop Merkley stated, "The Sprit of God has told me not to talk to you."

find answers I'll gladly share them.[62]

---

[62] Letter to Lee Baker from President Lorin M. Lund, Columbia, Maryland Stake Presidency, September 2005. See appendix A document number 27. As of January 2010, President Lorin M. Lund has not provided a single comment, suggestion, thought, or answer to any of the questions provided to him back in 2005.

CHAPTER SIX

Recovery and Rededication

Recovery from any serious illness or injury is a blessing worthy of celebration. I have worked with and prayed for many of my family and friends who have courageously battled potentially life-threatening illnesses. Recovery from such a serious illness can change forever the way one views every remaining aspect of life. I do not carelessly intend to insult any member or investigator of the Church of Jesus Christ of Latter-day Saints, but there is an unmistakable comparison between such a physical recovery and my spiritual journey out of the Mormon Church. I come from a family where our genetic history of cancer is disproportionately high and seldom offers the gift of recovery. Early recognition and immediate application is paramount, as our time to act on what we have learned may be very limited. The same is true with the discovery of a religious or spiritual truth. Common sense and good judgment tells us that as with a recently detected cancer, religious deception does not simply fade away or lose the ability to destroy us if we irrationally choose to disregard it.

As documented within the collection of letters and e-mails that chronicle my journey toward discovering the truth, my beliefs, my testimony, and my understanding of my own church changed over time.[63] Indeed, I did not start this course with the intent to leave the Church of Jesus Christ of Latter-day Saints. In fact, the darkest and most depressing days of my existence on this earth were the weeks just after I had come to recognize that Jesus Christ could *not* have approved, much less been the *Author* of, several of the primary doctrines of Mormonism. At this point, everything I had previously understood about the Mormon Church was beginning to unravel. It was not that the

---

[63] See the progression of knowledge and subtle changes in the author's faith in the Mormon Church as reflected within the several letters, e-mails, and documents found in appendix A.

facts had been hidden so deeply; it was simply that until then, I had no reason to question anything about the church, for what I had been taught was exceptionally admirable. My wife and I had built our family values around the good teachings of the Mormon Church, and yet it became clear that the leadership of the church did not share those same values. *Recovery* is one of those extraordinary words that can hide its true value and meaning. Recovery is not a gift; it is not a reward that one can give to another. True recovery always comes at a cost, sometimes as a penalty, but most often true recovery refills and replenishes much more than what was originally thought to have been lost. To know the true character of the Lord, to know of His unconditional love, and to know precisely how much He cares about my dear wife and me—this and so much more has been completely restored to us.

During the years we were just average members of the Church of Jesus Christ of Latter-day Saints, we unquestionably knew of the Lord's love and compassion for us. Based on that sure knowledge, combined with our faith and devotion to His teachings, we gratefully served wherever we were needed, yet we served in ignorance. Important changes came when we began to study the lives of the Mormon Prophets, to read their sermons and understand *all* their teachings, which are the very foundation of Mormonism. As much as I truthfully wanted to dismiss the perverse history of the Mormon Church, I could not, because as a Mormon I too owned a small part of that legacy. I had joined a church; the church had not joined me. It was of little significance that the Mormons I had known were all extraordinarily honorable and good friends, neighbors, coworkers, and spiritual companions. I knew in my heart that they too were blissfully unaware of the true history of the church. Much later, I was crushed to learn that several of them were intentionally and most deliberately unaware and selectively ignorant of exactly what I had come to know about our church.

I soon began to learn of the deeper and more powerful characteristics of a true religious discovery and the following recovery that is not so easily described. As with the very personal and intense initial journey to come to know the Lord, any genuine effort to fully, completely, and honestly return to Him can be equally as moving. It was as if the celebration of my recovery was more exciting to me because I had just recovered, not from a physical illness or injury, but from a much more serious religious illness with potentially eternal consequences.

Within a very short time, I came to understand that the Lord had never abandoned me throughout this agonizing ordeal. Despite my Mormon detractors, it was clear that He Himself had guided me, and, along with my self-respect, I had recovered the essential elements of His *true* character. No longer would my Savior and Redeemer endure the Mormon title of a secret polygamist who required men to share their wives among other men. No longer in my life would His teachings be perverted and distorted by men who claimed that sacrificial murder, racial bigotry, political lies, and religious deceit were all necessary for His holy purposes. After many hours of prayer, I now believe that the principal reason for this book is to bring glory to the Lord by removing from Him the disgrace and the scandal that the leadership of the Mormon Church has placed upon Him. The Lord has laid this work upon my heart, and I cannot turn from it. To stand and bear testimony of His love, His kindness, and His compassion is to deny and reject that with which the leadership of the Mormon Church infected my heart, mind, and soul for so many years. One cannot come to know the true character of Jesus Christ if one believes His character traits are those taught by Joseph Smith and Brigham Young. No Latter-day Saint will ever come to know the true depth of His grace, mercy, and love, if His true character is hidden behind the shadowy intentions of corrupt and hypocritical leaders.

The First Steps of Recovery

Nothing I had ever experienced in my fifty-plus years of life even remotely prepared me to seemingly abandon my family, my faith, and potentially my salvation for only a "feeling" that something was terribly wrong.

Within the pages of this book I have been able to communicate what I have studied, what I have learned, and what I have personally experienced on this, the most important journey of my life. What I cannot do here is to tell you with any degree of certainty what will happen to you if you decide to ask questions or seek answers for these same issues. What I can do with all conviction and clarity is to tell you that *God loves you* and that He knows well the strengths and weaknesses of your heart, as well as the many trials and blessings of your life thus far and the trials and blessings that yet await you. I can tell you that my wife and I have found the warmth and acceptance of the wider Christian community to be genuine, refreshing, and compassionate beyond anything we had imagined.

Without question those first few steps of recovery, particularly the attempt to find a new church, were very intimidating. As a former Latter-day Saint, much less a Bishop and High Priest of that faith, I was totally unprepared for the variety of services, the wide range of worship music, and even the different ways others observed the sacrament. And yet one of the most encouraging events of our life has been the incredible experience of fellowshipping with such a diverse collection of communities who truly love the Lord. Without fail each congregation met us with friendly smiles, warm hearts, and serving hands. We reflected on the composition of the early Christian churches, and we were encouraged to see the open and unrestrained fellowshipping of entire congregations. We felt very welcome among the several churches we visited, but the spirit of Paul's narrative below was strongest within Chapel in the Hills, a small, Bible-believing nondenominational church not far from our home.

> *Now therefore ye are no more strangers and foreigners, but fellow citizens with the saints, and of the household of God. And are built upon the foundation of the Apostles and Prophets, Jesus Christ himself being the chief cornerstone. (Eph. 2: 19-20)*

As we began to worship, study, and pray with this humble congregation of true Christ-followers, we were most impressed with their knowledge of the Scriptures and their unassuming nature. Having taken our first few steps toward recovery and rededication, we realized that all we had come to cherish regarding the teachings of Jesus Christ had come with us. All of our devotion and deep gratitude for His mission, His message, and His sacrifice remained with us. The veil of secrecy and corruption had been removed from between the Lord and ourselves.

Although I had considered my participation in certain rituals within the Mormon temples as offensive to the Lord, I can now look back with some measure of satisfaction, knowing this was the reason I left the Mormon Church. It is better to offend the leadership of any and all churches than to offend the Lord. In view of that standard, I can unequivocally state that Mormon Stake President Michael D. Jones got *one* thing right on December 10, 2008, when he wrote, "Brother Baker . . . you are excommunicated for conduct contrary to the laws of the Church of Jesus Christ of Latter-day Saints."[64] I did ask several important questions, and I did deliberately disobey and violate the laws of a *church*, but not of the *Lord*. I can live with that.

I now know the reason I did not get any answers to my serious questions from the leadership of the Church of Jesus Christ of Latter-day Saints during the most spiritually devastating period of my life. It was simply because the Lord Himself was leading me down a path to find the truth, the complete truth, with only my wife at my side. Upon serious reflection, as an active High Priest and an ordained Bishop in the Mormon faith, it could have happened in no other way. We have left the Mormon Church, and we have found the light of Christ within the wider Christian community brighter and stronger than we ever imagined it could be. We have been reminded that the Lord, through the Holy Scriptures, has guaranteed us His personal assurance as we pursue the truth in

---

[64] See appendix A document number 7.

Christ. He never said the pursuit would be easy; He only said it would be worth it.

It has come to my attention that a significant number of former members of the Mormon Faith feel that if they could have been so completely and utterly deceived by Mormonism, that maybe the core teaching of Christianity itself should be questioned. This is a critical mistake in judgment with potentially lethal eternal consequences.

When one leaves the Mormon Church based on a confident witness that the very Doctrine of that Church is *not* in harmony with the teachings of Jesus Christ, then that realization and the action that one takes on behalf of that commitment is only the first step to a closer more personal and certainly a more correct relationship with Jesus Christ. Exposing the spiritual malice and personal deception in Mormonism is not in any context a confirmation that Christianity itself is wrong, only that the Mormon's distorted version of Christianity is wrong. In fact, it is the exceptionally tender and legitimate teachings of Christ Himself that will expose the enormous errors of Mormonism. These very teachings, chief among them; *His Atonement for us* – and not Brigham Young's teaching of Blood Atonement, and *His Grace* – and not just the good works of the Mormon Pioneers, stand as the example of His divine Mission on our behalf. The fact remains that if we, as former Mormons, were blinded for a time and yet remained believers in Him, then we have lost nothing. For He never left us and we never left Him. His guidance for us was only momentarily distorted by the teachings of Mormonism.

The Fundamental Conclusions of This Book

It is not an insignificant undertaking to leave a church. But neither is it an insignificant undertaking to dedicate your life to God and to follow the teachings of His Son. Even the simple formation of the obvious question, "Do I follow the church or the Lord?" is spiritually ridiculous. My intent has been to present a true, honest, and firsthand account of both the extraordinarily corrupt history of the Church of Jesus Christ of Latter-day Saints and examples of how that history is defended, justified, and perpetuated at all costs to this very day.

I believe I have demonstrated a very simple fact of life: you cannot know what you do not know if you do not ask. Is that not precisely how we all initially come to the Lord? Ask, study, ponder, and pray is how the missionaries of the Mormon Church encourage both new members and any investigators of the church to come to know the truth. In time, those very same activities will lead to excommunication if they are directed outside of the "accepted" subjects to be questioned by the membership of that same church.

I have at times been somewhat bewildered that within the Church of Jesus Christ of Latter-day Saints there were not a higher percentage of spiritual giants ready to step forward to help with our questions. I have for many years been asked to cushion the other members of our church from the trials and struggles of this world so that they will not become overwhelmed and disheartened. We have cut grass, painted homes, fixed cars, trimmed trees and moved truck loads of furniture across town to ensure that others are not excessively beleaguered by the physical and emotional challenges of this world. This same service has been rendered to my family and me for which, I am grateful.

It has been my experience that the Mormon community is supremely capable of responding to nearly any "Physical" request for support and yet they are completely inadequate in responding to virtually any request for "Spiritual" support. If the Mormon reader views this harsh assessment as a wild exaggeration, then test it, try it, and ask your leadership any of the many questions noted within this book.

I have documented the fact that the "restored gospel of Jesus Christ" as taught by the Prophets, Seers, and Revelators of the Church of Jesus Christ of Latter-day Saints includes polygamy, polyandry, blood atonement, bigotry, sexual discrimination, political lies, and religious deceit and dishonesty as a matter of official Mormon doctrine, policy, practice, and Scripture.

I have lived through and documented the deceit and dishonesty of the current leadership of the Mormon Church. I have dedicated this work to the Lord and to both those who have endured similar experiences and to those who may find the strength to yet endure similar experiences. I pray that within these pages have been found the tender promptings of the Spirit of Truth to give comfort and moral encouragement to do the right thing before the Lord. My final testimony is this: after five years of painful uncertainty, spiritual depression, and an intense search for the truth, it was all worth it. I would have done it a thousand more times if required by the Lord. Because the truth does matter.

May God bless you, and may you keep an open heart and an open mind to His guidance, through the gentle promptings of the Holy Spirit.

Lee B. Baker

APPENDIX A:

IMPORTANT DOCUMENTS

The Church of Jesus Christ of Latter-Day Saints

Bishop's Certificate

We, the First Presidency of
The Church of Jesus Christ of Latter-day Saints, do hereby certify

that on the _Fifteenth_ day of _April_ _A.D. 1990_ was

LEE BARRY BAKER

Ordained and Set Apart

by _Stanley Y. Q. Ho_ as

Bishop of the _Mililani Second_ Ward

of the _Mililani Hawaii_ Stake

of The Church of Jesus Christ of Latter-day Saints. In testimony whereof,
we hereunto subscribe our names this _Thirtieth_ day

of _May_ _A.D. 1990_

THE FIRST PRESIDENCY

Elder
Certificate of Ordination

This certifies that Lee Barry Baker

of the Misawa Servicemen's Ward/Branch Japan Sendai Stake/Mission

was ordained to the office of Elder in the Melchizedek Priesthood in The Church of Jesus Christ of Latter-day Saints

on the 26th day of February Nineteen-hundred and Seventy-eight

whose priesthood office is Elder

Ordination performed by Brent Cecil Overson

Clerk Lee B Baker Stake/Mission/District President Brent Overson

THE CHURCH OF
JESUS CHRIST
OF LATTER-DAY
SAINTS

Document 2B

THE CHURCH OF JESUS CHRIST OF LATTER-DAY SAINTS

Priesthood Authority Line

Historical Department, Member Services
50 East North Temple Street
Salt Lake City, Utah 84150

Name	Was ordained	On
By: Lee Barry Baker	Who was ordained a High Priest	On May 17, 1987
By: Charles Peter Warnick	Who was ordained a High Priest	On September 12, 1976
By: Thomas S. Monson	Who was ordained an Apostle	On October 10, 1963
By: Joseph Fielding Smith	Who was ordained an Apostle	On April 7, 1910
By: Joseph F. Smith	Who was ordained an Apostle	On July 1, 1866
By: Brigham Young	Who was ordained (see below)	On

Brigham Young was ordained an Apostle on 14 February, 1835 under the hands of the Three Witnesses - Oliver Cowdery, David Whitmer, and Martin Harris (see Joseph Smith, *History of the Church of Jesus Christ of Latter-Day Saints*, vol. 2, P. 187)

The Three Witnesses were called by revelation to choose the Twelve Apostles, and on 14 February, 1835 were "blessed by the laying on of hands of the Presidency,"- Joseph Smith Jr., Sidney Rigdon, and Frederick G. Williams - to ordain the Twelve Apostles (see *History of the Church*, vol. 2, Pp 185-189)

Joseph Smith, Jr. and Oliver Cowdery received the Melchizedek Priesthood in 1829 under the hands of Peter, James, and John (see *History of the Church*, vol. 1, pp. 40-41).

Peter, James and John were ordained Apostles by the Lord Jesus Christ (see John 15:16)

PFH0164 3.87 Printed in USA

Document 3

MELCHIZEDEK PRIESTHOOD ORDINATION CERTIFICATE

This certifies that **LEE BARRY BAKER**

was ordained to the office of **HIGH PRIEST**

in The Church of Jesus Christ of Latter-day Saints

whose priesthood office is   HIGH PRIEST   in the Melchizedek Priesthood

by CHARLES P. WARNICK   17 MAY 19 87

THE CHURCH OF JESUS CHRIST OF LATTER-DAY SAINTS

Ward/Branch   SIERRA VISTA 4TH

Sierra Vista Arizona

Stake/Mission

Clerk

Stake/Mission president (District president where authorized)

Document 4

ARVADA COLORADO STAKE

Lee and Kathryn Baker
10844 Diane Dr.
Golden, CO 80403

April 24, 2008

Brother & Sister Baker,

I wanted to express my sincere apology for the hurt and heartache I caused you. My intention was to lift and help you, never to imply that you had made any particular comment. Nevertheless, I take full responsibility for my actions and your subsequent pain.

As I promised, I have spoken to all but one individual personally who was part of the original email (the last one is out of the country through Sunday evening). I have explained that the words used to describe my experience were mine alone.

Thank you for bringing this to my attention.

Sincerely,

President Jones

Document 5

THE CHURCH OF
JESUS CHRIST
OF LATTER-DAY SAINTS

ARVADA COLORADO STAKE
Lee and Kathryn Baker
10844 Diane Dr.
Golden, CO 80403

April 25, 2008

Brother & Sister Baker,

I am not pleased with the outcome of our last meeting. Revelation and reconciliation does not come in an environment charged with emotion. In my note to you both dated April 24, 2008, I now recognize how my comments were interpreted by you that I used words in my email, which implied they were yours. As such, I understand my part in the environment, and how we got off on the wrong foot.

My Counsel
As your priesthood leader, I first want to express my desire to help. Despite your comments of my inattentiveness to your needs, I am anxious to serve you. I reiterate here what I asked you to do since our very first meeting together, and again when we met at the Alkire building in late March - that you both release any feelings of anger and frustration towards any person/leader who you feel have mistreated, abandoned, or have been critical of you. Plead with Heavenly Father for the strength and ability to let those feelings go. The spirit can bring neither peace nor answers to questions in an environment of such feelings.

The 11 Questions
I have counseled the bishop, the high priest group leader, and others to whom you have given the packet to carefully consider before they decided to answer the questions as you have them. Nevertheless, I have told them that they can do as they choose. As you have seen, some have engaged in discussion with you. I have never asked them to withhold their support in any way.

Why would I counsel them about the questions in such a manner? As I have explained previously, I disagree with the premise and structure of the inquiry. What do I mean about the *premise and structure of the question*?

I view that many of the questions posed draw a conclusion, and demand a response to that conclusion. They are narrow in context. Some are based in historical hypothesis. Others are judgmental in nature. They require a speculative response. Such an answer won't bring peace. I understand that you and I do not agree on this point. Answers that are not drawn from revelation, are not supported by scripture, nor substantiated from current prophets, seers or revelators incites confusion, and invites the adversary.

You've complained that many priesthood leaders have said they would review the questions, and then get back to you. Then, for some reason, they recant. They step back and refuse. I won't speak for them, but only for myself. Once I looked at the questions, and began to study them, my conclusion to not proceed was clear, as I have explained above. But I have never abandoned the Baker family.

Again, as your priesthood leader, one who loves you, and prays for you, the first step is what I have outlined above in my counsel. If you truly seek the peace of mind and heart, I ask you to start there. May I invite you to join with me in a special fast on May 4, 2008? I will invite Bishop Doman, and Brother Tarullo as well. Would you be agreeable to that?

Let me conclude with two scriptures. The first found in Mosiah 4:9. The second from Jacob 4:8-12. These teach us about the nature of God, his power, and his source for answers to any question.

Believe in God; believe that he is, and that he created all things, both in heaven and in earth; believe that he has all wisdom, and all power, both in heaven and in earth; believe that man doth not comprehend all the things which the Lord can comprehend. ~ Mosiah 4:9

Behold, great and marvelous are the works of the Lord. How unsearchable are the depths of the mysteries of him; and it is impossible that man should find out all his ways. And no man knoweth of his ways save it be revealed unto him; wherefore, brethren, despise not the revelations of God.
For behold, by the power of his word man came upon the face of the earth, which earth was created by the power of his word. Wherefore, if God being able to speak and the world was, and to speak and man was created, O then, why not able to command the earth, or the workmanship of his hands upon the face of it, according to his will and pleasure?
Wherefore, brethren, seek not to counsel the Lord, but to take counsel from his hand. For behold, ye yourselves know that he counseleth in wisdom, and in justice, and in great mercy, over all his works.
Wherefore, beloved brethren, be reconciled unto him through the atonement of Christ, his Only Begotten Son, and ye may obtain a resurrection, according to the power of the resurrection which is in Christ, and be presented as the first-fruits of Christ unto God, having faith, and obtained a good hope of glory in him before he manifesteth himself in the flesh.
And now, beloved, marvel not that I tell you these things; for why not speak of the atonement of Christ, and attain to a perfect knowledge of him, as to attain to the knowledge of a resurrection and the world to come? ~ Jacob 4:8-12.

Sincerely yours,

President Jones

Document 6

THE CHURCH OF
JESUS CHRIST
OF LATTER-DAY SAINTS

ARVADA COLORADO STAKE

Lee B. Baker
10844 Diane Dr.
Golden, Co. 80403

Brother Baker,

The Stake Presidency is considering formal disciplinary action on your behalf, including the possibility of disfellowshipment or excommunication, because of being in apostasy.

You are invited to attend this disciplinary council to give your response and , if you wish, to provide witnesses and other evidence in your behalf.

This council will be held at 7:15 am on December 7, 2008 in the high council room. Please come through our Stake office doors on the south side of the building to meet with the Presidency at 7:00 am. There is a couch and chairs where you may wait during the proceedings of this Council.

Michael D. Jones
Stake President
Arvada Colorado Stake

Document 7

ARVADA COLORADO STAKE

December 10, 2008

Lee B. Baker
10844 Diane Drive
Golden, Colorado 80403

Brother Baker,

As a result of the disciplinary council held on December 7, 2008, you are excommunicated for conduct contrary to the laws of the Church of Jesus Christ of Latter-day Saints. As noted in the council, the conditions of your excommunication are as follows:

- Your name is removed from the membership records of the Church.
- You do not have any privileges of Church membership.
- Your temple blessings are revoked.
- You may not wear temple garments.
- You may not pay tithes and offerings
- You may not attend any church meeting, or any church activity.

You may contact me or your bishop by phone, mail, or email, provided your communications are respectful. Additionally, we warn against any acts of additional retribution or retaliation.

You have the right to appeal. Should you desire to do so, you have 30 days in which to provide such notice to me in writing, specifying the alleged errors or unfairness in the procedure or decision.

Sincerely,

Michael D. Jones
Arvada Colorado Stake President

Document 8

Michael D. Jones
15802 West 79th Place
Arvada, CO 80007

15 December 2008

Dear President Michael D. Jones,

With respect to your letter of 10 December 2008, concerning my written notice of excommunication, I indeed would like to exercise my right to appeal.

I do not appeal the judgment or findings of the procedure, only the specificity of the charge "for conduct contrary to the laws of the Church".

On the grounds of fairness noted both in your letter and as stipulated during the Disciplinary Council of 7 December 2008, I request a detailed written list of my conduct which was found to be contrary to the specific laws of the Church which were violated.

What I have provided in written form to both members and non-members of the Church has been well documented as truthful. This would include what you have provided to me as an Authorized Representative of the Church of Jesus Christ of Latter-day Saints, which refers to the Jewish Holocaust as an example of how the Leadership of the Mormon Church could "Lie for the Lord."

Thank you in advance for your respect of my right to this information.

Lee B. Baker

CC: w/letter from M. Jones, 10 Dec

Office of the First Presidency

DeVon Doman

- 265 -

Document 9

ARVADA COLORADO STAKE

December 27, 2008

Lee B. Baker
10844 Diane Dr
Golden, CO 80403

Lee,

On December 7, 2008, you were excommunicated as a member of the church for being in apostasy, which is contrary to the laws and order of the church. You have asked for clarification as to what laws were broken, and what were the specific actions that led to the decision of the council.

What follows is a brief summary of the information that was considered at your disciplinary council.
1. You acted in clear, open, and deliberate public opposition to the Church and its leaders.

Example: You took it upon yourself to denigrate and discredit the reputations of fellow priesthood brethren with their professional collegues, establishing a predatory pattern of conduct against leaders of the Church in both Maryland and Colorado.

2. You persisted in teaching as Church doctrine information that is not Church doctrine after you had been corrected by me and your bishop.

Example: You distributed packets of statements which contained information that is not Church doctrine on multiple occasions, in various forms and to broad audiences despite warnings and your personal commitment to stop doing so.

On the basis of these actions, you were excommunicated from the Church.

Sincerely,

Michael D. Jones
President, Arvada Colorado Stake
cc: Bishop Devon Doman

Document 10

POLYGAMY, PROPHETS, AND PREVARICATION: FREQUENTLY AND RARELY ASKED QUESTIONS ABOUT THE INITIATION, PRACTICE, AND CESSATION OF PLURAL MARRIAGE IN THE CHURCH OF JESUS CHRIST OF LATTER-DAY SAINTS

by Gregory L. Smith, M.D.

The Foundation for Apologetic Information & Research

The concept of "civil disobedience" is essential to understanding those occasions in which Joseph Smith or other Church members were not forthright about the practice of polygamy.

Like obedience to civil law, honesty and integrity are foundational values to the Church of Jesus Christ. Indeed, the success which critics have in troubling members of the Church with tales of polygamy and its deceptive circumstances is, in a way, a compliment to the Church. If the Church as an institution typically taught its members to have a casual disregard for the truth, a discovery that Joseph Smith had deceived others about polygamy would not be troubling to most. But, because the Church (contrary to the suggestions of some critics) really *does* teach its members to aspire to live elevated lives of moral rectitude, the discovery that deception was involved with polygamy can come as something of a shock. Disillusionment can ensue if we follow the critics in assuming that because Joseph occasionally misled others in this specific context, he must therefore have lied about everything else, and been absolutely unworthy of trust.

But, as we have seen, the practice of polygamy must be viewed in its moral context as an act of religious devotion which the Saints were unwilling to forego simply because the state or society disapproved.

Lying About Polygamy during the Nauvoo Era

The "lying" about polygamy that occurred in the Nauvoo period is partly related to this same civil disobedience. A real-life example is helpful. Suppose a Church member is living in Holland in the 1940s. Established laws command the deportation of all Jews to a grisly fate. A Church member might (as many brave Dutch did) decide that such a law has no moral force—indeed, it would be immoral to obey it. The Church member might further decide that he is morally bound to hide a family of Jews in his attic. One day, an SS team arrives, knocks at the door, and demands to know if the Church member knows of the whereabouts of any Jews.

The member has several choices:

1. he can decide that "honesty" is the highest moral value, and reveal the location of his Jewish guests.

2. he can refuse to answer the question, by remaining silent.

3. he can declare that he is not willing to comply with the request, and will not answer the question

4. he can lie to the German SS, and may also have to lie to his friends and neighbors to keep them from revealing the secret

Which is the correct moral choice? It is difficult to see how honesty can trump the lives of the Jews—so, option (1) is out. The SS officer is unlikely to go meekly on his way should one remain silent or verbally refuse to answer, so choosing either (2) or (3) will simply result in the Jews being found and the Church member and his family suffering the consequences of their disobedience to civil law. It seems to me that the most moral option—fulfilling the member's duty to his Jewish guests, his conscience, and his family—requires that the member lie to the SS.

Remember, someone who opts for civil disobedience must accept the risk of punishment. The Dutch who were caught harboring Jews suffered greatly for their integrity—but, they apparently considered the risk of that suffering to be worth retaining that integrity. One cannot complain if one's deception of the civil authorities is found out and punished—that is the price of civil disobedience on moral grounds. But, one is not morally obligated to participate in the prosecution of oneself or others for breaking laws one considers immoral.

An analogy to modern Church practice may illustrate some of the difficulties. Let us presume that current members of the Church have made covenants in the temple—but, not only do they covenant not to disclose certain concepts, but they promise not to disclose even the existence of the temple endowment itself. What would a Church member do if confronted publicly by an apostate with questions about matters they have promised to keep secret? Silence or a decision to "plead the Fifth" will simply play into their enemies' hands by effectively confirming the story that the member will not deny. They cannot remain true to their covenants if they answer in the affirmative; to deny what the apostate is saying is to be deceptive.

It was in exactly this position that some Nauvoo-era members of the Church were placed. They had no ideal choices, and so did their best to follow God despite circumstances beyond their control.

Didn't Joseph Deceive Church Members?

Some are quick to point out that Joseph Smith didn't just lie to the government or to non-members, but also deceived members of the Church. This objection ignores, of course, the point that to make the announcement publicly to the Church is the same as telling everyone.

field for deception. It is not difficult for historians to quote LDS leaders and members in statements justifying, denying, or deploring deception in furtherance of this religious practice."

Elder Oaks then reaches the key point: there will be times when moral imperatives clash. Do you save your family and the Jews you are hiding, or do you tell the Nazis the truth? Do you break up polygamous families, abandon wives without support, or tell the whole truth? One cannot do both—that is not an option. Elder Oaks notes:

My heart breaks when I read of circumstances in which wives and children were presented with the terrible choice of lying about the whereabouts or existence of a husband or father on the one hand or telling the truth and seeing him go to jail on the other. These were not academic dilemmas. A father in jail took food off the table and fuel from the hearth. Those hard choices involved collisions between such fundamental emotions and needs as a commitment to the truth versus the need for loving companionship and relief from cold and hunger.

My heart also goes out to the Church leaders who were squeezed between their devotion to the truth and their devotion to their wives and children and to one another. To tell the truth could mean to betray a confidence or a cause or to send a brother to prison. There is no academic exercise in that choice!⁸⁰

The actions of wicked people may place the Saints in conditions in which they cannot fulfill all the ethical demands upon them. In such difficult circumstances, only revelation—to the Church collectively and to individuals—can hope to show us what God would have us do. Judging such cases is extremely difficult; it is also hypocritical for Church critics to point out such instances without providing the context which underlay their choices, and which made them so wrenching. As Elder Oaks continued:

I do not know what to think of all of this, except I am glad I was not faced with the pressures those good people faced. My heart goes out to them for their bravery and their sacrifices, of which I am a direct beneficiary. I will not judge them. That judgment belongs to the Lord, who knows all of the circumstances and the hearts of the actors, a level of comprehension and wisdom not approached by even the most knowledgeable historians.⁸¹

Each case must be judged on its merits. Did some Church members or leaders make wrong choices? Probably—they and we do not claim any inerrancy. In the main, however, I think it clear that Church members did not "lie" or "deceive" because it was convenient, or because it would advance "the cause." They lied because moral duties conflicted, and they chose the option which did the least harm to their ethical sense. Happily, they had personal revelation to guide them. Concludes Elder Oaks:

I ask myself, "If some of these Mormon leaders or members lied, therefore, what?" I reject a "therefore" which asserts or implies that this example shows that lying is morally permissible or that lying is a tradition or even a tolerated condition in the Mormon community or among the leaders of our church. That is not so.⁸²

Given the fact that some Church leaders did deceive others concerning polygamy, it is reasonable to wonder whether such leaders also lied about other matters. Fortunately, a key doctrine of the Church is that no one should have to take anyone else's word for something—"that man should not council his fellow man, neither trust in the arm of flesh—but that every man might speak in the name of God the Lord, even the savior of the world."⁸³ This doesn't apply to polygamy alone; every discussion of testimony includes it. Joseph made numerous other claims that might make us skeptical: appearances of God and Jesus, angels, gold plates, and everything else. Said he:

Search the scriptures—search the revelations which we publish, and ask your Heavenly Father, in the name of His Son Jesus Christ, to manifest the truth unto you, and if you do it with an eye single to His glory nothing doubting, He will answer you by the power of His Holy Spirit. You will then know for yourselves and not for another. You will not then be dependent on man for the knowledge of God; nor will there be any room for speculation.⁸⁴

No Church member is obliged to blindly believe leaders, past or present, but we ought to at least consider their decisions with a hint of charity, and recognize the many factors that may have contributed to their choices, especially when we know so little about some of them.

Lying About Polygamy in Utah, Prior to 1890

Gandhi pointed out that a moral civil disobedience campaign required an atmosphere of relative safety:

Document 11

A Formal Request for Spiritual Support and Assistance
December 2007

Purpose:

In the past five years the most discouraging and frustrating aspect of my life has been, without question, my relationship with my own Church. Specifically, it has become painfully clear that, during the most important spiritual challenge in my life, the level of genuine concern is debatable at best, while the amount of actual support is simply depressing.

Little or no support at all has been, a very sobering, yet solid confirmation of the truthfulness and impact of the questions I have. As with each of these requests for support, nothing has or will ever happen without my repeated and embarrassing request for help. Anyone on the "outside" of this dysfunctional religious relationship might mistakenly consider such support to be a common consideration provided by one's own Church.

I completely understand that it would be much easier if I were to simply fade into that 35% of our inactive membership who may have serious issues, but no hope of conclusion or discussions. By comparison, some might consider me a very active member, yet I, like them, have only minimal expectations of any resolution.

One of the core problems for us with questions is, that there is no time and no forum within the entire curriculum of the Church to discuss issues. Not only is there no forum for open discussion in the Church, but that awkward silence in our classes when even the most basic of questions are asked... is a reflection that we all know that there is just one set of "acceptable" answers. So we must rapidly evaluate the audience, restrain some comments and then estimate the probability that our answer is the right one or stay quiet, as is most often the case. Or we can actually ask for help, as I have, and then wait for many weeks, then several months and now years.

Even within the Temple there are only "acceptable" answers. A few months ago my wife and I had a very simple question for the Temple President. Privately, in his office I asked about D&C 132 and multiple sealings for male members after the death of a sealed spouse... "I don't know about that, I think we will have to wait until we pass through the veil to know." An excellent example of an "acceptable", but useless answer.

I know all too well what my responsibilities are, but what exactly am I to expect from my Church? What is expected of me has been clearly provided in hundreds of meetings, manuals, pamphlets, lectures, scriptures, in leadership training, Conference talks and Temple or Priesthood interviews. But just exactly what support am I to expect from my Church? Well... now... that's just a bit hazy, and much more flexible.

1

In view of my years of frustration and intensity, my wife has asked if it was likely that the spirit of the adversary was driving my research and my thoughts on these subjects. I have told her, as I might ask you… I am only "researching" these subjects concerning the true history of the Church and it's Leaders… and yes, I do feel the immorality of these events… but what "spirit" drove these Brethren to actually teach or do these things?

Background:

As a convert of the Church, I have been troubled at how casually the general membership can maintain a testimony through a deliberately incomplete and shallow knowledge of Church history.

I am asking once more for spiritual and emotional support from my Church. I now consider my 30 years of service to the Church as a Bishop, High Counselor, Stake Young Men's President, High Priest Group Leader, Elders Quorum President and a host of other positions as both spiritual and emotional exploitation, a true one-way street.

I have defended the Church for the last time. I have come to realize that over 90% of the "anti-Mormon" information about the Church is actually true… simply true. Anyone can deal with the lies, but the *Truth* will challenge even the most passionate defenders of the Church, as I once was.

Throughout my entire association with the Restored Gospel my testimony has, and remains centered on my personal pillars of the True Church: Salvation for the Dead, Authority in the Priesthood, a Living Prophet, the Organization of the Church and Lost or Missing Scripture. But, I now need to know if there is room for me in this Church, if I believe with all my heart that a number of the critical doctrines and teachings of the Latter-day Prophets, which have effected the lives of millions, were at times absolutely wrong.

Take no comfort in the thought that "Brother Baker should not spend so much time focusing on these issues", in that, I have committed vast amounts of my time to the study of all the Scriptures over the past 30 years. At the requests of Stake Presidents, Mission Presidents and Bishops, I have spoken at numerous Stake Meetings, Firesides, Zone and Ward Conferences as well as Reactivation and Missionary Training events. I love the Gospel and Mission of Jesus Christ. I have given lectures on the Restoration of the Gospel, the importance of the Counsel of Nicea, the History of the Bible and my five pillars of the True Church… all centered on just why and how this Church is True.

The point is this… it is Spiritual and Emotional suicide to assume a personal course of action, that as a Member of the Church of Jesus Christ of Latter-day Saints, we must be enthusiastically dedicated to take and defend the entire history Church and every action of it's Leadership as right, true and just. But, that is precisely what we are trained each year to do. No wonder such an astounding number of the Church is inactive or disappears entirely.

2

Request:

Within the next two months, I would ask that you read, study, ponder and pray and provide me your answers to the eleven questions attached. I have provided both the Gospel Principal, which applies to each of the questions and sufficient references and examples to establish the validity of the question.

This collection will represent only a few of the references available, but sufficient for your consideration. If you would like to see the original documents or more such examples of the same point, please let me know. I have become extremely frustrated that this has been reduced to a written format to request your support, as what might be explained in a few short meetings has now required many hours to prepare.

You are intelligent and spiritual men, and I would ask you to consider the direction from President Boyd K. Packer: "Willingly defend the history of the Church.", General Conference Addresses, *Ensign*, November 2006 page 88. But to defend the history of the Church, you must know the history of the Church, and that could be dangerous. I would also ask that you do not embarrass yourself by simply stating: "I don't know about that", or "Well, that's not important to me." Well, it is very important to me, so please let me know if that alone is insufficient to solicit your support.

If my sister a Catholic knows, and my coworker a Lutheran knows, and my boss a Baptist knows... it's ok if we know. Although this past week, I did ask my boss to stop asking about the Church, because I figure... if I can't get answers, then why should he.

It has been annoying to watch how adult members of the Church who maintain and manage volumes of detailed information on sports, politics, their profession or personal hobbies of every description, but when asked about specific events in Church history or from the lives of the Prophets... "Well, I just don't know about that." is always a good enough answer.

Distractions:

It is critical that your efforts remain focused on the attached questions and not on my support in "other" areas. Your answer to these questions is exactly and specifically what I need. I do not need to become an assignment for someone to fellowship or befriend. As a former Bishop, I clearly understand the potential for committees, assignments and reports, which could result from a letter such as this.

A recent distraction was when my leadership recognized the needs of my wife, who has thus far been the **only** true and consistent support to me. Although I was the one who had sent several letters to the First Presidency and formally asked my Bishop for clear and direct assistance, it was "The burden on my Wife's shoulders" which attracted the devoted attention of my Leadership.

3

Offensive as this course was, she explained that she in fact did have a burden on her shoulders, which was the total lack of support I had received over these several years. I believe this tactic to have been to a clear message to me rather than of genuine concern for my wife. The message was obviously that the leadership cares more about my wife than I do. I have considered this just a pointless effort to drive a wedge between my wife and I. Testimony to this conclusion is the fact that no effort whatever, was made to minister to my wife or lift her "burden" which was so plainly recognized by our leadership. To ensure we had fully "communicated" my Bishop, added his advice that if I were to continue with these questions: "your Temple Recommend may be at risk". Strange, I only seek the Truth.

Again, I would only ask for your honest and detailed answers to the questions provided, in that action alone is your true support to both my wife and I. Additionally, you may find some personal value in this effort. One day these same questions may come to your home, through your sons or daughters. The sincere reality is, that as long as we share the Church, we share its history as well. I have learned the hard way that simply denying some truth can be more destructive to your total testimony.

I have lied several times to both new members and investigators concerning my true feelings on the several subjects in this packet. I now want to know how you would do it... how you will answer these questions, to help my testimony.

Your answers and comments are in fact to help me feel more a part of the Ward specifically and the Church in general. Without your answers, it will be impossible for me to evaluate just how I fit within a group that apparently has no issues, no thoughts and no disagreements with the subjects listed here.

In view of the fact some of these subjects may be too sensitive for some, I do understand that a few questions may be dismissed, selectively rejected or found to be not at all relevant within the specific version of the Church some have shaped for themselves, but I would ask for your consideration of these questions if only for the sort-term.

Thank you in advance for your integrity and your time.

Lee B. Baker
Ordained Bishop
High Priest after the Order of Melchizedek
Active Member of the Church of Jesus Christ of Latter-day Saints

4

Document 12

The Church of Jesus Christ of Latter-Day Saints
Office of the First Presidency
President Thomas S. Monson
50 East North Temple Street
Salt Lake City, Utah 84150

30 January 2006

Dear President Monson,

After 30 years of faithful service... I only ask for 30 minutes of consideration by someone, anyone in authority who could answer one personal question. Thus far the silence concerning this question has been very demoralizing.

Over the past two years it has become obvious, both when sharing the Gospel and now on a personal level... that a number of subjects found to be in the "anti-"Mormon" category, are in fact, True and Accurate accounts of the actual teachings of the Prophets and General Authorities as documented within authorized Church publications.

As only one example, the Journal of Discourses (issued under the authority of the First Presidency) has long been the single most referenced source of General Conference talks and official teachings of the early Prophets, Apostles and General Authorities.

How am I to explain or understand the selective use of the Journal of Discourses, in contrast to the simultaneous rejection of "some" of the teachings from the same Prophet or Apostle during the same time on the same subject presumably under the same inspiration of the Spirit also recorded in the Journal of Discourses?

With sincerity and respect.

Brother Lee B. Baker
High Priest
Membership Nr. 000-3443-8033 (Provide for identification purposes)

Document 13

Office of the First Presidency
President Thomas S. Monson
50 East North Temple Street
Salt Lake City, Utah 84150

26 July 2007

Dear President Monson,

I have been an exceptionally active convert-member for over 30 years. I have written you in the past (see attached) with a heartfelt desire for guidance. In response to my sincere letter of genuine concern, my Stake President was _instructed_ to read me a letter from "Salt Lake" which harshly stated that I should simply "Follow the Prophet" and not concern myself with the past.

The guidance to follow the Prophet and the examples of the Brethren is exactly my concern. How are we to know when our leadership speaks as a man or on behalf of God, when at times, their words and/or actions appear to be at odds with the teachings of Christ? Are some of these teachings intended to just simply fade away? If so, which ones and when?

If we are not permitted to _or_ choose not to educate ourselves, ask questions, study, ponder and pray, then Church History and its Doctrine will become _whatever_ we want, or more dangerous "need" it to be.

I really do want to know the truth, follow the truth and teach the truth. Yet, without any comment, discussions or guidance from our leadership, the general membership is left only to each others opinions on a number of critical issues. My own Bishop has been absolutely silent for eight months now after I have clearly asked for his help.

If my roof leaked I could get help, if sick I could get a blessing within an hour, but if I have a major spiritual challenge that seriously impacts my testimony… I am on my own.

With the utmost honesty and seriousness, I would ask if you consider the following in harmony with the teachings of the Lord Jesus Christ:

The Prophet Joseph Smith "tested" members of the Church by requiring their wives as his own, and then actually took a significant number of them. He married three sets of sisters, a mother and daughter as well as two 14 years-old girls when he was 37.

Joseph taught that the practice of Polygamy / Polyandry was the only way to the highest degree of Heaven and then publicly _denied_ his own participation in the doctrine.

In the 1840's the doctrine of Polygamy forced many to leave the Church because they would not support it. Then in the 1890's the doctrine of Polygamy forced many to leave the Church because they would not stop it. The Eternal destiny of millions hangs on the truthfulness and authority of this doctrine as well as the examples of its criminal practice by the Prophets, which was not in harmony with the Doctrine and Covenants.

Brigham Young taught the Doctrine of Blood Atonement, he taught that to become a God one must participate in Polygamy, that the "mixing" of a white man and a black woman would forever result in death on the spot, that all Blacks were cursed and very much a lesser race and that men lived on both the Moon and the Sun.

The Apostle Orson Hyde taught in General Conference that Jesus Christ had several wives and was the father of children on this earth.

John Taylor taught that the Black race exists to represent the powers of Satan.

As an Area Authority of the Church, Elder J.W. Marriott Jr. currently profits significantly from the daily sale of alcohol and the rental of pornography.

I do not see the hand of Jesus the Christ in these things.

Please help me to understand, my testimony hangs in the balance.

Sincerely,

Lee B, Baker

CC: Bishop Richard Merkley

- 276 -

Document 14

The Church of Jesus Christ of Latter-Day Saints
Office of the First Presidency
President Thomas S. Monson
50 East North Temple Street
Salt Lake City, Utah 84150

30 March 2008

Dear President Monson,

All I have ever asked for was for someone to talk to...

Too much to ask for? Well..... here we are now 5 years later with only a few "meetings" to evaluate my motivations, assess my loyalties and of course calculate my "Spirit" because our fine Church only assists those with a pleasant "Spirit", even if anything short of that is after many years of abuse within that Church.

Each of these short meetings has been surpassed by the many Leadership strategies, secret phone calls, broken promises, and a number of reported meetings and reports about... but not to... Brother Baker.

President Jones has even told me that he has spent more time on my issues than on any other member of the Stake. Strange... I have spent only about an hour and a half with him and in that time, not a single question of the 11 (although he said he would work on them), has ever been addressed. But, I now fully understand that I have just traded away my right to ask any of these questions for my right to hold a Temple Recommend.

Sister Baker believes that I should be more respectful, as this letter is addressed to the President of the Church. I have explained to her that the President of the Church has a large staff of assistants (one of them is reading this letter right now), who also read my previous letters -- all very respectful -- but all with no impact, no change in my Life, no change in the support from my Church Leadership, and no change with my daily struggles... the only thing that changes... is the growing void of compassion, friendship or concern (ya know like we read about on Sunday)... and into this void the adversary is only too delighted to pour options and opportunities, none of them good... but each of them very public and powerful.

It has been surreal to live in two worlds. One in which, after over 30 years of decorated service with the National Security Agency, I have earned the friendship, trust and respect of senior General Officers and Members of Congress. And in the other world... my Church Leaders say one thing and then do another. Where my desperate, sincere and honest request for support have been rejected by strategy and delays born of insincerity.

If something were to happen to me, I have forwarded two sealed package to my most trusted associates. These packages are complete copies of not only each of the many letters and questions to my Church Leadership over the past five years, but each packet includes a detailed and very comprehensive support appendix.

The appendix (not provided here), documents some 215 pages of letters, emails, meeting notes and dates, all key to establishing a creditable audit trail of the Church's purpose and intent.

I have explained to these gentlemen, that totally unsympathetic to more than 30 years of faithful service and well over a quarter of a million dollars of donations, these 11 questions alone… place my membership in jeopardy.

To ensure a clear understanding, specific to the true magnitude of my dilemma, I have explained in great detail the very unique Mormon application of two key beliefs and practices at work here:

Actions taken or required to protect the Good Name of the Church

This practice is paramount above all other concerns for the individual and is passionately employed at all levels within the Church.

The Loss of a Temple Recommend

There is no comparison within the Christian community they are familiar with. In Mormon society, the loss of a Temple Recommend does not simply imply that you may not attend the Temple itself. Without a recommend, a Father or a Mother cannot attend the wedding of a Child and the basic Family Unit itself is at risk for All Eternity.

This understanding is key to fully comprehend the impact of the following conversation:

Sunday, March 9th, 3:35 pm, Hallway then Bishop's Office within the Standley Lake Ward of the Church of Church of Jesus Christ of Latter-Day Saints, Alkire Building, 12995 West 72nd Ave. Arvada, Colorado – 80005 (Transcript Condensed)

Bishop Doman: "Well, what can we do for the Bakers?" (Lee and Kathy)
Bakers: "We are here for Temple Recommend interviews."
Bishop Doman: "I think we need to talk about your packet first"
  - Conversation moves into the Bishop's Office –
Lee Baker: "Why would the packet of questions have any bearing on our worthiness to hold a Temple Recommend?"
Bishop Doman: "Well, you have called President Gordon B. Hinckley a SCURRILOUS man."

Lee Baker:	"I have never said, written or communicated any such opinion, where would you have got that idea from? No such comment or impression is in my packet of questions."
Bishop Doman:	"Ok, maybe you did not, I have only read through your packet once."

The totally fabricated and unfounded, but clear accusation of speaking ill of the Lord's Prophet is a violation of our Temple Covenants. This false incrimination, from my Bishop himself just prior to a Temple Recommend Interview speaks volumes specific to both the intent and design of my Leadership's strategy. A short history of the life and accomplishments of President Hinckley were provided (supplement to the Ensign) to give some depth of understanding of the true force of the accusation for the non-member reader.

A very similar verbal attack was documented just minutes prior to the second phase (Stake Level) of the Recommend Interview with Stake President Jones on 16 March within the same facility.

So... what does Brother Baker really want? Again... and yet again... nothing more than that which was personally promised to me, face-to-face in my hour of need. Now just a mockery of my pain... the simple act of support that each of these "Leaders" of my faith had committed to... to provide me, in person their best and most honest answers to each of these questions. That's all and it's over!

They each said they would do just that...but now all three of them... who made that promise to me... now treasure their secret yet unauthorized reprieve, their pardon, and their acquittal of any responsibility to me. Stake President Jones told them he would deal with it, he has not... he secretly released them without even the integrity to tell me of his deceiving plan.

So... Dear assistant to the President... make a copy of this for the "special file" and one for the "legal department", then tell your team here what your guidance is... or just wait for me to make the next move... I can handle that as well. You might do better if you do some homework... read everything you have been given and then ask your team what it really meant when they say: "We have worked with Brother Baker". Ask them out of his 18 months in the Ward, how diligent of a Home Teacher was Brother Baker? And, how many times was he and his wife visited in that same time? Did he and his wife serve well in their callings? My team knows the answers to these and several other key questions to establish credibility.

Your ever faithful yet mistreated servant.

Lee B. Baker

Document 15

The Church of Jesus Christ of Latter-Day Saints
Office of the First Presidency
President Thomas S. Monson
50 East North Temple Street
Salt Lake City Utah, 84150

12 May 2008

Dear President Monson.

It may be more appropriate to address the reader of this letter as the Assistant of the Assistant to President Monson. Ya know... one day you should actually let the President of the Church read some of these letters, as the suggestions and instruction you guys have been passing down, are not working so well.

I am very concerned about the Arvada, Colorado Stake President. Michael Jones. who might need some emotional and mental help.

It seems he has experienced some short-term memory loss. Many, who might not know and love him as I do. would perhaps classify his memory loss as a simple lie... I prefer to think of it as a new Stake President that would rather report his challenges in the best possible light for the Church, while making the member in question (Hello... that would be me) appear to be possessed by the devil.

To assist with his memory loss, I would like to help however I can. I thought that a short segment from one of several recorded conversations might provide just the right method (his own voice) to correct the written account he has sent to both you and I.

At this point in time I might ask again, is <u>this</u> really easier than just answering our 11 questions? Oh... well, its ok with me.

In his tender letter dated, April 25th, he states: "<u>I have never asked them to withhold their support in any way</u>." and, "Why would I counsel them about the questions in such a manner?" It is very impressive and powerful that the <u>only</u> line of the entire letter which is <u>underlined</u>... is the **lie** itself, on Official Church Letterhead... how nice... with the name of the Lord Jesus Christ at the top... now that's something to be proud of.

It must have slipped his mind that not only did I question him about his actions (see the transcript and audio tape). but I also provided him the <u>original</u> letter from Bishop Richard Merkley in which he states:

"At the request of our Stake President, Michael Jones, I will not be responding to your individual questions with independent answers. Pres. Jones indicated that he would like you to work through him on this matter."

1

Sister Baker, and I also told him that both Bishop Doman and the High Priest Group Leader, Brother Tarullo reported the same instructions to stop. Ah yes... the power of a Subpoena... it's a wonderful thing to help with short-term memory loss.

What is so obtuse and corrupt, is that within the very same letter in which, he **lies** to you and I, in this... a letter from an Authorized Representative of the Lord Jesus Christ, he makes the following deceiving statements:

"As your priesthood leader, I first want to express my desire to help."
"I am anxious to serve you."

The above statements are particularly deceiving in view of his self-declaration of release on page 2 from any further support on the questions: "Once I looked at the questions, and began to study them, my conclusion to not proceed was clear, as I have explained above."

And what exactly was the driving force for him to stop any support from my Priesthood Leadership, then lie about it... and then release himself as well? Obviously it was the all important and most critical "Premise" and "Structure of the inquiry.

So, after Sister Baker and I have asked for help and communicated many times both in writing and also in very passionate personal interviews that... **"These Questions represent the single most critical and discouraging challenge to our membership in the Church."**, it should be completely understandable and deeply inspirational that the Lord's Representative in our Stake, under the direction of the Spirit of the Living God, after spending "more time in prayer for the Bakers than any one else in the Stake." would simply declare:

"I disagree with the premise and structure of the inquiry."

How deep and encouraging... how so very optimistic. Then it came to me... How silly of me not to have seen it before, maybe President Jones was simply employing a strategy on you and I, which he had explained to Sister Baker and I a few weeks ago.

I can only hypothetically think of his instruction in the form of a Newspaper Headline:

"Tape Reveals Local Mormon Leader Teaches its Ok to Lie for the Lord"

I suspect that no such report of the teaching of this unique Mormon practice by President Jones to Sister Baker, I and maybe others, has yet made it to Salt Lake. Again, let me help out where I can, just in case of any unexpected memory loss.

President Jones, just moments prior to our Sunday School Class, authoritatively and proudly provided me with a packet of documentation which justified the early

Church of Jesus Christ of Latter-Day Saints practice of "Lying for the Lord" especially to the United States Government.

He later explained in his office (you will love this recording) some of the specific conditions to which this practice was or is acceptable, including:

1. Identification or locations of the Church Leadership – sounds like the FLDS
2. Underage Marriages among the Church Leadership – sounds like the FLDS
3. Marriages to the Sisters, Daughters and Wives of the Church Leadership among and between the Church Leadership– sounds like the FLDS
4. Identifying specific assets, funds and land holdings– sounds like the FLDS
5. Details concerning the Doctrine of Blood Atonement – sounds like the FLDS
6. Judgment that the United States Government can not be trusted and is directly compared, within the very packet provided to me by President Jones, to the evil Government persecutions of Nazi Germany – sounds like the FLDS

It should be noted that when challenged on this practice, as it is one of our 11 questions (12th Article of Faith), President Jones clearly states several times that he too would have employed such a tactic. And it is my understanding, given that he is an Authorized Representative of the Church of Jesus Christ of Latter-Day Saints and my Senior Priesthood Leader who has provided this instruction and the supporting documentation to us in his office… that he would not hesitate to employ such a tactic today. After all… it's for the Lord.

In closing and totally indifferent to any plausible memory loss… President Jones should become well educated specific to the legal threshold of Defamation of Character and Slander. Although his several emails and letters are both slanderous and malicious… it seems that not everyone he has spoken to about the Bakers… knows how to keep secrets very well… Ah yes… the power of a Subpoena… it's a wonderful thing to help with short-term memory loss.

In a letter dated April 24th President Jones tells Sister Baker and I that:

"Nevertheless, I take full responsibility for my actions and your subsequent pain."

Ok… that's a good thing right? But wait… what is the real-world procedure of taking full responsibility? He should know that Church policy, manuals and actions will provide him no protection whatever… within the sphere of Defamation of Character and Slander he as so cheerfully jumped into to impress those around him.

Or is this the just the empty political version of taking "full responsibility", that is the total and complete dedication… of only the 3.5 seconds it takes to type those 18 letters on a piece of paper? Why would I ask so sarcastically? Well, we see… that he **will take** full responsibility for the pain he has caused us…but… wait… wait… wait just a minute… the very next day he declares that he **will not** address the 11 Questions which are so important to the Bakers.

That was very convincing, very sincere and certainly confirms the fact that both letters were written more for you than for me. They each contain all the selective key points you would want to see, as an act of repentance and apology, yet they retain the clear message for me that he is done with the questions before he even started, because of the all important "**premise and structure of the inquiry**".

Remember dear Assistant to the Assistant, I am here for you... if you truly need to know what all (not just part) of what has been happening here in the Colorado, please don't hesitate to call... you see... I do not have short-term memory issues, I have recordings.

Once more, I might ask... is this really easier than just answering our 11 questions? Oh... well, its ok with me. Because it is not just the Church of President Michael Jones, it is not just your Church, it is the Lord's Church and it is our Church as well. How many thousands have renounced the struggle to understand their Membership or their Church just because they could not stomach the cold hard bureaucracy, the strategies, the policies and procedures of men who are motivated by any and all tactics possible to defend not the Truth... not the Gospel of Jesus Christ which we have come to love, cherish and teach to our children and grandchildren... but the "Good Name of the Church".

Don't you just miss the good old days when you could dispatch the Danites, and the problem children in the Church would simply "vanish". I am not yet ready to drink the Kool-Aid, but I am certainly ready for the next level.

Sincerely,

Lee B. Baker

CC:

4

Document 16

Open and Public Testimony

Of

Lee B. Baker, High Priest and Ordained Bishop

After over 30-years of faithful service, my Leaders have questioned my loyalty to the Church as well as the depth of my understanding and commitment to the "Restored" Gospel of Jesus Christ. The following is my Public Testimony of what I recognize as the teachings of Jesus and a few, which I do not believe to be His teachings.

If my testimony of these subjects is found to be <u>not</u> acceptable to the Church of Jesus Christ of Latter-day Saints, then this Public document may serve as the foundation for any disciplinary action, for this is what I sincerely believe and I will accept the consequences of it:

I believe that the Lord Jesus Christ is the literal Son of the living God. That through His Atonement in the garden and on the cross, he has provided all mankind the only path to Salvation which is through our personal acceptance of Him as our Lord and Savior, in that we would have Faith in Him, Repent of our sins and follow both His Commandments and His example.

I believe that Joseph Smith Jr., was called of the one and only true God to restore both His Church and the Priesthood to the earth. I believe that through that Priesthood, he organized the only true Church on the earth with its authorized Ordinances, Blessings and Organization as with the ancient Church established by Christ Himself.

I believe that Joseph Smith Jr., did, under the direction of the Holy Ghost and by Divine Powers of revelation and discernment, did translate the Book of Mormon for the benefit of all mankind as a true Second Witness of the mission of the Lord Jesus Christ.

I believe that Thomas S. Monson is the living Prophet of God on the earth today and as such, that he holds all the restored keys of the Priesthood necessary to guide and direct the Lord's Church on the earth.

I believe that the Prophet Joseph Smith Jr., did not follow the Laws of Plural Marriage as recorded in the Canonized Scriptures of the Church, specifically: D&C 132: 61-64. His several plural marriages without the <u>consent or even the knowledge</u> of his first wife (Emma) were equally unlawful due to the fact that many of these women were at the time and then remained, the wives of <u>other men</u>. Both actions by Joseph Smith are clearly prohibited and are explicitly forbidden by the Scriptures.

Additionally, I believe that, as accurately recorded in the Official History of the Church, Vol. 6 page 411, in May of 1844 the Prophet Joseph Smith Jr., did publicly and deliberately <u>lie</u> about his 13-year participation in the practice of polygamy to avoid legal accountability. Joseph Smith Jr. confidently stated: "What a thing it is for a man to be accused of committing adultery, and having seven wives, when I can only find <u>one</u>." The unquestionable point of fact is, that he had at least <u>thirty-three</u> wives in May of 1844.

1

I believe that the Atonement of Jesus Christ was universal and available for all who would repent of their sins, and accept Him alone as their personal Savior. As such, I do not believe the teachings of the Prophet Brigham Young specific to the need for or the practice of <u>Blood Atonement</u>, in that a member's own blood must be spilt on the ground to atone for their sins in this world, nor do I believe that such a principle was ever a Commandment, Teaching or Doctrine from Jesus Christ.

I believe that some teachings of the Prophets and/or Quorum of the Twelve Apostles have <u>not been inspired or directed by the Holy Ghost</u> as Doctrine from the Lord Jesus Christ.

Concerning such teachings, I believe that the far <u>greater</u> responsibility for the <u>impact</u> of such misleading sermons and teachings falls directly on the Leadership of the Church themselves, rather than with Spirit of Discernment from within the very congregations, whom, have in good faith sustained these leaders as Prophets, Seers and Revelators, to guide and direct them back into the presents of the Father and the Son.

By virtue of their Position and Authority within the Church, this responsibility would reasonably extend to the Leadership of the Church as <u>examples to the world</u> in general and the members of the Church specifically, as pertaining to the Honoring and Sustaining the Laws of the Land as well as maintaining the high Moral Standards of the Church.

Examples of what I definitely believe to be <u>false teachings or hypocritical actions</u> by the Leadership of the Church, both today and in the early days of the Church would include:

That a Temple oath of vengeance against the United States of America was from Christ.
That God the Father had sexual intercourse with Mary to conceive Jesus the Christ.
That Satan himself has guided the Government of the United States of America.
That Nigger jokes are appropriate in Official Church Publications or Sermons.
That a Temple oath of Blood Atonement against members was from Christ.
That Jesus the Christ took multiple wives and had children on this earth.
That if a white man has sex with a black woman he will die instantly.
That only those who participate in polygamy will become Gods.
That the Black Race is on the earth to properly represent Satan.
That apostates or dissenters of the Church should be killed.
That profiting from the sale of Pornography is acceptable.
That the Laws of God are superior to the Laws of Man.
That the Moon and the Sun are both truly inhabited.
That lying for the Lord is completely acceptable.

Lee B. Baker, High Priest & Bishop – The Church of Jesus Christ of Latter-day Saints

2

Document 17

Listing of Ordnances, Endowments, Callings and Ordinations
for
Bishop Lee B. Baker

Church Record Number   000-3443-8033

Baptism Date	17 February 1977
Confirmation Date	17 February 1977
Ordained to the Office of a Priest	27 February 1977
Ordained to the Office of an Elder	26 February 1978
Endowment Date and Temple	10 March 1979, Wash. D.C.
Patriarchal Blessing	24 August 1980
Ordained to the Office of High Priest	17 May 1987
Ordained to the Office of Bishop	15 April 1990
Excommunicated from the Church	07 December 2008

Callings and Positions held within the Church of Jesus Christ of Latter-day Saints

Bishop	Hawaii
Bishop's 1st and 2nd Counselor	Arizona
Stake High Counselor	Arizona, Colorado
Stake Young Men's President	Colorado
Stake Young Single Adult Advisor	Maryland
High Priests Group Leader	Maryland
Elder's Quorum President	Germany, Maryland
Ward Young Men's President	Hawaii
Sunday School Teacher	Colorado, England, Georgia
Ward Activities Leader	England
Ward Financial Clerk	Germany
Ward Historical Clerk	Texas
Assistant Scout Master and Cub Master	Maryland, Hawaii
Explorer Post Advisor	Maryland
Home Teacher	All locations for 32 years

Document 18

Dear Fellow Brother or Sister,

July 2008

As a convert to the Church, I have often relied on the knowledge of others who can draw from years of Church experience as well as an extensive personal or family history in the Church to clarify potential issues.

I have myself, hesitated at some of these questions from family, coworkers, new members and close neighbors, but I sincerely feel that they should not be dismissed without a genuine effort to be answered. I am encouraged and have great confidence in your support, which is best described in a paragraph from the *Principles and Practices of the Restored Gospel*, by Victor L. Ludlow:

"The Church is a God-given vehicle for perfecting the imperfect Saints through instruction, fellowship, support, and love. It will not fail us. When we strive to lift others, we all become unified and strengthened in Christ's work. As Paul told the Hebrews, "Both he that sanctifieth and they who are sanctified are all of one." (Heb. 2:11). This unity is the hallmark of the true Church of Christ. It is felt among our people throughout the world. As we are one, we are His. Thus, we must overcome diversity and weakness and help our fellow Saints to grow if we wish to be true members of Christ's fold."

As Sister Baker and I prepare to continue our Missionary Service, we are truly excited at the prospect that you might be able to provide some insight concerning these few questions. I believe with all my heart and with all that I know to be true, that the Spirit has directed me to present these questions in this format, that you might be able to "Strive to lift another, as we all become unified and strengthened in Christ's work."

For those whom I do not know personally, I have included a few background documents to establish the sincerity of my request.

We are completely and at times painfully aware that some of these questions are in fact controversial or at best, very sensitive. Nevertheless, they are important and valid to some whom the Lord has placed in our paths. Although it may be difficult, we continue to stand and teach the Truth to the World and we do not shrink from it, nor do we apologize for it.

As we support each other in the Church, my spirit is encourage by the wisdom and prophetic guidance of President Joseph Fielding Smith:

"We have been commanded by the Lord to study the standard works. The scriptures are replete with the admonishment to gain knowledge and an understanding of Gospel Principles. The glory of God is intelligence, or, in other words, light and truth. (D&C 93:36)"

1

Thank you so very much for your time and your thoughts on any or all of what follows.

May the Lord Bless you for your efforts to bring the Gospel of Jesus Christ to others that you may not yet know, but are genuinely seeking the Truth.

Sincerely,

Lee B. Baker
Former Bishop of the Mililani Second Ward, Mililani Stake, Hawaii

Contact Information:

Lee and Kathy Baker
10844 Diane Drive
Golden, CO 80403

Home:
Work:
Fax:
Email: leebbaker@hotmail.com

For the best use of your time, I have done some of the fundamental research on each question and I have provided, where possible, the appropriate and authoritative references for your review.

Additionally, I ask that you, as I have, considered both the merit and the basis of each question to ensure some measure of sincerity within the very foundation of the question. I think that you will agree that the clearly absurd "All Mormons have horns." class of questions or comments will not be represented here. Again, Thank You for your efforts.

2

Document 19

From: jsrockwood@msn.com
To: leebbaker@hotmail.com
Subject: RE: How are you?
Date: Fri, 17 Oct 2008 08:33:47 -0600

Lee,

I am truly sorry to hear of the affect your questions are having on you and your family. While I know these questions are very important to you, I am sure you are considering if they are worth the pain they seem to be causing. Their fruits don't seem to be the fruit of the Spirit as described in Galatians and Ephesians.

I have learned that it is important to become source sensitive. What are the sources of our questions and answers? I also know that the Lord always requires faith as we seek after truth, so I wonder if it is worth considering that perhaps the great purpose in this whole process is to exercise your faith and move on, follow the counsel of your leaders and friends, trusting that the questions have been answered or will be answered in due time, but not to let them cause harm to you in the mean time. I had an experience six years ago that I still don't understand, still doesn't make sense to me, still seems very wrong, but I had to drop it before I let it consume me. I still don't have the answers, but I am at least not entangled with the pain and the consequences of that pain anymore. I learned that what the Lord was not going to give me the answers I wanted and instead was going to require me to drop it and exercise my faith, let it go, and in due time perhaps I might get the answers and justification I seek. The confusion, anger and inequity of the situation still creep into my mind once in awhile, but I have to remember to leave it alone, it does me absolutely no good, no matter how I feel about it. I can't tell you how free I felt when I forgave the individuals and the situation involved and finally realized my personal role, responsibility and contribution to the situation and let it go. There are so many examples of how rather then resist something or relentlessly pursue something that doesn't seem to bring forth good fruit, no mater how important or right it seems to be to us at the moment, we need to just let them go and trust that the Lord in his wisdom will reveal to us the why's and how's when he deems fit.

In regards to the scripture you mention. I don't view those three things as absolute conditions. I view them as one example of many possible scenarios. In that context it all makes sense to me. I also concentrate on verse 60. Since it is not mine to know everything that went on in those infant years of the Church, I know that Joseph was sustained and justified by God and that the fruits of his works the last 170 years since then prove to me that Joseph was a prophet of God in good standing with God and therefore should be with me. Evidently, as he struggled to fulfill his mission assigned to him by God, he had challenges, mistakes, struggles, and triumphs along the way, but in the end seemed to satisfy is Father and therefore deserves nothing less than my satisfaction and thanks.

I am praying that peace will come to you and that you will stay close and united with the gospel and the saints whom you love and who love you.

My sincerest hopes,
Steve

From: leebbaker@hotmail.com
To: jsrockwood@msn.com
Subject: RE: How are you?
Date: Wed, 15 Oct 2008 20:01:58 -0600

Steve,

Thank you for the email and the offer.

How are things?

The very worst year of my life, and Kathy's and now also for my four Children.

What can you do for me?

Simple, tell me again how what is clearly called a Law in the canonized Scriptures of the Church, became diluted into something... anything less.

As clearly recorded by Joseph Smith in D&C 132: 61-64, the Lord sets three conditions (under the heading of a Law) which are required for a member of the Priesthood who desires to take other wives: She must be 1) "a virgin", 2) "the first give her consent", and 3) "vowed to no other man", "belongeth unto him and to no one else.

"All these principles that I have treated upon, pertaining to eternal marriage, the very moment that they are admitted to be true, it brings in plurality of marriage, and if plurality of marriage is not true or in other words, if a man has no divine right to marry two wives or more in this world, then marriage for eternity is not true, and your faith is all vain, and all the sealing ordinances and powers, pertaining to marriages for eternity are vain, worthless, good for nothing; for as sure as one is true the other also must be true. Amen.   Apostle Orson Pratt, 18 July 1880, Tabernacle Salt Lake, JoD, v21, p.286

Thanks again for your thoughtfulness... but I really do believe that even with your kind heart and true consideration... it is not your calling nor your responsibility to address my Spiritual issues. But I am very interested in your thoughts on the above items, as they seem to me to be clear and free from any need of analysis or debate as do the vast majority of my questions.

Thanks again.

Lee

From: jsrockwood@msn.com
To: leebbaker@hotmail.com
Subject: How are you?
Date: Wed, 15 Oct 2008 16:05:58 -0600

Hi Lee,

I haven't seen you for awhile. How are things and is there anything I can do for you?

Steve

Document 20

General Administration

The Lord guides His covenant people today through the President of the Church, whom we sustain as prophet, seer, and revelator. The President of the Church presides over the entire Church. He and his counselors, who are also prophets, seers, and revelators, form the Quorum of the First Presidency.

Members of the Quorum of the Twelve Apostles are also prophets, seers, and revelators. They, along with the First Presidency, are "special witnesses of the name of Christ in all the world" (D&C 107:23). They act under the direction of the First Presidency "to build up the church, and regulate all the affairs of the same in all nations" (D&C 107:33). They "open the door [to the nations] by the proclamation of the gospel of Jesus Christ" (D&C 107:35).

Members of the Quorums of the Seventy are called to proclaim the gospel and build up the Church. They work under the direction of the Twelve Apostles and the leadership of seven brethren who are called to serve as the Presidency of the Seventy. Members of the First and Second Quorums of the Seventy are designated General Authorities, and they may be called to serve anywhere in the world.

The Presiding Bishopric is the presidency of the Aaronic Priesthood throughout the Church. The Presiding Bishop and his counselors serve under the direction of the First Presidency to administer the temporal affairs of the Church.

The Young Men, Relief Society, Young Women, Primary, and Sunday School organizations all have presidencies on the general level to provide instruction and direction.

Area Administration

An area is the largest geographic division of the Church. The First Presidency assigns the Presidency of the Seventy to directly supervise selected areas of the Church under the direction of the Quorum of the Twelve Apostles. In other areas of the Church, the First Presidency assigns Area Presidencies to preside. An Area Presidency consists of a president, who is usually assigned from the First or Second Quorum of the Seventy, and two counselors, who may be assigned from any Quorum of the Seventy. Area Presidencies serve under the direction of the First Presidency, the Quorum of the Twelve, and the Presidency of the Seventy.

Some brethren are ordained to the office of Seventy but do not serve as General Authorities. They are called Area Seventies, and they are assigned to quorums other than the First or Second Quorums of the Seventy, according to geographic location. Their jurisdiction is limited to the general region in which they live. Some Area Seventies serve in Area Presidencies.

Local Administration

Wards and Branches. Members of the Church are organized into congregations that meet together frequently for spiritual and social enrichment. Large congregations are called wards. Each ward is presided over by a bishop, assisted by two counselors. Small congregations are called branches. Each branch is presided over by a branch president, assisted by two counselors. A branch may be organized when at least two member families live in an area and one of the members is a worthy Melchizedek Priesthood holder or a worthy priest in the Aaronic Priesthood. A stake, mission, or district presidency organizes and supervises the branch. A branch can develop into a ward if it is located within a stake.

Each ward or branch comprises a specific geographic area. Different organizations in the ward or branch contribute to the Lord's work: high priests groups; elders quorums; the Relief Society, for women ages 18 years and older; Aaronic Priesthood quorums, for young men ages 12 through 17; the Young Women program, for young women ages 12 through 17; Primary, for children ages 18 months to 11 years; and the Sunday School, for all Church members ages 12 and older. Each of these organizations fulfills important roles in teaching the gospel, giving service, and supporting parents in their sacred duty to help their children become converted to the gospel of Jesus Christ. These organizations also work together to help members share the gospel with others.

Stakes, Missions, and Districts. Most geographic areas where the Church is organized are divided into stakes. The term stake comes from the prophet Isaiah, who prophesied that the latter-day Church would be like a tent, held secure by stakes (see Isaiah 33:20; 54:2). There are usually 5 to 12 wards and branches in a stake. Each stake is presided over by a stake president, assisted by two counselors. Stake presidents report to and receive direction from the Presidency of the Seventy or the Area Presidency.

A mission is a unit of the Church that normally covers an area much larger than that covered by a stake. Each mission is presided over by a mission president, assisted by two counselors. Mission presidents are directly accountable to General Authorities.

Just as a branch is a smaller version of a ward, a district is a smaller version of a stake. A district is organized when there are a sufficient number of branches located in an area, permitting easy communication and convenient travel to district meetings. A district president is called to preside over it, with the help of two counselors. The district president reports to the mission presidency. A district can develop into a stake.

(See: lds.org)

Document 21

CERTIFICATE OF RETIREMENT

FROM THE ARMED FORCES OF THE UNITED STATES OF AMERICA

TO ALL WHO SHALL SEE THESE PRESENTS, GREETING:

THIS IS TO CERTIFY THAT

BAKER, LEE BARRY, ███████████, CHIEF WARRANT OFFICER THREE, REGULAR ARMY, MILITARY INTELLIGENCE

HAVING SERVED FAITHFULLY AND HONORABLY, WAS RETIRED FROM THE

UNITED STATES ARMY

ON THE TWENTY-NINTH DAY OF FEBRUARY

ONE THOUSAND NINE HUNDRED AND NINTY-SIX

WASHINGTON, D. C.

GENERAL, UNITED STATES ARMY,
CHIEF OF STAFF

Document 22

THE UNITED STATES OF AMERICA

TO ALL WHO SHALL SEE THESE PRESENTS, GREETING: THIS IS TO CERTIFY THAT THE PRESIDENT OF THE UNITED STATES OF AMERICA AUTHORIZED BY ACT OF CONGRESS 20 JULY 1942 HAS AWARDED

THE LEGION OF MERIT

TO   CHIEF WARRANT OFFICER THREE LEE B. BAKER, UNITED STATES ARMY

FOR   distinguishing himself by exceptionally meritorious conduct in the performance of outstanding services in numerous key positions at Department of the Army, Joint Service, and Field Station levels from February 1986 to February 1996. He sought and achieved operational intelligence excellence which significantly impacted upon the research and development of the new United States Army doctrine, the establishment of the Kunia Regional Signal Intelligence Operations Center, and the streamlining of Aerospace Data Facility functions and organizations. Chief Warrant Officer Baker's distinguished performance of duty throughout this period represents outstanding accomplishments in the most cherished traditions of the United States Army and reflects utmost credit upon him and the military service.

GIVEN UNDER MY HAND IN THE CITY OF WASHINGTON
THIS   18th   DAY OF   January   19   96

Brigadier General, USA
Commanding

SECRETARY OF THE ARMY

DA FORM 4086, 11 APR 81

- 294 -

Document 23

January 2008

Dear Lee,

I received your packet last month (December 2007) that details the various questions about the history of the church that you have been researching. At the request of our Stake President, Michael Jones. I will not be responding to your individual questions with independent answers. Pres. Jones indicated that he would like you to work through him on this matter.

My general observations would be for you to consider the following:

- It is important to remember that the First Principles and Ordinances of the Gospel are: first. Faith in the Lord Jesus Christ, second, Repentance. third, Baptism by immersion for the remission of sins, fourth. Laying on of hands for the gift of the Holy Ghost.

- The Book of Mormon is the keystone of our religion, meaning it is central to our religion. There are certainly many facets/facts/teachings in the church - but the Book of Mormon is at the very center of the gospel. Other things can be on the periphery - and should be treated as such.

- As friends, family, or others come to you with questions (as they have in the past), consider whether they are searching to find the best way to place their Faith in the Lord Jesus Christ, or are they trying to draw on information from history that may or may not be factual – with no real definitive way of determining the authenticity of those claims, with the end result being the undermining or destroying of Faith in the Lord Jesus Christ. (Moroni 7: 16-17)

- It is not necessary for any of us to explain/justify the actions of another. We are each responsible for our own salvation. It is not our place to judge the actions of others. In your own words in a letter to a Stake President (Pres. Johnson), you said: *"You should not have to explain, excuse or justify his actions."*

Lee. I encourage you to work with President Jones on this. He is a good, humble man that really is interested in helping you. Both you and your wife are wonderful, talented, capable people. Both of you have received the necessary ordinances that are needed to obtain eternal life. Keeping those covenants is now your charge. I encourage to do just that.

Sincerely,

Richard Merkley

Document 24

August 2008

Hello Lee,

Several weeks ago you handed me a copy of an April 25, 2008 letter you received from Pres. Jones. You asked that I respond to the highlighted sentence in that letter. This is my response.

The sentence says "I have never asked them to withhold their support in any way."

I agree with that sentence. Pres. Jones has not asked that support be withheld – rather, he asked that you work with him, and through him, on this matter. In an earlier paragraph he says "I have counseled...others...to carefully consider before they decide to answer the questions as you have them...as you have seen, some have engaged in discussion with you." Pres. Jones goes on to say that the questions posed, draw a conclusion, and demand a response to that conclusion.

Lee, my response to you is this:

God the Father, and His Son Jesus Christ personally appeared to Joseph Smith as a boy. They personally called him to be the prophet of the restoration. The remainder of his life was dedicated to that end. Joseph Smith never professed to be a perfect man. He had limitations, made mistakes, and had need for repentance, just as we all do. Jesus Christ is the only man who walked the earth as a perfect individual. Joseph Smith carried out the mission he was called to do being taught by inspiration, revelation, and in many cases, visions. He knew more about God, and his overall plan than anyone else on earth. He learned these things directly from heavenly beings.

Lee, I know that most of the questions you pose deal directly with the prophet Joseph and things he did, or did not do. My testimony is that Joseph did what he was supposed to do. My faith is in Jesus Christ. He is the one who called Joseph Smith to accomplish the work that was done. He could have called someone else, but he didn't. That's good enough for me. I'm certainly not in a position to second guess the Savior, and I don't believe anyone else is either.

After all that Joseph Smith did, or did not do - where does he stand in the eternities?

We have a very clear understanding of that by reading the Doctrine and Covenants, Section 138 - the vision given to the President of the Church in 1918 - Joseph F. Smith. Reading the entire section puts things in context, but looking at verses 38 and after, speak about the "great and mighty ones" starting with Adam and going on... verses 53 - 55 speak about Joseph Smith, Hyrum and others who were chosen to be....rulers in the Church of God.

This vision, received in 1918, was 74 years after the death of Joseph and Hyrum in 1844. This vision specifically states that they have their place among the noble and great ones. Jesus Christ is the one who makes that judgment - based on their works. I place my faith in Jesus Christ. And He has placed Joseph Smith among the noble and great ones - and therefore, I accept all that Joseph Smith did in completing the mission he was called to accomplish. That is where Joseph Smith stands in the eternities. Because of that, the questions that you pose are not a concern to me - and I hope, that you can trust in Christ to the point where they will not be a concern to you. Our safety comes when we place our trust in Jesus Christ - and those He has chosen. He chose Joseph Smith, and placed him among the noble and great ones following his death. That's good enough for me.

I hope my response has been helpful.

Sincerely,

Richard Merkley

Document 25

Subject: RE: Letter from Kathy Baker
Date: Mon, 31 Mar 2008 10:26:39 -0600
From: mjones@sonsio.com
To: leebbaker@hotmail.com
CC: jsrockwood@msn.com; rodtarullo@yahoo.com; rdmerkley@msn.com;

Sister Baker,

Thank you for your note. I feel very deeply about your struggles.

While I would like to answer all of your questions, email probably isn't the best, or even the most appropriate forum. Regardless, I will, and I know Bishop Doman will make ourselves to meet with you and your husband. Notwithstanding, let me clarify and reiterate a few things we've already discussed.

When we met last week, my invitation was that if you harbored any feelings of anger and frustration towards any person/leader who you feel have mistreated, abandoned, or have been critical of you and your husband, that you let those feelings go. The spirit can neither bring peace nor answers to questions in an environment of such feelings.

When your husband kindly and generously embraced me at the end our interview, I felt a spirit of understanding and reconciliation. Can I build on that moment?

Having doubts and asking questions are not wrong or a sign of weakness. Didn't Joseph Smith himself doubt and question as he learned? One time he said, "In the midst of this war of words and tumult of opinions, I often said to myself: What is to be done? Who of all these parties are right; or, are they all wrong together? If any one of them be right, which is it, and how shall I know it?" (Joseph Smith - History 1:10) Having doubts is not evidence of wrongdoing; attempting resolve doubt can be a step toward right. Asking questions is not a sign of weakness, but a sign of growth. "Prove all things," and "hold fast that which is good" (1 Thessalonians 5:21) the scriptures teach.

Let me share with you again my own personal journey through the questions posed regarding Joseph Smith. My petition to the Lord was not whether Joseph was some fallen and conniving con man who stole other men's wives, or a well-meaning, but libidinous prophet who preyed on people's faith; I asked Heavenly Father "where does he stand as prophet of the restoration?"

The answer I received, as I shared with you and your husband, was that I saw in my mind's eye, Joseph Smith, standing in the heavens, glorious and exalted. There was a beauty and grandeur that I can only poorly express. I saw those who came in judgment of him, and when they entered his presence, they shrank in horror and shame receiving for themselves a full view of the man and of themselves. Now, I don't know whether Joseph misapplied the law of eternal marriage, or if he broke the commandments for his own selfishness (though I believe that he did not), or if his unrighteous actions caused others to stumble and fall. I only know how the Lord regards him today, and for the eternities to come...and for me, it is enough and to spare. Having this knowledge, the other questions are meaningless to me. My grateful testimony is that Joseph Smith is a prophet of God.

How each member works through this or any other question is a very personal, and holy matter. While my answer might help you, it won't satisfy you. It is similar to an investigator who is looking to know the truth. Your testimony will inspire and bless, but until the person has their own personal witness, your testimony won't sustain them.

Now there are a number of other things you have mentioned that I haven't addressed. As I mentioned earlier, those items would be better addressed in person.

Be safe in your trip, and I look forward to speaking with you on your return.

--Michael Jones

Document 26

The Law of the Gospel

A Portion of the Sacred Mormon Temple Endowment Ceremony

The following is a segment of the then sacred and most secret Church of Jesus Christ of Latter-day Saint's Endowment Ceremony as practiced by the author himself within Mormon Temples throughout the world. It was not until many years later that the direct and repulsive connection between the penalty phase of the Endowment Ceremony and Brigham Young's teaching of the Doctrine of Blood Atonement would be understood. The Endowment itself is presented as an instructional video, although within the Salt Lake Temple the presentation is acted out by Temple Workers without the aid of costumes or visual props.

"We are required to give unto you the Law of the Gospel as contained in the Holy Scriptures; to give unto you also a charge to avoid all light mindedness, loud laughter, evil speaking of the Lord's anointed, the taking of the name of God in vain, and every other unholy and impure practice, and to cause you to receive these by covenant."

"You and each of you covenant and promise before God, angels, and these witnesses at this altar, that you will observe and keep the Law of the Gospel and this charge as it has been explained to you. Each of you bow your head and say yes."

"The execution of the Penalty is represented by placing the thumb under the left ear, the palm of the hand down, and by drawing the thumb quickly across the throat to the right ear, and dropping the hand to the side."

The officiator in the pre-1990 version, after demonstrating the sign and execution of the penalty, would say to the congregation within the Temple Endowment Room:

"I will now explain the covenant and obligation of secrecy which are associated with this token, its name, sign and penalty, and which you will be required to take upon yourselves. If I were receiving my own Endowment today, and had been given the name of "John" as my New Name, I would repeat in my mind these words, after making the sign, at the same time representing the execution of the penalty: I, John, covenant that I will never reveal the First Token of the Aaronic Priesthood, with its accompanying name, sign, and penalty. *(The Officiator demonstrates the execution of the penalty.)* Rather than do so, I would suffer my life to be taken."

Document 27

Lee,

Your letter arrived Tuesday and its tone was quite a surprise to me. I harbor none of the ill feelings you concluded I must feel towards you nor any of the intentions you ascribed to my actions in your letter. As I have mentioned in previous conversations, I consider you a friend and someone with many admirable attributes; in particular I think you are very compassionate and hardworking.

My delay in finding authoritative answers to the questions you sent results from two factors: several unexpected family events on top of a known very busy period and the fact that the questions are interesting to me but I don't feel an urgency to resolve them immediately. This has been my perspective all along and perhaps, if I have not been clear on that perspective, I may have left you with the wrong expectation about how rapidly I might find some answers. You have worked on them for some time now and they remain unresolved so I'm assuming its going to take some substantial effort to find the answer. One of the questions, the one citing a verse in an earlier edition of the Book of Mormon about people becoming "a white and delightsome people", I think I do know the answer to, but have not been able locate the source yet. Which brings me back to the unexpected family events. Since we spoke about the questions my father's health has deteriorated and he recently had back surgery, my sister's first child was born 7 weeks early and her husband is unemployed, one of my nieces was hit by a car, etc. and all of this was on top of painting bedrooms and halls, planning all of the stake activities, YM activities, YW activities, combined YM/YW activities, Primary activities for 2006, preparing several talks and training meetings in English and Spanish, having very limited internet access for the past month, and working extra hours in the evening for some special taskings from work. Thus, when something had to give, it was time that might have gone to other projects and activities such as the questions you shared.

Hopefully this provides sufficient explanation of my actions to demonstrate that my intentions and actions have all been forthright, open, and without malice or deceptive intent. I continue to be interested in understanding the answer to the questions and will continue to pursue them. As I find answers I'll gladly share them. I'm interested in the answers you find if you find one before I do. Your letter contained accusations and conclusions that I ascribe to misaligned expectations and those probably resulted from a lack of clarity on my part in communicating my perspective. I apologize for that and ask your forgiveness.

You remain someone I consider a friend and one with many attributes worth emulating. I hope that our future holds many warm and intriguing conversations on gospel and other topics.

Lorin Lund

Document 28

26 September 2005

Dear Stake President,

This letter is to serve as formal notification that as a previous Bishop myself, that I find it personally offensive and damaging to the good name of the Church that Elder J. W. Marriott, Jr. would participate in the dissemination of pornography for commercial gain.

In direct violation of the General Handbook of Instructions – dissemination of pornography – and in view of abundant counsel such as: Elder Dallin H. Oaks, General Conference, 3 April 2005, "For many years our Church leaders have warned against the dangers of images and words intended to arouse sexual desires. Now the corrupting influence of pornography, produced and disseminated for commercial gain, is sweeping over our society like an avalanche of evil."

With all do respect to Elder Marriott's Vice-President for Communications, why would Adult Movies be needed to provide the revenues for Good Movies... when the Good Movies are not provided for Free? Additionally, it would take a monumental accounting effort to ensure that Tithing funds from the dissemination and commercial gain of such pornography was not provided to Church Offices under normal contributions from Elder Marriott.

If Church policies, standards and guidelines are not to be applied to our business or commercial activities, then I stand corrected and this letter may be destroyed.

Sincerely,

Lee B. Baker
Membership Record Number: 000-3443-8033 (Provided for authentication purposes)

Document 28B

J.W. Marriott Jr.
CEO and Chairman
One Marriott Drive
Washington, D.C. 20058

30 August 2005

Dear Elder Marriott,

I have seen your photograph prominently displayed both in your exquisite Hotels and Resorts as well as within the High Counsel Room of our Stake Center. I have often pondered if your shirt or maybe your tie in those photos was purchased through your family sales and distribution of Pornography.

As a member of your Rewards Program (Silver Elite – 519 355 226), I have attempted for three years, without comment from your offices, to gain some insight through normal business channels (Corporate Headquarters and On-Line Member Services), specific to your personal choice and practice of renting "Adult Movies". On both business and personal travel, I have found it confusing that on top of the nightstand that holds the Book of Mormon, is an "entertainment" guide, which includes in-room Pornography.

I have made some preliminary contacts with your industry regulatory officials... and it would appear that the sale and distribution of Pornography is not, as far as I can tell a business requirement. Additionally, I assume that you would not provide your 2,600 properties across 66 countries as an elegant showcase for those who would profit from the sexual abuse and degradation of women... free of charge.

In view of my past requests for information concerning this preferred business practice, all of which have gone unanswered, I wish to be removed from your Rewards Program and as a High Priest and Member of the Church of Jesus Christ of Latter-Day Saints, let me say that you are Wrong to continue profiting from the sales and distribution of Pornography.

Please be assured that if this letter is to go unanswered... I will exercise the most public of forums to bring this hypocritical activity to the attention of your guests, your shareholders and to Church Officers at whatever level required.

Most Sincerely,

Lee B. Baker

Document 29

Marriott International, Inc.
Corporate Headquarters

Marriott Drive
Washington, D.C. 20058

Roger W. Conner
VP, Communications
301/380-5605
301/897-9014 Fax
Email: roger.conner@marriott.com

September 23, 2005

Mr. Lee Baker
7064 Cedar Avenue
Elkridge, MD 21075-6307

Dear Mr. Baker,

I want to thank you very much for taking the time to share your concerns about adult movies in some of our hotel rooms. I certainly respect and appreciate your views on this subject, and so does Mr. Marriott.

The material you reference is part of a wide variety of programming offered by all major hotel chains. As you know, it's also offered as an option on nearly all residential cable and satellite services, as well as the Internet. Clearly, this is a matter of adult choice that must be selected and paid for separately from all regular television. That certainly is the case in all our hotel rooms. Guests can quickly and easily block the offering of this material by calling the front desk or using the TV remote control.

Please know that Marriott is in no way involved with the production of adult television programming or in-room-movie programming shown in our rooms. Also, please understand that we manage these hotels and do not own them. The adult movies provide the revenue to pay for the good movies and our owners refuse to change the formula as the economic impact to their hotels would be substantial.

Once again, I appreciate the time you have taken to express your feelings. Your views are important to us.

Sincerely,

Roger Conner.

cc: J.W. Marriott, Jr.

- 303 -

Document 30

Please do not feel that you need to write me a letter concerning my issues specific to the current business practices of Elder Marriott. You should not have to explain, excuse or justify <u>his</u> actions.

I know too well how it feels to explain, excuse or justify some of the peculiar actions or teachings of Joseph Smith and Brigham Young... especially knowing full well that they themselves would <u>not</u> want others to create any apology for them.

For many years I have enjoyed sharing the gospel, but it seems harder now (specific to some Church History issues) as it would appear that a well organized active "Clean-up" effort has now relegated some of the past authorized and fundamental teachings of the Church into the general "Anti-Mormon" category of today, even though they may be true. Those of us who would attempt to answer potentially difficult questions are left utterly to our own point of view. Several Missionaries have pointed out that even the Preach My Gospel manual does not contain a single word of guidance specific to questions concerning Polygamy or Blacks and the Priesthood.

It is as if when confronted with questions based on indisputably true and factual events or teachings, which may be embarrassing, we should simply "move-on" to find a <u>less</u> well-informed potential convert. If such information is <u>true</u>, it is a grave disservice and potentially damaging to our Members to have them learn of such things from <u>outside</u> the Church.

When discussing such subjects, over a year ago, President Lund told me "There is an answer for everything." That is only true if you completely avoid those non-members who know... what you don't. Especially if what they know has been selected <u>entirely</u> from the Official Church website or the Journal of Discourses, both hardly Anti-Mormon sources.

I have a very strong testimony of the Gospel and of the Church in its <u>full</u> and true version. But, am I too concerned about this general "Clean-up" of history, manuals and teachings? As President Lund pointed out, it is inappropriate and unacceptable to hang in our Chapel, a painting of the Lord Jesus Christ, the Son of the Living God, Our Savior, He who stands at the very head of this Church. That may be why I find it confusing that a photograph of Elder J. W. Marriott Jr. is hanging in the very room where Official Church Disciplinary Courts are held, potentially dealing with the issue of pornography, when <u>he</u> continues to profit from the sale and distribution of pornography.

It is reasonably simple to me... if you are a Member <u>and</u> a Billionaire... not all the rules apply.

Lee B. Baker

APPENDIX B

Mormon History – A Short Chronology of Significant Events

The principal outline for this short review of the history of the Mormon Church has been taken from the official Web site of the Church of Jesus Christ of Latter-day Saints and other authoritative historical documentation. The purpose of this chronology is to give the reader who may be unfamiliar with Mormon history a synopsis of some of the more significant events that have shaped the Church of Jesus Christ of Latter-day Saints.

Overview

At the age of fourteen, Joseph Smith Jr. retired to the woods near his home in Palmyra, New York in 1820 to offer a prayer to God Himself, asking direction concerning which church he should join. His spiritual bewilderment came during the height of a religious revival period in the early nineteenth century often called the Second Great Awakening. His claims of visions, heavenly visitations, and the discovery and translation of the Book of Mormon would set into motion a series of events that would build the foundation for the Church of Jesus Christ of Latter-day Saints.

The distinctive doctrines and practices of this uniquely American religion would persuade many to believe that it was the single greatest threat to the political, moral, and ethical fabric of the nation. Others would consider it to be the only true church on the earth today, precisely because of those same distinctive doctrines and practices.

Significant Events in Mormon History

1820 At the age of fourteen, Joseph Smith reports a vision of God the Father and Jesus Christ. Jesus Christ tells Smith that all Christian denominations have become corrupt and that he is not to join any church.

1827 After several visits from the Angel Moroni, Joseph Smith is given the gold plates from within the Hill Cumorah. Within two years the gold plates are translated into English and known as the Book of Mormon.

1830 The church, first known as the Church of Christ, is formally organized in Fayette Township, New York, with about thirty believers in attendance.

1831 As recorded within modern Mormon Scripture, Doctrine and Covenants 132, the practice of polygamy (and polyandry) begins in secret within the first year of the church.

In stark contrast, the official Mormon Scriptures of the day actually reject the practice from 1835 to 1876.

1833 The Mormons begin to flee Jackson County, Missouri, across the Missouri River because of intense and violent persecutions.

1838 The name of the church is changed from the Church of Christ (1830), to the Church of the Latter Day Saints (1834) to The Church of Jesus Christ of Latter Day Saints (1838), with the hyphen in "Latter-day" added a century later to be grammatically correct. More recently (1990s), the Mormon Church has significantly increased the font of the words "Jesus Christ" within the church's name on all official publications and buildings.

1840 The doctrine of Mormon baptism for the dead is publicly announced by Joseph Smith. The church begins the controversial practice of baptizing the dead by proxy, which requires the need for significant family genealogy research.

1844 Joseph Smith, as the mayor of Nauvoo, Illinois and the commanding general of the Nauvoo Legion (nearly 3,000 troops) and Prophet of the Lord, also runs for president of the United States.

1844 Joseph Smith, secretly practicing "plural marriage" has taken some thirty-three wives, eleven being the wives of other men. His former longtime friend and counselor in the church, William Law, and others issue a local newspaper (the

Nauvoo Expositor), declaring that Smith attempted to seduce their wives as part of "plural marriage."

1844 Joseph Smith and his brother Hyrum are arrested and jailed in Carthage, Illinois. The two brothers are charged with treason and, although promised protection by Governor Thomas Ford, an anti-Mormon mob storms the building and murders them on June 27th. Official Mormon records indicate that Smith was armed with a six-shot pistol smuggled to him by Cyrus Wheelock and that Smith himself shot three of his assailants that afternoon[65]. Not even remotely the defenseless and feeble death Smith predicted as recorded in Mormon Scripture[66]: "I am going like a lamb to the slaughter". The Mormon Church is thrown into turmoil and split into several rival groups.

1847 Brigham Young's pioneer company of Mormons leaves the United States for the Salt Lake valley, then a territory of Mexico.

1849 After the War with Mexico (1846-1848), Brigham Young petitions the United States Congress for the massive state of Deseret, which would have been nearly all of the land lost by Mexico to the United States. The request is denied, and the territory of Utah is created in 1851.

1852 The Mormon Church officially and openly acknowledges the doctrine of "plural marriage," and the legal, political, and social impact of polygamy comes to the attention of the American public.

1857 President James Buchanan sends one third of the United States Army to put down what was known as the "Mormon Rebellion" in Utah and to replace Brigham Young as the governor of the territory.

1857 During the elevated tensions of the "Mormon Rebellion," and as an apparent reprisal for years of persecution,

---

[65] Church History in the Fulness of Times, Church of Jesus Christ of Latter-day Saints, Salt Lake City, Copyright 1989, page 281.

[66] Doctrine and Covenants, Section 135, Verse 4, Church of Jesus Christ of Latter-day Saints, Salt Lake City, Copyright 1981.

Mormon leaders plan, execute, and cover up the murder of some 120 white men, women, and children. In what became known as the "Mountain Meadows Massacre," a wagon train from Arkansas is tricked into willingly disarming themselves under a white flag of truce. The members of the party are then shot execution-style at point-blank range.

1862 President Abraham Lincoln signs the Morrill Anti-Bigamy Act. The federal law targets polygamy, which Lincoln had called one of the "twin relics of barbarism." The act banned bigamy in the United States and limited any church or nonprofit ownership of any assets within the territories to $50,000.

1876 Although secretly practiced for some forty-five years and illegal in the United States, the formal doctrine of "plural marriage" is published for the first time by the Mormon Church in the updated version of Doctrine and Covenants.

1882 The United States Congress passes the Edmunds Bill, making plural marriage a felony and prohibiting polygamists from voting, holding public office, or performing jury duty.

1887 The United States Congress passes the Edmunds-Tucker Act, another anti-polygamy law, allowing the federal government to confiscate much of the church's real estate.

1887 As a practicing polygamist at the age of seventy-eight, the third Prophet of the Mormon Church, John Taylor, dies as a fugitive while in hiding from United States federal officials in the small town of Kaysville, Utah.

1890 The fourth Prophet of the Mormon Church, Wilford Woodruff receives a "revelation" from the Lord ending the practice of plural marriages. It is known as the "First Manifesto." The split in the church over the practice of polygamy continues among the mainstream Mormons for at least the next fifteen years. Woodruff's guidance is considered ambiguous.

1904 The fifth Prophet of the Mormon Church, Joseph F. Smith, issues the "Second Manifesto," which further clarifies and reiterates the church's position against polygamy. Mormons, even the most senior leadership of the church, are now excommunicated for the practice.

1904 The United States Congress begins three years of public hearings concerning the nomination of Reed Smoot as senator from Utah. Because he is one of the Twelve Apostles of the Mormon Church, the Reed Smoot hearings examine every detail of controversial Mormon doctrine.

1978 The Mormon Prophet Spencer W. Kimball receives the "revelation" that all worthy members of the church, without regard for race or color, may obtain the blessings of the Mormon priesthood.

1981 New editions of the Book of Mormon, Doctrine and Covenants, Pearl of Great Price, and the LDS edition of the King James Bible with study aids are published. Non-Mormons consider some changes to the Mormon Scriptures controversial.

1990 The "penalty" portion of the secret Mormon temple ceremony, a clear reference to the doctrine of "blood atonement," is removed under direction of the First Presidency of the Church.

2010 Worldwide membership in the Church of Jesus Christ of Latter-day Saints reaches 13.5 million.

Bibliography

Official Mormon Church Publications and Resources

Book of Mormon, Doctrine and Covenants, Pearl of Great Price. Salt Lake City: Intellectual Reserve Inc, 1979.

Ensign. Salt Lake City: Intellectual Reserve, Inc. An official magazine of the Church of Jesus Christ of Latter-day Saints.

LDS Collectors Library 2005. CD-ROM. Salt Lake City: LDS Media and Deseret Book, 2004. Primary resource for official reporting of the various sermons, talks, speeches, and teachings of the authorities of the Church of Jesus Christ of Latter-day Saints, as recorded during the official general conferences of the church, and the *Journal of Discourses* of the several Prophets, Seers, and Revelators of the church.)

Teachings of Presidents of the Church: Joseph Smith, Brigham Young, John Taylor, Wilford Woodruff, Heber J. Grant, David O. McKay, Harold B. Lee, and Spencer W. Kimball, and other official lesson manuals, study guides, books, and pamphlets published by the Church of Jesus Christ of Latter-day Saints. Salt Lake City: Intellectual Reserve Inc.

www.lds.org. The official Website of The Church of Jesus Christ of Latter-day Saints.

Non-Mormon Church Publications and Resources

Bagley, Will. *Blood of the Prophets: Brigham Young and the Massacre at Mountain Meadows.* Norman, OK: University of Oklahoma Press, 2002.

Compton, Todd. *In Sacred Loneliness: The Plural Wives of Joseph Smith.* Salt Lake City: Signature Books, 1997.

Denton, Sally. *American Massacre: The Tragedy at*

Mountain Meadows, September 1857. New York: Vintage Books, a Division of Random House, Inc., 2003.

Hirshson, Stanley P. *The Lion of the Lord: A Biography of Brigham Young.* New York: Knopf Press, 1969.

Krakauer, Jon. *Under the Banner of Heaven: A Story of Violent Faith.* New York: Doubleday, a Division of Random House, Inc., 2003.

Paulos, Michael Harold. *The Mormon Church on Trial: Transcripts of the Reed Smoot Hearings.* Salt Lake City: Signature Books, 2007.

Widtsoe, John A. *Discourses of Brigham Young.* Salt Lake City: Deseret Book Company, 1941.

Outstanding On-Line Resources

Witnesses For Jesus, Inc.
http://4mormon.org/

Tri-Grace Ministries
http://web.me.com/igniteUT4Christ/Trigrace/Home.html

CPSIA information can be obtained
at www.ICGtesting.com
Printed in the USA
FFOW03n2328280515
13676FF

9 781937 520755